The Bristol and Gloucestershire Archaeological Society
Gloucestershire Record Series

Hon. General Editor

David J.H. Smith, M.A., F.S.A.
County and Diocesan Archivist of Gloucestershire

Hon. Editorial Advisors

Christopher Elrington, M.A., F.S.A., F.R.Hist.S.
formerly General Editor of the
Victoria History of the Counties of England

Brian S. Smith, M.A., F.S.A., F.R.Hist.S.
formerly Secretary to the
Royal Commission on Historical Manuscripts

Volume 7

Tewkesbury Churchwardens' Accounts, 1563–1624
ed. C.J. Litzenberger

TEWKESBURY CHURCHWARDENS' ACCOUNTS, 1563–1624

Edited by C.J. Litzenberger

The Bristol and Gloucestershire Archaeological Society

1994

The Bristol and Gloucestershire Archaeological Society
Gloucestershire Record Series

© The Bristol and Gloucestershire Archaeological Society

ISBN 0 900197 39 X

Produced for the Society by Alan Sutton Publishing Ltd., Stroud, Gloucestershire
Printed in Great Britain

CONTENTS

PLATE

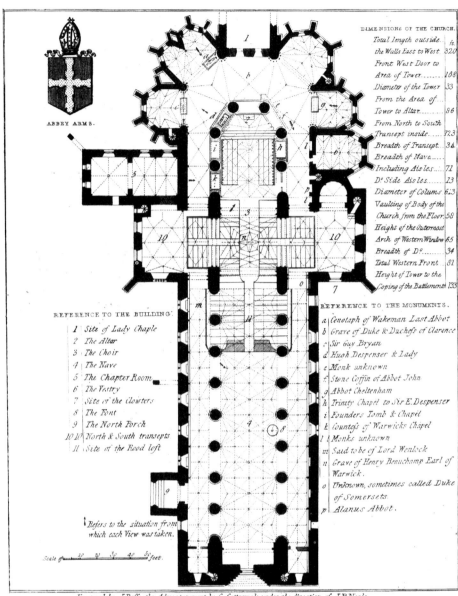

Proof copy of a plate published in J.P. Neale and J. Le Keux, *Views of the most interesting collegiate and parochial churches in Great Britain* vol. 1, 1825.

INTRODUCTION

The Parish and Town of Tewkesbury

The parish church of St. Mary's, Tewkesbury, which is situated on the bank of the River Severn in Gloucestershire, is a commanding edifice visible from some distance away. In the sixteenth and seventeenth centuries it was the only church in the market town of Tewkesbury, located just above the confluence of the Severn and Avon rivers approximately ten miles up-river from the city of Gloucester. Long and narrow, bounded on three sides by water, the town owed much of its livelihood to fishing and water-borne trades, and to its leatherworking industry. The church itself had been consecrated in 1121 as the abbey church of a Benedictine monastery established by the Normans. Looking more like a cathedral than a parish church, it is huge and cruciform in shape, with an imposing central tower and massive pillars rising to support its high roof in both the nave and the chancel. In fact, the ambulatory plan and the elevation of the nave are quite similar to those of its sister church, St. Peter's Abbey, Gloucester, which became the cathedral of the new diocese of Gloucester in 1541.[1]

Tewkesbury Abbey was one of the major monasteries dissolved by the crown in 1539, and was scheduled for demolition. The people of the town intervened to save it, however, as it was the traditional place of worship for the parish. In June 1543 'the bailiffs, burgesses and commonalty of the borough and town of Tewkesbury' raised £483 and purchased 'the said abbey church with the bells etc. and the churchyard etc.' from the king 'to be used for ever there after by the bailiffs, burgesses and commanlty and other parishioners as their parish church and churchyard'.[2]

The close relationship between the parish and the town, exemplified by the town's purchase of the church, would continue well into the seventeenth century. The churchwardens regularly presented their accounts 'in the parishe churche . . . [to the] bailiffs of Tewkesbury and to other [of] the burgesies and commonaltie of the same towne then present'.[3] Further, the bailiffs' interest was more than *pro forma*; on

---

[1] D. Verey, *Gloucestershire: The Vale and the Forest of Dean,* 2nd edn. (1976; reprint, Harmondsworth, 1992), 357.

[2] Gloucestershire Record Office (hereafter GRO), Tewkesbury Borough Records (hereafter TBR) B2/1, 1. David Knowles declares that the survival of the 'whole fabric' of the church at Tewkesbury was particularly remarkable. At Bolton, Pershore and Malmesbury parishioners or patrons also purchased abbey churches for use by their parishes, but in each case the 'monastic portion had been shorn off', whereas at Tewkesbury it remained. This was contrary to the instructions given to the commissioners responsible for the dissolution, who were to pull down all such churches, as well as other monastic structures. D. Knowles, *The Religious Orders of England; The Tudor Age* (Cambridge, 1959), vol. 3, 384–6.

[3] See below, *passim.*

occasion they assumed responsibilities normally reserved for the churchwardens. In 1576 they financed alterations to the church house and sold church goods, depositing the proceeds in the town chest, rather than that of the parish. Three years later, church leads were used for gutters on the town's new boothall.[1]

The Churchwardens

The office of churchwarden, the premier position of lay leadership within the sixteenth-century English parish church, had evolved in a rather *ad hoc* fashion from the early thirteenth century.[2] At that time responsibility for the parish was officially divided between the rector and the parishioners with the rector having the care of the chancel while the parishioners were to maintain the nave and churchyard. Shortly thereafter, the parishioners were also given responsibility for providing a long list of ornaments, liturgical items and books. These obligations, however, were not combined with any rights; possession of church property or goods by parishioners was expressly forbidden. Nonetheless, a sense of corporate responsibility developed over the following three centuries in response to the obligations (both material and financial) imposed on parishioners by those in positions of authority. Also, beginning in the thirteenth century individuals were endowing prayers and other memorials for the dead with land and tenements, and since such gifts needed to be managed, parish representatives soon took on that role as well. Thus, parish communities gained a corporate identity and churchwardens' responsibilities grew to meet emerging needs, rather than as a result of either official sanction or encouragement.

In fact, surviving parish accounts show that as early as 1349 parishioners were filling a diverse set of financially based roles, and approximately a century later the term 'churchwarden' appeared in parish records. What were the obligations of early parish leaders? Churchwardens bought, sold and maintained church property, administered bequests, organized collections on feast days, and raised money to pay subsidies. They also financed repair work, purchased ornaments and liturgical books, and paid salaries. In addition, they sometimes maintained lights before images, brewed ale, traded cattle or bees, supervised major parish construction projects, looked after churchyards, and defended their parishes against negligent rectors. Long before 1571 when it was required by statute, churchwardens also represented their parishes in ecclesiastical visitations, reporting on both the moral transgressions of the laity and the physical condition of parish buildings.[3]

Those who held the office of churchwarden from earliest times to the Reformation generally came from the middle levels of society and were quite competent. The men and women chosen to lead Elizabethan and Jacobean parishes were the more prosperous and successful husbandmen, yeomen, artisans and merchants. From 1563 to 1624 the parish of Tewkesbury fits this pattern: the churchwardens were members of the town's ruling elite drawn mainly from successful merchants and leaders of craft guilds. However, Tewkesbury was atypical in that those parish leaders appear to have ranked as equals with the town's bailiffs. In most urban parishes, the position of churchwarden ranked below most of the officials of the town.

---

[1] GRO, TBR A1/1, ff. 11, 12v.

[2] For a more thorough discussion of the evolution of the office of churchwarden in the English parish church see B.A. Kumin, 'The Late-Medieval English Parish *c.* 1400–1560' (Ph.D. Thesis, University of Cambridge, 1992).

[3] R. H. Helmholz, *Roman Canon Law in Reformation England* (Cambridge, 1990), 106.

Churchwardens, nonetheless, provided the vital link between the state and ecclesiastical hierarchy, on the one hand, and the people in the parish, on the other. As John Craig has pointed out, 'Churchwardens stood in a position overlapped by two worlds'.[1] They were the stewards of the parish resources, but they were also responsible for implementing and enforcing official policy, both religious and social. They provided information to the authorities on a number of matters, ranging from lists of those receiving poor relief to the names of those who refused to receive Easter communion. The churchwardens were under oath to present all offenders. However, there has been much disagreement as to the reliability of these officials as agents of ecclesiastical policy, particularly with regard to reporting transgressors who ranked above them socially, or were their close friends or neighbours. If the churchwardens had some doubt as to whether or not an offence had been committed, they might have neglected to report it, or they might have reported it without naming those who were guilty. This happened frequently in the reporting of those who absented themselves from Gloucestershire parishes in the 1570s.[2] This tendency may have changed, however, following the revisions of the canons on 1604. Canon 115 protected churchwardens from defamation suits which might have arisen as a result of presentments brought against parishioners.[3]

Meanwhile, they may have been less reliable in their implementation of changing religious policy. While some churchwardens promptly introduced the prescribed changes to protestantism, such as lowering the altar area and replacing the altar with a table, or replacing all wall-paintings of images with scriptural passages, others did only the minimum. They might have purchased the requisite communion book and books of homilies, but no more.[4] Tewkesbury is an example of the minimalist approach to the introduction of protestantism. Nonetheless in 1563, the churchwardens identified prominent fellow-parishioners who had violated official religious policy, signalling their willingness to fulfill their sworn responsibility, at least to some extent.[5]

Certainly, the Tewkesbury churchwardens could not be faulted with regard to their other ongoing responsibility, which was to oversee the material needs of the parish. In particular, the maintenance of the fabric of the nave of the church was a substantial responsibility in the case of Tewkesbury Abbey. Other Elizabethan churchwardens may have used their limited funds to introduce protestantism more fully, but Tewkesbury gave first priority to their large and venerable building.[6] They repaired it and improved it. Most notably, they added a large new chancel window in the mid-1560s.[7]

A comparison of Tewkesbury's expenditures with those of the parish of St. Michael's in the nearby city of Gloucester sheds additional light on the pattern of

---

[1] J.S. Craig, 'Co-operation and initiatives: Elizabethan churchwardens and the parish accounts of Mildenhall', *Social History* 18 (1993), 359.

[2] GRO, Gloucester Diocesan Records (hereafter GDR) 44, *passim*.

[3] Helmholz, *Roman Canon Law*, 66, 107.

[4] For a more thorough discussion of the Reformation in Gloucestershire see Caroline Litzenberger, *The English Reformation and the Laity: Gloucestershire, 1540–1580* (Cambridge, forthcoming).

[5] GRO, GDR 20, 44.

[6] St. Michael's and St. Aldate's in Gloucester and the parishes of Dursley and Lechlade all spent substantial sums to enhance their protestant worship. They all whitewashed their walls to cover images of the saints, and St. Michael's and Lechlade both painted scriptural texts on the walls. They all purchased a large number of books: large bibles, the *Paraphrases* of Erasmus, psalters and extra communion books (that is, Books of Common Prayer). GRO P124 CW 2/4, *passim*; GRO P154/6 CW 1, *passim*; GRO P154/14 CW 1, *passim*; GRO P197 CW 2/1, *passim*.

[7] See below, pp. 10–12.

expenditure seen in the Tewkesbury churchwardens' accounts. For instance, during the period from 1563 to 1580 when Elizabethan protestantism was being introduced, 20% of St. Michael's expenses were for the accoutrements of worship, while during the same period Tewkesbury spent only the minimum required to obtain the mandatory Prayer Book and the Book of Homilies. Most of Tewkesbury's expenditure was, as noted above, for maintenance and improvement of the fabric of the parish. Further, the related patterns of revenues and expenses were much more erratic at Tewkesbury than at St. Michael's. At St. Michael's, the two aspects of the annual accounts appear to be related: when expenses increased either nominally or extraordinarily, revenues increased correspondingly. Such was not the case at Tewkesbury where there appears to be very little correlation between the two. Also, while both parishes relied on seat money and rental income as steady sources of revenue, additional sources of income at Tewkesbury seem to have been rather *ad hoc*. For instance, the pattern of church ales seems sporadic, and there were several years in which much of the revenue came from a few large (unexplained) donations from parishioners. The Tewkesbury accounts do not exhibit the pattern of introducing new rates or special collections such as 'Easter money' and then continuing them for several years, as is evident in those of St. Michael's. The size and diversity of the parish of Tewkesbury seem to have enabled the leadership there to respond to demands for additional funds in a less systematic manner than was feasible in smaller, more homogenous parishes. However, Tewkesbury's sluggishness in meeting the requirements of Elizabethan religious policy also eased the burden on parish finances.

The Reformation in Tewkesbury

The advent of protestantism in England elicited a chilly reception in Tewkesbury. Wills from the period 1541 to 1558 demonstrate a marked resistance to change, as testators continued to leave money for such traditional, pre-Reformation remembrances as lights before altars and provisions for prayers for the dead. Further, it appears that the parish leadership did not divest itself of the trappings of traditional worship during the reign of Edward VI, as the protestant bishop of Gloucester, John Hooper, had ordered. Rather, lay piety and traditional worship continued as long as possible according to customary practice. Apart from the use of the prescribed Book of Common Prayer in Edward VI's reign, traditional religion continued basically unchanged until the accession of Elizabeth in November 1558.[1]

Elizabeth's reign began with a loud crash, as the beautiful, lead-clad steeple which topped the tower fell on Easter Day 1559.[2] Whether this event was providential or not, the next fifteen years certainly give evidence of increasing religious discord. Parish dissension would crescendo to something of a climax by the mid-1570s. During the first few years of Elizabeth's reign, worship gradually returned to the minimalist conformity of the Edwardian years. In 1563 the churchwardens purchased the required Book of Homilies and Communion Book (or Prayer Book), and the latter was being used frequently enough to need re-gluing just two years later.[3] That same year, 1565, a number of prominent parishioners were presented for publicly demonstrating their displeasure with the pace or direction of religious change. Most

---

[1] The first Prayer Book was used from the summer of 1549 until it was replaced in the autumn of 1552. The latter was then used until shortly after Edward's death in July 1553.

[2] See below, p. 93.

[3] See below, pp. 1, 4.

notably, the churchwardens presented the town bailiffs and one of the other burgesses for walking 'with their cappes on ther heades at the tyme of the holy communion before the chauncell doore', that is, at the front of the nave where a door led into the chancel where the holy communion was being celebrated.[1]

The bailiffs and their fellow-burgess seem to have been objecting to protestant forms of worship, but others may have wanted more rather than less change. Further, the parish leadership itself may have been unsure of the ultimate doctrine and policies of the Elizabethan Church. The same presentments which reported the transgressions noted above also listed 'not defaced reliques', including a pax, crosses, candlesticks, censers, incense, a Mass book, processionals, and two 'clappers to go about with on Good Friday', all items which should have been destroyed or at least sold following the return to protestantism under Elizabeth.[2]

Parish expenditure did nothing to dissuade those who preferred the Old Religion from their hopes for a return to catholicism. While other parishes were spending their revenues on implementing Elizabethan protestantism, Tewkesbury was not. True, the requisite books and surplices were being purchased, used and mended, and both the walls and the windows were being whitewashed to cover offending images, but no church goods were being sold, the altar area was not revamped, and most of the parish funds were being spent on either maintenance or improvements to parish buildings, rather than on liturgical change.[3] If religious change was indeed coming to Tewkesbury, it was only coming slowly and hesitantly.

In the mid-1570s there was still less rather than more conformity in Tewkesbury. A metropolitan visitation to the diocese of Gloucester was held in 1576, and Tewkesbury was found wanting. A chalice rather than the requisite communion cup was still being used, and the parish lacked an English Bible. In addition, several individuals were still clinging openly to the Old Religion. One was accused of using a rosary, while it was alleged that another 'useth a papist primer in churche'. Furthermore, a number of parishioners had not received Easter communion as was required.[4] A year later the parish still had a tall candlestick, 'one riche coape, . . . vij albes', and 'a pece of imagerye', possibly a statue of St. Mary. Further, they had just sold a piece of velvet, some 'fryng and white sylke', old vestments and pieces of vestments, and 'vij stepes of steyer', probably the stairs to the rood loft which would have been free-standing at Tewkesbury because of the distance between the pillars at the entrance to the chancel.[5] The rood loft (and in this case presumably the stairs, as well) had been ordered removed early in Elizabeth's reign.

Things had not changed much even eight years later. An inventory presented to diocesan visitors on 4 May 1585 lists 'the best coope of tynsell with redd roses', 'iij Awbes of lynnen', 'one Amyce', 'the best pawll for the communyon boorde', one other payll of redd and grene satten with a fringe', 'one other of checker worcke', 'a table clothe with a frynge of golde', 'a black pawll of velvytt', and cushions of velvet and satin.[6] Of those items, the use of the cope, albs and amice had been prohibited, and they ought to have been destroyed no later than 1576. The various palls and tablecloths, on the other hand, conformed to the requirement of an attractively covered communion table replacing the pre-Reformation altar in the Elizabethan church. Thus as late as twenty-five years into Elizabeth's reign, the parish of Tewkesbury was still reluctant to shed all vestiges of Catholic worship, although they were probably no longer using the illicit items, and were abiding by some aspects of

---

[1] GRO, GDR 20, 44.
[2] GRO, GDR 20, 44–45.
[3] See below, *passim*.

[4] GRO, GDR 40, f. 47.
[5] See below, pp. 35–36, 40
[6] See below, p. 58.

official religious policy. Tewkesbury's response to official religious policy was typical of a number of Gloucestershire churches, and illustrates one of the many manifestations of reluctant, conservative conformity to Elizabethan protestantism which could be found in the late-sixteenth century. Reluctant and minimal conformity was, however, just one point among many along the spectrum of local responses to the established church.

Customs and Culture in Tewkesbury

The customs and culture of Elizabethan and Jacobean Tewkesbury also suggest the continuation of traditional practices. Under pressure from the 'hotter sort of protestants', variously referred to as the godly and as Puritans, municipal authorities across much of England had begun to curtail dramatic presentations during Elizabeth's reign.[1] Not so in Tewkesbury. There the parish 'players gere' continued to be hired out and refurbished right through to the end of Elizabeth's reign. It was usually rented to parishioners and the plays were often performed in the parish church. The costumes were loaned frequently in the 1570s, and were even rented out twice during 1576, the very year of the archiepiscopal visitation. At that time the collection included 'five players gownes, 4 jackets, 4 beardes, [and] twoo heades'.[2] Over the next eight years it was refurbished and augmented to include eight gowns, seven jerkins, four caps of green silk, eight 'heades of heare for the apostles', ten beards, a 'thunder heade', a 'face or vysor for the devyll', and 'Christes garments' made from six sheepskins. Clearly, this 'players gere' was intended for use in religious plays, the type of drama which most upset the godly. The costumes and props were used, maintained and expanded at least into the early 1600s, when a series of three plays was performed in the church to raise money for a stone battlement to replace the steeple which had fallen on Easter Day 1559.[3] References to the 'players gere' disappear from the Tewkesbury churchwardens' accounts after 1601, probably as a result of the prohibition in the canons of 1603.

Another distinctive local custom, but one with fewer obvious religious overtones, was the churchwardens' control of the assignment of seats in Tewkesbury parish church. Payment for a 'rome' in a pew appears to have been made only when the place was first assigned, and there seems to have been an informal custom of inheritance whereby the heir or heirs had first claim to the seat previously held by their surviving parent. By a similar procedure permission was occasionally granted to an individual to construct his own pew in return for a fee several times larger than that paid for pre-existing seats.[4] Each year a few people asked for seats and paid the fee or

[1] E.K. Chambers, *The Elizabethan Stage* (Oxford, 1923), vol. 1, 278–88; H.C. Gardiner, *Mysteries End: An investigation of the last days of the medieval religious stage* (New Haven, CT, 1946), 74–75, 83–86. However, travelling companies of players were quite popular throughout the realm at least through to the end of Elizabeth's reign, and the corporation records give evidence of play productions in Gloucester as late as 1640/1. Chambers, *The Elizabethan Stage*, 331–36; *Records of Early English Drama: Cumberland, Westmorland, Gloucestershire*, eds. A. Douglas and P. Greenfield (Toronto, Buffalo and London, 1986), 253, in which all entries referring to players in the Tewkesbury churchwardens' accounts are also printed and discussed.

[2] See below, pp. 15, 26, 36, 37, 40, 43.

[3] See below, pp. 48, 49, 53, 54, 56, 93, 94. The play productions and associated festivities suffered a huge net loss of over £21, below p. 94.

[4] See below, pp. 3–44 *passim*. Alfred Heales, the noted authority on pew seating customs and laws, describes a similar procedure in the parish of Ludlow as 'very curious and probably unique'. A. Heales, *The History and law of church seats or pews, Book I – History* (London, 1872), 84.

rent, often specifying with whom they wished to sit. However, in 1576, many parishioners relinquished their old places and sought 'roomes' in the new pews constructed just after the town received its new charter.[1] When such a request for a change in seat assignment was granted, the individual or couple made a new payment and the churchwardens duly noted the relinquishing of the old seat. When seats were reassigned, the particular positions occupied by the town oligarchy were partially revealed by the language used in their requests for seats. For instance, we know that in 1576 the elite of the parish were seated in the foremost pews, while those who probably ranked just below them socially requested the seats just vacated by their betters. In 1595 row and seat numbers were introduced into the entries for pew rentals, making seating patterns self-evident.[2]

Status was not the only factor which determined where people sat. Gender could also be a factor. In most sixteenth and early-seventeenth century English parishes women and men occupied separate areas of the church, typically but not always with the women on the north side and the men on the south. Further, unmarried women usually sat in a separate area from the married women and widows, while young men normally sat at the rear of the church. However, in Tewkesbury there were numerous exceptions to that pattern, as husbands and wives sometimes sat together, and sometimes husbands requested that their wives be placed in a pew with a particular older male parishioner. Gender-segregated seating does not appear to have been a conscious policy in Tewkesbury much before 1595. But by that time it appears that women were sitting separate from men, and that the wives' seats were assigned to them through their husbands. The churchwardens declared

> That uppon decease of any wife in the towne it shalbe in the churchwardens by consent of the bailiffs (if nede so requier) to place any other woman in the same rome fit for that place there to keepe suche rome upon a quarteres rent to the churche until the husband of the decessed woman shall mary againe, and then she to take suche place as in meane tyme no husband to challenge the place.[3]

At that point Tewkesbury was simply following the pattern found elsewhere in England. As with religious change, however, they had only slowly conformed to those practices.

The Accounts

The Tewkesbury churchwardens' accounts for the years 1563 to 1624 are in reasonably good condition. They are bound in a long narrow book with pages measuring approximately four inches in width and fifteen and a half inches in length. A few pages show some evidence of water damage, and thousands of thumbs and fingers grasping the lower right corners of pages to turn them have virtually obliterated the amounts for some entries. However, most of the volume is quite legible. The first six pages have been designated as pages i–vi, and contain brief notes in an eighteenth-century hand concerning the volume's contents and significant events from the period covered by the accounts. They are not included in this edition. Churchwardens' accounts from 1563 into the eighteenth century occupy most of the

---

[1] See below, pp. 35–37. James Bennett, *The History of Tewkesbury* (1830; reprint, Gloucester, 1976), 42–43.

[2] See below, p. 76.

[3] See below, p. 75.

remainder of the book with only a few missing years. In particular, for the period from 1563 to 1624, the accounts for 1610 and 1611 are missing. Also included in the volume are two copies of the will of Mr. Cooke, a prominent benefactor of the church. After p 472 the pagination is mixed with occasional foliation for approximately fifty pages. The rest of the volume runs for thirty-three pages, beginning at the back of book (upside down), and includes the length and weight of each of eight bell ropes in 1703, minutes from some parish meetings from 1638 and later, and additional eighteenth-century churchwardens' accounts.

The accounts are generally divided into separate sections for revenues and expenses for the term of each pair of churchwardens (usually but not always approximately one year). Sources of revenue and objects of expenditure are generally specified. Revenues include rents of houses, land and pews, payments for burials and the ringing of bells, and proceeds from church ales and the sale of church goods. Expenses cover maintenance of the fabric of the parish, major renovations to parish buildings, purchase of the accoutrements of worship (whether catholic or protestant), and payments relating to diocesan administration.

Editorial Conventions

All accounts and attendant narrative have been transcribed in full and *verbatim*, with the following exceptions. The words 'Item pd' which precede every entry for expenses have been omitted. Most abbreviations have been expanded, and spelling has not been modernized except for the use of i or j, u or v and use of initial capital letters. Amounts, which appear in the accounts in lower-case Roman numerals with superscript designations of pounds, shillings and pence, appear here as Arabic numerals with column headings for pounds, shillings and pence. Incomplete entries have been indicated by [ ] illegible portions of text by [...] cancellations by ⟨ ⟩ and illegible cancellations by ⟨...⟩. During the period covered by these accounts the calendar year began on 25 March. To prevent confusion with modern convention, dates falling between 1 January and 24 March are given with both relevant years (for example, 2 February 1611[/2]).

Caroline Litzenberger
University of West Virginia
August 1994

GLOSSARY

The aim of the glossary is to render the text accessible to the general reader without the need for constant consultation of works of reference. It therefore includes technical or archaic terms deemed to be beyond, or on the verge of, the range of current usage.

The decision to present the text in its original form adds a complication: at this period spelling was phonetic; indeed, the concept that there is a correct way to spell words only developed with the spread of literacy and did not obtain general currency until the use of dictionaries in schools became widespread in the nineteenth century. In this text, therefore, many words appear in unusual forms, sometimes compounded by the broader speech of local dialect. Unfamiliar spellings of some common words have been included e.g. *myese* (mice), but for reasons of space most have not; the reader is therefore required to identify (e.g.) *ynch* (inch), *ierne* (iron), *ile* or *yell* (aisle) and many others.

Where the combined resources of the editor, general editor and experts generous with their special knowledge have been insufficient to establish a meaning with reasonable certainty, the strength of editorial conviction concerning the explanation offered may be gauged by the use of '*perhaps*', '*presumably*' or '*probably*'.

albe	alb: a long vestment of white linen, worn girdled, with long close sleeves.
amyce	amice: a broad oblong piece of linen worn on the shoulders beneath the alb with one edge surrounding the neck like a collar.
baldericke	baldric: the strap by which the bell-clapper was hung. *Also* baldrick, baldricke, baldrigg, baldryck, baldryke, baldwricke, ballride, ballwrick, ballwricke, ballwryck, balricke, balrige, balrigge, balrudge, balwrick, balwricke, balwrike, balwrycke, baudericke, baudricke, bauldericke, bawdericke, bawdrick, bawdricke, bawdrycke, bawlricke, bawlrycke, bawlryge, buldricke.
beare	bier: the moveable stand on which a corpse is placed before burial. *Also*, bere, beere.
beasome	besom: a broom, usually made of a bunch of twigs bound together around a handle. *Also*, beassome, beesom, beesome, beessome, beosome, besomme, bysome.
bord clothe	tablecloth.
bord naill	a common type of nail used for boards or planks. *Also*, bord nayle, bordnayle.
borden	burden: a 'load' considered as a measure of quantity for dry goods.

xv

bowble	bow bell: *possibly* the sanctus bell, situated between the chancel and the nave and not part of the main peal.
bowster	bolster: the horizontal member from which a bell is hung.
braggette	bracket.
bryeringe	briering, briaring: protecting newly planted trees, etc. with dead thorn bushes. *Also*, bryringe and thorneing.
buckerine	buckram.
buttes	butts: targets for archery practice. The duty of maintenance probably belonged to the constable.
caliver	a light kind of musket introduced in the 16th century.
casement	a window frame.
chusshinge	cushion. *Also*, cussion, cwisshin, cwosshyn.
corslette	corslet: a garment or item of body armour (usually tight-fitting) covering the torso but not the limbs.
coule	cowl: a garment with a hood or a cloak, in either case covering the head and shoulders and being without sleeves.
cradle	a frame in which to carry glass.
creaste	crest: tiles shaped to cover the crest or ridge of a roof or to form the bottom of a gutter. *Also*, cresse, creste.
dex, dexte	desk: sloped reading stand without legs; it rested on a table or pulpit.
diaper	a linen fabric woven in a small simple pattern consisting of lines crossing diamondwise.
dogge	dog: *possibly* a mechanical device having a projection or tooth which can act as a brake; *perhaps* used for the clock chimes.
dyece	dais: the raised platform on which the lectern holding the Bible is located.
ell	measure of length, 45 inches.
eves bords	eaves boards: boards at the edge of the roof which tilted the slates in order to shed water.
fant, faunt	font.
fore bell	*possibly* the foremost bell of the peal, i.e. the treble, usually termed the 'little bell'.
frogge locke	*possibly* a suspended or detachable lock, a padlock (cf. horse lock).
gatt, gatte	gate.
gigg	gig: device to secure the church gate.
grate	*presumably* a form of cattle grid. The church grate was situated close to the churchyard gate, and comprised metal bars set at or below ground level supported on timber. There are regular payments for cleaning and emptying it and in 1609 it was re-dug (p. 118).
gret bell	great bell: the tenor. The other three bells in the peal are usually termed the 'little bell' (i.e. the treble), the '2 bell' and the '3 bell'.
gudgeon	pivot, usually of metal, fixed on or placed into the end of a beam spindle, and on which a wheel turns or a bell swings. *Also*, gudgin, gugeon.
gues boord	*possibly* eavesboard.
gymmowes	gimmels: hinges.
gyste	joist.
hach nayles	hatch nails: door nails. *Also*, hatch nayle, hatche nayle.

hacke	*probably*, hatch.
halior	halyard: a rope or tackle used to raise or lower a bell. *Also*, hallier, hallior.
harntz	*probably*, harness, i.e. armour.
haire	hair lime: a kind of wall plaster made by adding hair to lime to bind the mixture closely together. *Also,* heaire, hear lyme, hear, heare lyme, heer, heer lyme, heere, heir, heire, her lyme, here lyme, here lyem, here, herlyme, herre.
hoges heed	hogshead: a large cask for liquids, etc. of a particular capacity which varied according to the contents and locality. *Also*, hogges heade, hoggesheade.
holland	holland cloth: a fine quality linen.
honey bage	honey bag: for making baldrics.
horsse lock	horse lock: padlock.
humely booke	homily Book. *Also*, nomyly booke.
jerkine	jerkin: a garment for the upper part of the body; a close-fitting jacket, jersey or short coat, often made of leather. *Also*, jirkyn.
kipe	the hide of a young animal, such as a calf or lamb. *Also*, kippe skine.
lathe nayles	lathe nails: nails used in roofing.
leker	liquor: lubricant for the bells. *Also*, liccor, licker, licor, licour, liquar, liquor, lucker, lycar, lycare, lycer, lycker, lycor, lycouer, lycour, lycoure, lyker.
little bell	the treble, *possibly* otherwise known as the 'fore bell'. It was recast at Worcester *c.* 1589.
maille	maul: a massive hammer. *Also*, male, malle, mayle.
munnelle	mullion: a vertical bar dividing the lights in a window. *Also*, muniall, monial.
murren	morion: a kind of helmet without a visor worn by soldiers in the 16th and 17th centuries.
myese	mice.
pargetinge	plastering. *Also*, parjetinge, parjettinge.
pargyter	plasterer. *Also*, pargytter, parjeter.
pareter	apparitor: official of the consistory court. *Also*, pariter, paritor, parretter, parriter, parritor.
pecing	piecing. *Also*, pecyng, peecing, pesyng.
pecke	peck: a measure of capacity for dry goods (the fourth part of a bushel or 2 gallons); a vessel used as a peck measure.
Pentecost Money	an offering made on Pentecost (or Whitsunday) to the cathedral. *Also*, Penticoste mone, Penticoste moneye, Penticoste monie, Pentycosse mony, Pentycost money, Pentycoste, Pentycote mone, smoke sylver, and *perhaps* sinage money.
pentise	penthouse: a small structure such as a porch or outhouse attached to the wall of a building.
peyse	peise: weight (for the clock).
picke	pyx: a vessel to hold the reserved sacrament.
planckinge stone	flat slab of stone.
plume house	building for storing or casting lead (*plumbum*), *perhaps* the building known earlier as the trasyng house (p. 11).
potle	pottle: a half gallon pot or measure for liquids. *Also*, Pottell.
prooader	*Probably* powder.

quarell	quarrel: stone obtained from a quarry. *Also*, quarrell.
quarell glass	diamond-shaped panes which made up stained glass windows.
quicke	quick: living plants.
quicksett	quickset: live slips of cuttings of plants set in the ground to grow, especially those of which hedges are made.
quininge	quoining: wedging or securing masonry. *Also*, quyninge.
quorum nomina	A form of writ used to collect unpaid taxes.
raffle money	*Possibly* revel money: *perhaps* for refreshments for workmen or *possibly* relating to a play.
rent bords	split boards.
ridle	riddle: a coarse-meshed sieve used for separating sand from gravel. *Also*, ryeng seve.
sancte bell	sanctus bell: bell rung at the elevation of the Host during the Mass. *Also*, sanctes, sanctus, saunce bell.
sarchand	sergeant.
sauter	psalter. *Also*, sawtere.
sclaitt	slate. *Also*, sclate, sclatte, sklat, sklatt, slatt.
seameinge	attaching sheets (of lead) by means of seams. *Also*, seamige, seaming, seaminge, seming.
shide	a piece of wood split off from timber. *Also*, shide, shids, shyd, shyde.
shotinge	shutting: splicing or welding two parts together. *Also*, shottyng, shutting, shuttinge.
shreedes	shreds, *possibly* to protect roof timber from the lead; moss was more often used for this purpose.
shutt	shut: a splice joining two pieces of rope.
simoing	cementing: *Also*, simoning.
sinage money	*possibly* synodals; *perhaps* the regular payment usually termed 'Pentecost Money'.
slipe	*probably*, slip: a long, narrow and relatively thin piece or strip of some material.
smoke sylver	see Pentecost Money.
soalderinge	soldering. *Also*, soderinge, soldringe, souderinge.
soder	solder. *Also*, souder, soulder, sowder.
sommer	summer pole: a pole decked with flowers and erected during a spring or summer festival; Maypole.
speek nayles	spikes: large long nails. *Also*, speek nailles, speekes, speke nayle, spicke, spyck naille.
spicing	splicing. *Also*, spicinge, spysing, spyce.
starre	a star hung in the church during Epiphany representing the star which drew the Magi to Bethlehem.
stonne lyme	stone-lime: lime made from limestone (as distinguished from chalk-lime).
strickle	A straight piece of wood with which to level or smooth the surface of a measure of grain or of something which is being cast or moulded.
stryck	strike: a measure of a quantity of grain or dry goods (usually 2 bushels). *Also*, strycke, stryke.
sirplece	surplice. *Also*, sirples, surpelesse, surples, surplesse, surplessis, surplesys, surplice, surplis, surplisse, surplusse, surplyce, syrplysse.
sutyng	sorting.

taske	tax.
thorneing	see bryeringe. *Also*, thorneinge.
tracyng howse	tracing-house: a house in which the plans of a building are traced. *Also*, trasyng howse. *Possibly* later called the plume house.
tresselles	trestles. *Also*, trisell.
tunbrell	*possibly* tumbrell: a cucking stool, a device for punishing scolds by ducking them in water.
vase	*probably*, an architectural ornament having the shape of a vase.
walplett	Wallplate: horizontal timber laid along the top of a wall to which rafters are joined.
whetlether	whiteleather: leather of a white or light colour. *Also*, whit leather, whit lether, white leather, white lether, whitlether, whitt leather, whytleather, whytleather, whytlether, whitlyme.
whiteinge	whitewashing. *Also*, whitinge, whitlyminge, whytlymyng, lyming, lyminge.
whoope	hoop: a circular band of metal, wood or other still material. *Also*, whope.
whop	hoop: a measure of grain or dry goods of varying capacity, depending on locality.
wyndles	windlass.
yat	gate. *Also*, yate, yatt, yatte, yeatte.

ACKOWLEDGEMENTS

I am indebted to a number of institutions and individuals for their support of the transcription of these churchwardens' accounts for the parish of Tewkesbury. First, I would like to thank the managers of the Archbishop Cranmer Fund for their financial support. For permission to publish the accounts I thank the Vicar and P.C.C. of Tewkesbury. In addition, this work could not have been accomplished without the gracious and knowledgeable assistance of the staff of the Gloucestershire Record Office, in particular Kate Haslem, and the other members of the Search Room staff. And finally, I am most indebted to David Smith, Honorary Secretary of the Bristol and Gloucestershire Archaeological Society, as well as County Archivist. He has provided invaluable guidance and encouragement throughout this project.

Caroline Litzenberger
University of West Virginia
August 1994

CHURCHWARDENS OF TEWKESBURY 1563–1624

1563–64	John Hewes	Edward Leight
1564–65	Humfrey Richardes	Thomas Grymer
1565–66	Giles Toney	Alexander Greene
1566–67	Nicholas Cleveley	James Phelpes
1567–68	Robert Smythe	Henry Dowle
1568–69	Roger Gilbert	John Wilkes
1569–70	Roger Turbell	John Leight
1570–72	Richard Rudgedale	Thomas Portar
1572–74	John Millington	Robert Davis
1574–75	William Leight	Edward Baston
1575–76	William Field	Thomas Malliard, Sr.
1576–77	Charles Stratford	William Johnsons
1577–78	John Bubbe	Richard Field
1578–80	Thomas Donne	Richard Rogers
1580–83	George Freebanck	Thomas Millichep
1583–84	Thomas Hilley	John Manne
1584–85	William Toney	Lawrence Moone
1585–89	John Field	George Morrey
1589–90	James Greene	Thomas Cowles
1590–92	William Cleveley	Thomas Sclicer
1592–94	William Phelpes	William Dunne (dec'd)
1594–96	William Gilbert	John Skullow
1596–99	Robert Jeynes	John Tommes
1599–1603	John Cooke	Thomas Deacons
1603–04	Frances Pace	John Raye
1604–07	William Hytches	Richard Bradford
1607–09	George Morrey	Thomas Gelfe
1609–10	William Cowles	Robert Jennings (dec'd)
1610–11	[accounts missing]	
1611–15	Thomas Hoare	William Dixon
1615–18	William Whitledge	Kenelme Merson
1618–22	Edward Millichep	Thomas Hale
1622–23	Edward Phelpes	Richard Mynce
1623–24	Michael Millington	William Wilson

Tewkesbury Churchwardens' Accounts 1563–1624

[Gloucestershire Record Office P329 CW 2/1]

1 **The true & just accompte of the aforesayd John Hewes & Edward Leyte of all souche somes of money as they have payd & layde forthe for the repayre & amending of the sayd churche of Tewkesbury & other thinges to the same churche aperteynynge, duryng the tyme of theyre offyce, 1563.**

	£	s	d
for the weying of the lead in the vestry to twoo men			8
to the somner for Pentecost money		3	6
for paper			1
to the somner at the archedeakons visitation			3
for ⟨a boke⟩ our byll of presentment			8
to Clemens for clensing the gutters in the over partes of the churche			8
for nayles			2
for the making of a staple			1
for a bell rope		5	1
for besoms to swepe the churche			1
for halfe a hyde of whytlether			18
for the making of 3 ierne pynnes			1
to the bysshopes clarke for makyng our byll of presentment & for the receipt of the same byll			17
the somner at the bysshopes visitation			6
for the makyng of the bawdrickes and dressing of the belles to John Cole		10	5
for the makyng of a copye of a commysion			2
for paper			1
for the mending of the frame of the sancte bell			12
for lathe nayles			4
for twoo bondell of lethe			6
for twoo sclatters for a dayes worke			20
more for besoms			1
for the mending of a dore			2
for this Regester boke		2	–
to Richard Rudgedale for an humely booke		2	10
for a boke of preyers for the plague			3
for the makyng of the eye of the clapper of the greate bell			[...]
for apece of lether for the clocke			4
for a roppe for the clocke		8	3
for the taske of the halfe acre of medow that lyethe in Aven hamm & perteynethe to the church			[...]
and the somner when he had the byll of names of all the howseholders within the town			[...]
more [for] besoms			[...]
for the mending of the ierne [...] that hange the greate bell			[...]

1

2 at Mr Chauncelors visitacyon to the somner & for our byll		10
for hanging of the greate bell and for nayles		12
for making of a bawdericke and for wyer for the clocke to John Coole		4
to Jerom for shottyng of the great bell clapper	2	–
to John Coole for the ringing of the bell	13	4
more for besoms		1
to John Wynall for a communyon booke	3	–
more to Clemens for clensing the gutters		8
to John Rekes for the mending of the locke and polly for the clocke		20
to Rekes for his workemanship in bracyng of the greate bell		3
for nayles for the churche dore		1
for a new key for the greate bell		7
to twoo sclatters for twoo dayes work & a halfe upon the churche	3	6
for lathe nayles		2
for three hundred of pynnes		3
for a loade of sclatte	7	4
for a barell of lyme		14
for the carieng of the barell to churche		1
for the leyng in of a rafter		3
for three hundred of lathe nayles		6
for twoo bondell of lathe		6
for nine hundred of pynnes		9
for caryeng of water to make morter		⟨...⟩
to twoo sclatters for four dayes worke & a halfe	6	–
to twoo sclatters for 5 dayes work	6	8
for seven hundred of lathe nayles		14
for four bondell of lathe		12
for 800 pynnes		8
for mending of the churche dore locke		2
to Mr Baylyffes	5	–
for the mending of the churche grate & caryeng awey of the donge there		4½
for clensing of the gutters after the sclatters		1
for Pentecost money this yere	3	6
for the wryting of this boke		12
for the wasshyng of the churche clothes		8
Summa totallis	5 5	11

And so the sayd John Hewes & Edward Leyte remayne indetted to the churche £4 16s 11d over & above the debtes or old arrereges.

3   And so there receyte dothe excede the some of theyre charge in stocke £4 16s 11d whiche they have delyverd unto Thomas Downebell & George Morey baylyffes then in the presence of the whoale parysshe & thereof the sayd churchemen John Hewes & Edward Leyte do stand acquyted & dyscharged.

[Signed] Thomas Downbell   Georg Morrey

Md That the sayd churche wardens dyd not accompte for the whoale arereges lefte behynd but onely for the arereges of William Reade, Arm. & John Butler as in the boke of the last accompte wrytten with Mr Pertes hand it doth appere. So that the resydew of the arereges it yet not accompted for are under wrytten & to be chargyd upon Humphrey Richarde & Thomas Grymer new electyd churche wardens as folowithe.

	£	s	d
Upon James Chester of Brystoll for one tonn of lead yet behynd	7	–	–
William Coole for certen money taken forthe of the stocke of the churche, as apperythe in the papers of the old accompt	12	50	–
by churchwardens & charges in the next accompte et debit[1]	9	–	–
Julian Wye for her arereges as in particulers apperythe		31	8
Richard Hawlye for the buryall of hys mother		6	8
Upon John Butler & Thomas Godwyn for the lead money recevyd of Sir Thomas Russell, knyght	10	10	–
Upon Alexander Browne for his uncles John Rogers legacies to be paid in 5 years, the first payment to begynn at Mychaelmas nexte in the yere of our Lord 1564	5	–	–
The wyfe of Thomas Alen deceassed for the legacyes of her husband		3	4

Md Delyveryd unto Humfrey Richardes & Thomas Grymer in stocke of money £4 16s 10 [...] charged in next yeres accompte.

4   [ ]

5   **Here folowithe the true & juste accompte of Humfrey Richardes & Thomas Grymer churche wardens of Tewkesbury for one whole yere & more that is to sey from the 16 daye of Aprell in the yere of our Lord 1564 unto the 30 daye of May in the yere of our Lord 1565 Then made & geven up in the parishe churche of Tewkesbury foresaid unto Henry Grene & Alexander Geste then baylyffes of the same towne & also to other the burgesies & communaltie of the same towne then presente.**

Arereges as yn the fote of the last yeres accompte apperithe   33   11   8

First a true & presette note of all somes of money as the above namyd Humfrey Richardes & Thomas Grymer have recevyd to the use of the same churche of Tewkesbury during the tyme of theire offyce.

	£	s	d
in the churche stocke in redye money	4	16	1
of Mr Cole at sondry tymes	3	–	–
of Mastres Smythe for the rent of halfe an acre of grasse in Aven hamm		3	4
of Kenelme Cotterell for a roume yn a seate for his wife			20
of Thomas Hutchins & Richard Bubbe for a seate			12
of George Holland for a place to sette a seate upon		2	4
of Humfrey Brushe for a seate for hym & his wyfe			12
of Humfrey Richardes for his roume yn a seate that was John Gases			20
of William Hyll for a roume yn a seate for his wife			20
of Henry Poller for a roume yn a seate for his wyfe			20
of John Hiche for a roume in a seate for his wyfe			20
of Roger Malyard for a roume yn a seate for his wife			16
of John Watson for a seate for hym & his wyfe		2	–
of Humfrey Hurste for a seate for hym & his wyfe		2	–
of Richard Mathew for the rent of his howse			30
of Mr Perte for ierne being halfe a hundred lacking seven pounds	2	4	–
Summa totallis of the charge with the foresaid arrerages	44	3	6

6   Here folowithe a true & presette note of all souche somes of money as the afore namyd Humfrey Richardes & Thomas Grymer have payd for the repayring & amending of the sayd parishe churche of Tewkesbury & other thinges belonging unto the same churche in the tyme of theire office.

---

1   Later insertion. Above the figure of £9 is 60s in the same hand.

for the weyeng of the lead in the vestry to twoo men			8
for a rope for the lyttle bell			3
for mending of the peyse of the clocke			1
for lycouer for the belles			2
for besoms for the churche			1
to John Cole for mending of a bawdricke			2
to Mr Downebell for the making of inventories of the churche goodes		2	–
for twoo psalter bokes for the churche		2	8
to Jeromm for mending of forebell clapper		2	8
for subsyde money			2½
for whitlether to make a bawdricke			3
for the making of the bawdricke			2
to Edward Jeromm for mending of the clocke & for nayles			6
for wyer for the clocke			1½
paid at Gloucester when we putte up our byll of presentment for expences			8
paid at Cheltenham for expences at that visitacyon			8
to John Cole for the ringing of the bell & keping of the clocke		6	8
for besoms for to swepe the churche			1
for lycouer for the belles			2
to Henry Smythe for the mending of twoo clappers that were broken		5	2
to Robert Joyner for mending of the whele of the greate bell			2
to Mr Morey for 27 pounds of ierne to mend the clappers withall		3	4
to the plomer for 9 dayes worke for him & his man at 2s 4d the daye		21	–
to hym for seven skore & syxe poundes of soulder at 10d the pounde	6	– 20	
for 1 pounds of rosen for the plomer			2
to Jeromm for making hundred lead nayles			3
to Clemens for clensing the stayers of the steple & the leades			11
to John Rekes for the braseing of the greate bell & of third bell			11
for the making of the nayles for the same			3
to Grettane for 6 dayes paving in the churche		4	–
for the glewing of the communyon boke			3
for lycouer for the belles			1
for besoms to swepe the churche			2
for the presenting of our boke at Gloucester			8
for making of a seate in the nether end of the churche & for mending of the belowes of the organs & for nayles for the same		3	6
to Henry Fylde for a hyde of whitlether		2	–
to Henry Smythe for making of hundred lead nayles			2
to John Smythe for the making of a locke & a keye & a bolte for a dore in the quyre			8
to Pers for mending of a locke & a key dore that goithe in to the steple			2
to John Cole for the ringing of the bell & keping of the clocke		6	8
to Clemens for clensing of the gutters			6
for smoke sylver		3	9
for the writing of this boke			16

(7 appears in the left margin beside "to John Rekes for the braseing of the greate bell & of third bell")

Summa totallis of alowances	9	16	–
& they do owe	34	7	11

Of the which

James Chester of Bristow merchante for his arrerages for the price of one tonne of lead yet not payd as aperithe yn the fote of the laste accompte	7	–	–

William Cole for certen moneye taken oute of the churche stocke over
    & besydes 60s payd this yere to the churche ⟨men⟩ wardens to the
    use of the churche as yn the fote of the laste accompte aperithe for
    his arreregis yet behynde unpayd   9   –   –
    (Whereof receved £5 by A Grene & G Toney so remayne Nicholas
    Cleveley £4 James Phelps Nichols Grenewood)
Richard Hyll in the right of Gylyan his wyfe executrix of the last will
    & testament of Gyles Wye for her arrerages as yn the fote of the
    laste accompte apperithe   31 [...]

8   Richard Hareley for the buryall of his mother as yn the laste accompte
    for his arrerages   6   8
Brydgette Rogers alias Smythe for the legacie of John Rogers hir late
    husband to be payd at 20s by yere for fyve yeres the firste payment
    to have byn begonn at Michaelmas 1564 whiche ys allegyd by her
    that Alexander Brownyng shuld paye for her arrerages as yn the
    laste accompte   5   –   –
    (too yeres past unpaid & for rest at £5)
John Butler & Thomas Godwyn late baylyffes for the price of certen
    leade receved of Sir Thomas Russell knyghte for theire arrerages
    as yn the last accompte   10   10   –
The wyfe of Thomas Alen for the legacies of her husband bequethid
    unto the churche as yn the last accompte for her arreregys   3   4
The sayd churche wardens for theire proper arrerages yet behynde
    unpayd with 4d receved of Alexander Dryver for the rent of a
    garden at Easter 1565   16   7
    (Which 16s 7d is delyveryd over to the new churchwardens to be
    unswered & charged to them upon theyre nexte accompte and be
    here undersigned elected & appointed

Alexander Grene [&] Gyles Toney – churchwardens

The weyghte of lead to them delyverd is a tonn & a halfe eyghte hundred & 14 pounds

The bras where of parte is gylte is halfe a hundred poundes

9   **Here folowethe the true & juste acompte of Gyles Toney & Alexander Grene churchwardens of the parishe churche of Tewkesbury for one yere That is to sey from the 20 daye of Maye in the yere of our Lord 1565 unto the 5 daye of Maye yn the yere of our Lord 1566 Then made & geven up in the parishe churche of Tewkesbury foresayd unto Thomas Ricardes & Robert Grene then baylyffes of the same towne of Tewkesbury and also to other of the burgesies & comynaltie of the sayd towne then present**

Arrerages as yn the fote of the last accompte yt dothe appere   34   7   11

First a note of all souche somes of money as as the above namyd Gyles Toney & Alexander [Grene] have recevyed to the use of the same churche of Tewkesbury duryng the tyme of theire office

	£	s	d
of Mr Baylyffes in the presence of the parishners at our election		16	7
of Mr Bayly Grene in the presence of Mr Downebell Mr Wyat & Mr Dogmore	5	–	–
of Mr Cole	4	–	–
of John Rekes & Thomas Mondy for a seate in Seyncte Nicholas Chapell			20

of Wyll Tyrret for a seate yn the same chapell		20
for standinges in the churche howse upon the feyer daye	5	–
of Thomas Dower for a place for his wyfe in a seate		12
more of Mr Bayly Grene	40	–
more of Mr Cole	20	–
of Richard Mathew for the rent of his howse in the hie strete	15	–
of Mastres Smythe for the rent of an halfe acre in Aven hamm	3	4
of Thomas Rudgedale for asete in the churche that was Antony Morrys	2	8
of Henry Poller for a place for his ⟨wyfe⟩ selfe yn a sete		12
of James Phelpes for 26lb of olde irone	2	3
of John Syrrell for a place in a seate that was Fraunces Bestes		16
of John Hewes for aplace in a seate that was John Fyldes		12
of Thomas Pygeon for the rent of a shop that he was behynde the last yere	2	–
of William Toney for a seate		20
of John Band for a seate	2	–
more of Mr Bayly Grene	6	8
of Andrew Severne for olde tymber		12
of Alexander Grene for a seate		12
of Mastres Pert for the burall of Mr Pert in the churche	6	8
of Maude Perlor for rynging		6
for standinges in the churche howse	2	[...]
of Richard Mathew for halfe a yeres rent of the howse in the highe strete		[...]
of Richard Fyld for halfe yeres rent of the churche howse		10
of Richard Bondy for a rome in a seat that was James Peynters		20
of Pygenn for the laste yeares rente of the shope in the chyrche hows	2	–
of William Boroson & John Fylde for a sete	2	4
of Alexander ⟨Grene⟩ Drywer for the rent of his garden		4

Summa	16	18	8

Here folowethe a true & preset note of all souche somes off money as the afore namyd Gyles Toney & Alexander Grene have payd & leyde forthe fore the reparyng & amending of the sayd parishe churche of Tewkesbury & other thinges belonging to the same churche in the tyme of theire office

	£	s	d
for paper			1
for one loade of sclatte		5	8
for the carryeng of the same to the churche			2
for two loade of sclatte		12	–
for weyeng of the lead			6
to John Cole for sutyng of the vestmentes			4
yn yernest for a rope for the fore bell			12
for a pere of hinges for a settle in the quyer			4½
more for the bell rope		5	4
for twoo bondell of lathes			6
for nayles			8
for a barrell of lyme			14
for the cariage of a loade of sclate to the churche			6
for mending of the bell ropes & grease for the belles			4
for the diging & carryeng of a loade of sand			12
for a hundred & a halfe of bordes		4	6
for the carryage of bordes & lyme			6
for four bondelles of lathes			12

10

to twoo sclatters for 3 dayes worke	4	6
to Rekes for a dayes worke & mending a dore		12
for nayles		4
for thirteen hundred of lathe nayles	2	2
for too hundred of bord nayles & 100 hatch nayle		16
for too borden of mosse		2
for too sclatters for 6 daye worke	9	–
to Rekes for too dayes worke		20
for an elmen bord		12
to Gowghe for thre dayes worke	2	–
for a barrell of lyme		15
for a bondell of lathes		3
11 for 1,000 lathe nayle & 300 of hatch nayles	2	6
to John Rekes for a dayes worke		10
to a laborer for four daye worke	2	8
for 6 borden of mosse		12
to twoo sclatters for ⟨13⟩ 5 dayes worke	7	6
for 20 bondelles of lathes	5	–
for ⟨the caryage⟩ 3 barelles of lyme & for the caryage of the same to the churche	4	–
for the carryag of twoo loade of sclatte to the churche		11
for twoo loade of sclatte to Mr Morey	12	–
to twoo sclatters for a wickes worke	8	2
to a laborer for too dayes worke		16
for lathe nayle & hatche nayle	2	6
to Thomas Smythe for 6 dayes worke	4	–
for a loade of sclatt & the carryage	5	8
for 7 bondell of mosse		14
for 1,000 lathe nayle & 200 hatche nayle	2	4
to Thomas Mondye & his man for for [*sic*] four dayes worke		6
to Thomas Smythe for four dayes worke	3	–
to Gowghe for thre dayes worke	2	–
to twoo sclatters for 6 dayes worke	9	–
to twoo carpenters for 6 dayes worke	10	2
to a laborer for 6 dayes worke	4	–
for a loade of sclatte & the caryage	6	–
for a pece of tymber & the sawing	4	8
for 6 borden of mosse		12
for the makyng of thre barres for the glas ⟨wyndo⟩ wyndowes		4
for 6 dayes worke to Thomas Smythe	4	–
for 6 borden of mosse		12
for lathe nayle & hatche nayle	4	10
for a loade of sclat & the carryage	5	8
for 1,000 lathe nayle 100 hatche nayle		14
to Rekes & Bradshaw for too dayes worke	4	–
for 5 bordes for the gutters		20
for planckes to ley the gutters	3	4
to thre sclatters for 5 dayes worke	11	6
to Gowghe for four dayes worke	2	8
for lathe nayles & hatche nayles	2	6
to Thomas Mondy & his man for 5 dayes worke	7	6
to a laborer for thre dayes worke	2	–
to Robert Collyns for 30 fote of glas	10	–
to Gowghe for a daye & a halfes worke		12
for to loade of sclat & the caryage in	12	2
to Thomas Smythe for 5 dayes worke	3	6

	to John Cole for a baudericke		4
	to Thomas Mondye for four dayes worke for hym & his man	6	–
	to Thomas Smythe for four dayes worke	2	7
	to a laborer for 3 dayes worke	2	–
12	for makyng cleane the gutters		8
	for the makyng of a key		2
	for thre borden of mosse		6
	for too crestes		2
	for 22 bondell of lathes	5	6
	for the halyng of a pece of tymber		4
	for a loade of sand		10
	for nayles		18
	for besoms		1
	to Thomas Tyncker for 6lb of sowder	5	4
	for the taske of the halfe acre		2½
	for halfe a strycke of coles		1½
	for lycouer for the belles & for besoms		3
	for our charges to my lord byshope		12
	to thre men for one dayes worke	2	–
	to Rekes for mending of the bere		2
	for too mattes		12
	for a bell rope	5	4
	for besoms		1
	to John Cole for candles	4	–
	to Rekes for worke		12
	for besoms		1
	for the hewing up of a shete of lead		3
	to Henry Backe ageyne for a rome in a sete that Mastres Cox ⟨dyed⟩		
	& he stryvyd for		16
	for lycouer for the belles		6
	for mending of the surples		2
	to John Cole for the rynging of the bell	13	4
	to Mondy & his man for 2 dayes worke	2	8
	for the paving of too graves & mending the barre of the chaunsell dore		8
	to Robert Collyns for 38 fote of glasse	12	8
	to Collyns & his man for a daye worke		12
	to Thomas Smythe for mending the wyndowes with stone	2	8
	for makyng a grave		3
	to Rekes for mending the dores		2
	to too workemen		8
	for the makyng cleane the gutters		8
	for Pentecost money	3	6
	for the makyng barres for the wyndow		4
	for the wryting of this accompte		20
	to Rikes for worke in the churche		2
	to Thomas Smythe for a dayes worke		8
	for whitlether		12
	to John Cole for too bawdryckes & for sutyng of the vestementes		9

	Summa	16	12	6

13 As to the whole arrereges of the last yeres accompte where withall Gyles Toncy and Alexander Grene were chargid withall They have receved no more but £5 of Mr Cole so that thei stand dyschargyd for theire whole accompte savyng for the arrereges whiche yet restythe behynd unpayd & to be chargid upon the accompte of the churche wardens under namyd 6d.

for the some of   29   7   11

[*In scribes hand*:]   Nicholas Cleveley   James Phelpes

Md The last churchewardens upon theire throw accompte made saving for the arrereges above namyd have delyverid over (whiche was the rest of theire accompte) unto the churche wardens above namyd 6s 2d yn stock

Md Where Henry Grene had delyveryd unto hym by Mr Perte £15 to the use of the churche be yt knowen that the sayd Henry Grene hathe payd unto Alexander Grene & Gyles Toney £7 6s 8d

Whereof they have made theyre accompte as before apperithe so that Nicholas Cleveley & James Phelpes stand chargid for the receipt of the resydew of the said some

	£	s	d
The sayd Henry Grene vid. for the some of	7	13	4
Mr Bayly Ricardes & Mr Butler for a seate yn the churche		5	–
to [sic] Mr Butler for the rest of a seate yn the churche this one yere		2	–
Wylliam Wyat for the rent of the churche howse			20
Kellam Cotterell for the buryall of his wyfe		6	5[...]

This also they stand chargid to receve

Md That Nicholas Cleveley & James Phelpes have recevyd the 21 daye of Maye anno domino 1566 of Henry Grene £7 8s 4d (part of payment of the some of £15 above specyfied & delyverid to hym by Mr Perte & so he remaynethe in det to the church 10s)

– Recevyd of William Cole		40 [...]
– Recevyd of Edmonde Floke for the buryall of Mr Gyles Wye	6	8

14   **Here folowethe the true & juste accompte of Nicholas Cleveley & James Phelpes churche wardens of the parishe churche of Tewkesbury foresaid for one yere. That is to saye from the 5 daye of May in the yere of our Lord 1566 unto the 25 of Aprell yn the yere of our Lord 1567 Then made & geven up yn the parishe churche of Tewkesbury foresaid unto Roger Malliard & Nicholas Grenewood then baylyffes of Tewkesbury & to other the burgesies & commonaltie of the same towne then present**

The arrereges as yn the fote of the last accompte it dothe appere ys £29 7s 11d And also the aforesaid Nicholas [Cleveley] & James Phelpes were charged with the receipte of these somes folowing

	£	s	d
of Henry Grene as it apperethe over the other syde of this leafe	7	13	4
of Mr Butler & Mr Ricards for a seate yn the churche		5	–
of Mr Butler for the rent of a seate for one yere		2	–
of Mr Wyat for the rent of the churche howse			20
of Kellam Cotterall for the buryall of his wife		6	8

So the whole arrerage is	37	16	7

First a note of all such somes of money as the foresaid Nicholas Clevely & James Phelpes have receved to the use of the parishe churche of Tewkesbury during the tyme of theire office as folowethe

	£	s	d
of Mr Bayliffes yn stocke		6	2
of Henry Grene	7	3	4
of Mr William Cole		40	–
for a quarter of malte geven to the churche by Robert Higgyns		14	8
in gaynes ⟨of⟩ of our churche ale at Whitsontide last	11	10	–
of Mr Ricards for a seate		5	–
of Edmond Floke for the buryall of Mr Gyles Wye		6	8
of Thomas Bryan for a seate in the churche			20
for standinges yn the churche howse at Bartlemew fayer		5	6
of the executors of Thomas Hiatte of Walton		3	4
of John Pers for the buryall of his mother in the churche		6	8
of Thomas Grenewood for olde ierne		2	10
of Rowland Lancaster for his rome & his wifes yn a seate			16
of John Wolridge for his wifes rome yn a seate			8
of Parrys of the Lode for a rome yn a seate at the nether end of the churche			8
of Mastres Smythe for the rent of halfe acre in Aven hamm		3	4
of Richard Mathew for halfe a yeres rent of the howse in the hie strete		15	–
of Thomas Crompe for his rome in a seate			12
of Kenelme Cotterell for the buryall of his wife		5	–
of George Frebaynke for a seate [for him & his] wyfe		3	–
of Mother Edwards of Walton geven to the reparacion of the churche		6	8
for a stone yn Seyncte Katherins Chapell		10	–
of Henry Taylor & Henry Poller for a seate yn the churche		2	8
for the standynges in the churche howse at Seyncte Mathias fayre		2	–

15 appears beside the Mother Edwards line.

It is to be noted that there is recevid of arrerages thys yere as before apperethe in these receiptes £10 [...]

The some of the charges by them receved to the use of the churche foresaid is £25 14s 2d whereof they have paid & leyd forthe as folowethe

Here after folowethe a note of all suche somes of money as the foresaid Nicholas Clevely & James Phelpes have leyde forthe & paid for the necessary reparations of the parishe churche of Tewkesbury aforesaid as folowethe

	£	s	d
for a loade of sclat & the carrieng of yt into the churche		5	6
for iron to mend the greate bell clapper & for the workemanship		2	8
to William Wood for thre lockes & for nayles to set them on the dores		2	4
for too loade of sclatte		10	8
for the carryeng of it into the iles			6
for the coppye of our charge at my lord bishops visitacion to the Regester			20
to Thomas Smythe & to Grubbe for too dayes worke			14
for nayles			4
for too loade of sclat		10	8
for the carryeng of it into the iles			6
to Father Hiatte the mason at his first commyng to se the worke of the chauncell wyndow		2	–
for thre loade of sclat		16	–
for the carryeng of it into the iles			9
for clensyng of the grate & for the mydle gyste of the grate & for 3 staples & too greate nayles & for the leyeng of the same ageyne			21
for 3 barrelles of lyme & for the caryeng of the same to the churche		4	–

to Thomas Burford for the holyng of seven thousand of sclat	5	10
to the somner for the delyvering up our byll at my lords bishops visitation		2
to Goughe for 3 dayes worke	2	–
to Robert Reve for the makyng of a dore for the store howse & annother for to go into the iles		8
for a locke for one of the dores & for nayles		16
for a small pere of gymmowes & for a dore hinge		7
for the carryage of the stone for the wyndow from the quarre	4	4
to four masons for a wickes worke	24	–
to Wylliam Hiche for the carryeng of a loade of sand		12
to hym for the carriage of an other loade of sand		14
16 for the carrieng of too loade of sand into the churche		4
to Robert Hicox for 3 barrell of lyme	3	6
to William Hiche for the carryeng of yt to the churche		4
for a pound of waxe & a pound of rosen		10
to Thomas Cobler for diging of sand		2
for cords to make the scaffolde		4
for nayles to William Fielde		2
for the windyng up of the greate stones		2
to John Rekes for the makyng of a scaffolde at the chauncell wyndow		8
to four masons for 4 dayes worke	16	–
to Hiat the mason for 45 fote of stone for the chauncell wyndow	45	–
for the mending of a surpelesse		2
for a ridle & a ryeng seve		4
to Thomas Smythe & Richard Goughe for a wickes worke	8	–
for besoms to swepe the churche		1
to Nicholas Myllard for the mending of a bell whele		1
to hym for mending the frame in the trasyng howse to cast lead		2
to John Watson for 2 loade of sand		21
for the carryeng of it into the churche		2
for the carryeng of a loade of sand up into the tracyng howse		2
for a boke of prayers agenst the Turke		4
for a frogge locke		6
for a 1,000 of lathe nayle		18
to Thomas Cobler for too dayes worke		12
for nayles to ley the planckes under the gutters		4
for a rope for the sanctus bell		16
to William Raynoldes for ridding of the gutters		8
to Richard Goughe for a wickes worke	4	–
to Thomas Smythe for 4 dayes worke	2	8
for too long planckes for the gutters sydes	2	8
for a seve to carry up sand		2
to Goughe for a wickes worke	4	–
to Thomas Smythe for a wickes worke	4	–
to John Shaw for too bondle of stone lathe		8
to Mr Morrey for a greate plancke	2	4
to William Fielde for a 100 hatche nayles		3
to Nicholas Myllard for makyng the tymber worke aboute the gutters & pecyng of the rafters		14
to a laborer to helpe the plomer for a wike	4	–
to William Field for 700 lathe nayle & for a hundred hatche nayle		22
to him for bord nayle & spickes		11
to the curat for wrytyng of a boke of all the names of them that have byn christened wedded & buryed in 3 yeres past & for the makyng of an inventory of the churche goodes	3	4

to the somner for delyvering the same boke of names to my lord		4
for 400 of lathe nayle & a 100 of hatche nayle		10
for 9 bondle of lathe	2	3
to Pers Somner for the makying of 12 claspes for the new pipes aboute the chauncell & for pesyng & makyng 22 small barres for the windowes		12
to Smythe & Goughe for a wickes worke	8	–

17

to Thomas Smythe & Richard Goughe for one wickes worke	8	–
to John Cole for the mending of too baudrickes for the belles & sortyng of the vestementes yn the vestry		6
to Mr Morrey for 4 barrelles of lyme	4	8
for the hawlyng of the lyme to the churche		4
to Thomas Smythe & to Goughe for a wickes worke	8	–
for 18 pounds of iron for the great bell clapper	2	3
for a quarter & 21 pounds of iron	5	10
for the makyng of the greate bell clapper	8	4
to too men for to helpe to strike with the smythe		8
to Thomas Smythe & Goughe for a wickes worke	8	–
for a hyde of whitlether to Thomas Bondy	2	4
for makyng of a new bawdricke & for the mending of too other bawdrickes		8
for the makyng of rivettes for the wyndowes & for a new eye to the bawdricke		8
to Mr Greves for the casting of 1500 of lead	30	–
to hym for 76 pounds of solder at 8d the pound	50	8
to Puddle to Mondy to Savage & to Smythe for thre dayes worke	8	–
to Goughe for a dayes worke		8
to Anne Redhed for 9 bondle of mosse		18
for eves bords aboute the iles		12
for the washing of 3 surplesses		4
for tymber to dubbe the rafters		14
to Anne Redhed for too burden of mosse		4
to Henry Rogers for too peces of tymber that we did cut at the makyng of the scaffold for the masons		4
to Thomas Smythe for stoppyng of the wyndowes in Seyncte Katheryns chappell & in the vestry		16
to John Sandiford for too rent bords to make the third bell whele		16
for the sawing of them		2
for a whope for the third bell whele		2
to Reve for the makyng of the same whele		12
to Robert Collyns for new settyng of a hundred & syxe fote of glasse	33	4
for the mending of the staple of the third bell whele		4
to John Cole for ryngyng of the bell upon Christmas yeven for that quarter	6	8
to William Felde for lathe nayle bord nayle hatch nayle & speke nayle	4	11
to William Baker for 10 bondle of lathe	2	6
to John Cole for ryngyng of the bell for Seyncte Mary quarter	6	8
to John Mason for clensing the chappelles		6
for 4 barrelles of lyme	4	2
for the carryeng of them to the churche		4
to Puddle & Goughe for a wickes worke	8	–
for the mending of the band of one of the surplesses & for the washing of the same		5
for besoms		1

18

for greace to greace the belles		8
to the Archedeacon for Pentecost money	3	6

to the plomer for setting up the pypes aboute the chauncell & for souder	12	–	
to a laborer for too dayes worke to helpe the plomer		16	
to Pers Somner for 3 keyes for the common coffer		10	
to the plomer for makyng of 2 grates of lead to set over the pipes & for			
2 pounds & a halfe of souder	2	–	
to Puddle & Savage for a wickes worke	8	–	
to the sawiers for sawing of a pece of tymber	2	–	
to Edward Adams & his man for theire worke	4	8	
for the wryting of our presentment at the Archedeacons visitacion		8	
for our charges at Gloucester at the delyveringy of hym up		10	
to William Baker for 5 bondell of lathe		15	
to William Felde for 900 of lathe nayle for borde nayle & spike nayle	3	–	
to the plomer	8	–	
for the makyng of thre long nayles		1	
to Thomas Mondy for the hewing of an hole yn the wall & for the			
settyng in of a stone to beare the greate beame over the quyer		4	
to a man to helpe the plomer		10	
to Richard Kynnard for crestes & gutter tile		16	
for the makyng clene of the gutters		8	
to John Cole for the makyng of too bawdrickes & mending of an other			
& for besoms		6	
for the writing of this boke of accompte	2	–	
to William Hiche for the hawlyng of too peces of tymber to the churche		4	
The whole some of theire allowances is	25	–	9
And they do owe	25	–	13
The which			
James Chester of Bristow merchant for his arrerages for one tone of			
leade yet not payd for as before apperethe	7	–	–
William Cole for his arreges for certen money taken oute of the			
churche stocke as before apperethe	40	–	–
Richard Hill as in the righte of Julyan his wife executrix of the last			
will and testament of Gyles Wye for her arrerages as before			
apperethe	⟨31	8⟩	
	25	–	
Richard Hareley for the buriall of his mother for his arrerages as before			
apperethe		6	8
Bridget Rogers alias Smythe for the legacie of John Rogers her late			
husband to be paid at 20s the yere for fyve yere the first payment to			
have byn begon at Michaellmas in the yere of our lord 1564 whiche			
is alleaged by her that Alexander Broune shulde pay it as before			
apperethe	5	–	–
John Butler ⟨& Thomas Godwyn⟩ late baylyffes for the price of certen			
leade receved of Sir Thomas Russell knyght for ⟨their⟩ his arrerages			
as before apperethe	4	10	–
the wife of Thomas Alen for the legacie of her husband bequethed unto			
the churche for her arrerages as before apperethe		3	4
Henry Grene for the some of £15 receved by him of Mr Perte for his			
arrerages as before apperethe		10	–
John Butler for the rent of a seate in the churche for one year		2	–
William Wiatte for one halfe yeres rent of the churche howse for his			
arrerages as before apperethe			20
Kenelme Cotterell for the buryall of his wife for his arrerages			20

19

the said churche wardens for theire proper arrerages yet behynd unpaid
    whiche they have redy to delyver up   ⟨13 5⟩
                                                    28 5

More over there are certen legacies & rentes due unto the churche for this last yere &
are not yet receved whiche are to be charged upon the next churche wardens as
folowethe

	£	s	d
Master Wiat for one yeres rent of the churche howse beside the halfe yeres rent afore expressed 3s 4d dew at St Mary Daye last paste whiche is in all		5	
Jone Smethesend of Walton for her husbands legacie to the churche		20	–
Richard Mathew for one halfe yeres rent of the house in the hie strete (Mr Cookes gift)		15	–
Thomas Pigeon for the hole yeres rent of his shop in the churche howse dew at the feast of St Michaell last past		2	–
Alexander Dryver for a yeres rent of his garden in the churche yard dew at Michaelmas last past			4
Mr Butler for money receved by him of Henry Slaughters wyfe		26	8

The whole arrerages above said where with the said Nicholas Cleveley & James
Phelpes were charged as before apperethe was £37 1s 6d whereof they have receved as
before apperethe £10 & so they are discharged of theire accompte

It is further to be noted that Thomas Godwyn is discharged of £6 of the £10 10s that
was betwene Mr Butler & him as above apperethe

by me Nicholas Grynwood [*signed*]

All thynges allowed the arrerages are now but   25 – 13

20   Md delyvered unto Robert Smythe & Henry Dowle elected & chosen churche wardens
the 4 day of Maye 1567 by Roger Malliard & Nicholas Grenwood the same daye in the
presence of the parishioners 28s 5d

Item The vestamentes & ornamentes, lead bras iron & other implementes perteynyng to
the parishe churche of Tewkesbury do appere in an inventory indentid whereof the one
parte remaynethe with the churche wardens aforesayd

**Here folowethe the true & just accompte of Robert Smythe & Henry Dowle
churche wardens of the parishe churche of Tewkesbury aforesaid for one yere that
is to sey from the 4 daye of Maye 1567 unto the 16 of Maye 1568 Then made &
geven up to the parishe churche of Tewkesbury unto William Wyat & William Hill
then Baylyffes of Tewkesbury in the presence of other burgeses & diverse of the
commynaltie of the same towne**

Arrerages as apperethe in the fote of the last accompte is all thinges
    allowed   25 – 13

First a note of all souche somes of money as the aforesaid Robert Smythe & Henry
Dowle have receved unto the use of the parishe churche of Tewkesbury duryng the
tyme of theire office

	£	s	d
at the handes of Roger Malliard & Nicholas Grenewood then baylyffes		28	5
in gaynes of the churche ale at Whitsontyde last	6	16	8

of Thomas Pigeon for the rent of his shoppe in the churche howse for one whole yere endyd at Michaelmas last past		2	–
of William Baker for a seate			16
of Kenelme Cotterell for a seate			16
of John Hodges for his rome		2	–
of William Smythe for a seate his wife		2	–
for four bousheles of leade ashes		2	–
of Jone Smethesend of Walton for her husbands bequest to the churche		20	–
of Band for an olde blocke			4
of Richard Mathoes for halfe yeres rent of the howse in the highe strete dewe at Michaelmas last		15	–
of Richard Tyrret for too seates		2	10
for the hier of the players gere			18
for a dore			18
of Thomas Cockes for a seate			14
of Richard Mathoes for halfe yeres rent dewe at Seyncte Mary Day last past		15	–
of Mr Bayly Wiatte for too yeres rent of the churche howse dew at Michaelmas last as apperethe by the bokes afore		6	4
of Mastres Smythe for the rent of the halfe acre in Aven hamm dew at Michaellmas last		3	4
for standynges in the churche howse the too fayere dayes		[	]
of Henry Dowle for his roume in a sete			8
of hym for a seate for his wife			12
of Alexander Dryver for too yeres rent of his garden in the churche yarde			8
for the standinges in the churche howse at the twoo faire dayes		6	5
The some of the charges by them recevyd to the use of the churche is	12	11	6
Of the whiche they have recevyd of arrerages whiche is to be set downe in this accompte		55	9

Here after folowethe a note of all suche somes of money as the foresaid Roberte Smythe & Henry Dowle have payd & leyed forthe for the reparacions & other charges of the same parishe churche of Tewkebury

	£	s	d
to the somner for the taske of the halfe acre in Aven hamm			3
to Clemence for worke			8
for wayeing of the lead		2	–
to Clemence for clensing the gutters			16
for lyker for the belles			4
for a bell roppe		6	2
for makyng of the inventory of the churche goodes			12
for lyker for the belles			4
for a hundred thre quarters & thre fote of oken bords		6	8
for the mendyng of the churche bokes			6
to Robert Gynes & his mann for too dayes worke			23
for the makyng of the bell clapper		5	4
for besoms			1
for 18 pounds of iron & makyng of the bell clapper		5	–
for nayles			6
for besoms			1
for the mending of a bawdricke			3
to Nicholas Hill			3
to the plomer		3	4

for halfe a hundred of bord nayles			3
more for nayles			2
for a sauter boke			12
to the smythe for worke			4
for wyer shides			2
for a halter			1
to Robert Gynes for makyng of the beere & for the tymber that went to yt		3	8
to John Cole for ryngyng of the bell		6	8
for wyer shides			2
for nayles			6
to Clemence for worke			4
to Robert Gyver for worke			20
to John Cole for the ryngynge of the bell		6	8
for the mendyng of a surplesse			4
for the clensyng of the gutters			6
for mendinges of the formes			6
for pavyng of the churche		8	4
for besoms			2
for nayles			4
for mendyng of a surplesse			4
for a locke			4
for a barrell of lyme			14
for lyker for the belles			3
for nayles			4
yn parte of payment for our tymber	4	–	8
to the Archedecon for Pentecost money		3	6
for the wryting of our presentment			8
at the delyveryng hym up			3
to Robert Gyver for worke			8
to spende goyng to Beawdcley aboute our tymber		2	–
for our dyner at the visitacion		2	–
for the wrytyng of this accompte			20

And so the whole some of theire allowance is	8	–	20

It is to be noted that the foresaid Robert Smythe & Henry Dowle have recevyd of the arrerages in the last accompte mencioned but onely 55s 9d

As it apperethe in the receypte afore declared the whiche they recevyd of Jone Smethesend 20s of Thomas Pigeon 2s & of Mr Wyat 5s of Mr Baylyffes 28s 5d & of Alexander Dryver 4d

23	So they do owe	26	15	2

of the whiche

James Chester of Bristow marchante fore his arrerages for one ton of lead yet not payd as before apperethe	7	–	–
William Cole for his arrerages for certen money taken forthe of the churche stocke as before apperethe		40	–
Received of this some the 6 of September 1568 20s			
Richard Hill is in the ryghte of Julyan his wife executrix of the last will & testament of Gyles Wie for her arrerages as before apperethe		25	–
Bridget Rogers alias Smythe for the legacie of her late husband John Rogers to be by part 20s the yere for 5 yeres & the first payment to have begonn at Michaellmas in the yere of our Lord 1564 whiche is aleged by her that Alexander Browne shoulde paye it	5	–	–

Richard Hareley for the buryall of his mother for his arrerages as appere before		11	8
John Butler for his arrerages for the price of certen lead recevid by him of Sir Thomas Russell as before apperethe	4	10	–
The wife of Thomas Alen for her arrerages as before apperethe		3	4
Henry Grene for the some of £15 recevid by him of Mr Perte for his arrerages		10	–
⟨John Butler for the rente of a seate in the churche for one yere 2s⟩		5	–
Kenelme Cotterell for his arrerages for the buriall of his wyfe			20
John Butler for his arrerages for money recevyd by him of Henry Slawters wyfe		26	8
The foresaid churche wardens for theire proper arrerages whiche they have redy to deyver up	4	9	10
Sum of the arrerages	26	15	2

More over Thomas Pygeon dothe owe one yeres rent for his shoppe dew at Michaellmas last		2	–
& Mr Bayly Wyat for halfe yeres rent of the churchehowse dew at seyncte Mary Daye last			20
Which is to be charged upon the next churche wardens to gether up & so the arrerages do amounte yn all unto	26	18	10

24   Md The churchemen aforesaid have boughte of one Lawrence Lake for the parishe churche of Tewkesbury too sommers of 40 fote long & 20 ynches one way & 18 ynches an other waye & 8 gystes of 40 fote long & 14 ynches one waye & 12 ynches another way whiche tymber the said Lawrence must delyver at the key of Tewkesbury before mydsomer daye next commyng & theire price is £7 whereof he hathe recevyd of the said churche wardens £4 as before apperethe

Thomas Pygeon hathe payd his arrerages 2s which apperethe in the fote of the last accompte	2	–
Mr Baylye Wiatte hathe paid for halfe yeres rent that he was behynde of the churche howse dew at St Marye daye last		20
Received more of Kenelme Cotterell		20
Received of Richarde Wakeman for his rowme in a seate		12
Paid of the same some for halfe a hide of whit lether		16
Paid for the makyng of twoo baldrickes		8
Paid to Lawrence Lake	20	–
Paid to the somner for subsidie		3

Md Robert Baker & Henry Dowle have delyvered unto Roger Gilberte & John Wilkes churche wardens newly elected £3 13s 11d

Here folowethe the true & just accompte of Roger Gylberte & John Wilkes churche wardens of the parishe churche of Tewkesbury foresaid for one yere lackyng 5 wickes that is to sey from the 16 daye of Maye in the yere of our Lorde 1568 unto the 12 daye of Aprell in the yere of our Lorde 1569 Then made & geven up in the parishe churche of Tewkesbury unto William Thornebie and Richard Pace then baylyffes of Tewkesbury yn the presence of dyverse other burgeyses & others of the comynaltie of the same towne

Arrerages as in the foote of the last accompte apperethe all thinges allowed is	26	–	7

Where of they have receved as here particularly shall appere in theire receiptes 51s 8d whiche also is discharged in the foresaid arrerages as there playnely apperethe

25   Firste a note of all suche somes of money as the sayd Roger Gilberte & John Wilkes have receved unto the use of the foresaid churche duryng the tyme of theire office

	£	s	d
of Mr Parye for a seate yn the churche		5	–
of the olde churche wardens as it apperethe before	3	13	11
of Mr Cole in parte of payment of his arrerages		20	–
of Mr Butler in parte payment of his arrerages for Henry Slawghters wife		26	8
More of Mr Butler for a seate		5	–
for the buryall of Stephen Webbe		6	8
for the buryall of Mr Whitehead		6	8
of Richard Sadler for his rome yn a seate		2	–
of the good wife Nutbie for her rome yn a seate			20
of William Barnard for his rome in a seate			8
for the buryall of Mastres Arkell		6	8
of Edmond Deken for one yeres rent of his howse dew at Seyncte Marie Daye last paste		30	–
for standinges in the churche howse of dyverse persons		4	–
of Mastres Smythe for the rente of an halfe acre of medowe for one yere ended at Mychaellmas last past		3	4
of Alexander Dryver for the rent of his garden in the churche yarde			4
of Humfrey Richards for his standing in the churche howse too faire dayes			16
of Pygeon for the rent of his shoppe yn the churche howse		2	–
of Richard Rudgdale for a seate			7
⟨The whole some of theire receiptes is	9	10	11⟩
of William Wiat for the rent of the churche howse		3	4
of My Baylie for a seate		5	–
The whole some of theire receiptes is	9	19	7

Here folowethe a note of all suche somes of money as the said Roger Gylberte & John Wilkes have payd & leyde forthe for the necessary reparing & a mending of the afore saide parishe churche

	£	s	d
to Clemence for the makynge cleane of the gutters			8
to Thomas Grenewood for lead nayles			12
to John Cole for helpyng to waye the lead & for volding up the vestementes			4

[two blank pages numbered 26 and 27]

28
to Thomas Grenewood for makyng of leade nayles			7
to Clemence for 6 dayes worke to helpe the plomer		3	–
to Mastres Cole for 14 pounds of ierne			21
to Henry Smythe for the makyng of leade mayles & mendyng of the braces buckles keyes & a clapper of the belles		2	8
to William Dickes for thre dayes worke		2	3
to Clemence for 4 dayes worke			18
to William Feilde for nayles			1

to Mr Wiatte for a pece of tymber			3
to Pers Smythe for the mending of a locke & a key			6
for meding [*sic*] of the clocke		7	4
for a borde			10
to the plomer for his worke		20	–
to hym for soulder		16	–
to Clemence for helpyng the plomer		3	–
for the fetchyng the tymber from the key & leyeng it in the churche		8	3
to the plomer for soulder		7	4
for his worke		4	6
to Clemence for helpyng the plomer thre dayes			14
for mending the beere			3
to Robert Baker for the tymber that came from Beawdeley		40	–
to John Cole for ryngyng of the bowbell		13	4
for the makyng of too bawderickes			4
for the makyng cleane of the grate			12
for ⟨the ma⟩ too bell ropes		12	–
for besoms			4
for woode			5
for the paving of too buryalles			4
for lyker for the belles			9
for writing of the names of the seates in the churche			6
for clensyng the gutters			6
for whitlether			20
for 4 bocles for the bawderickes			3
for the writing of this boke of accomptes			20
And so theire allowance is	7	16	4
It ys to be noted that the foresayd Roger Gilberte & John Wilkes have receved of the arrerages as before is mencioned		51	8
So that they do owe	21	10	3
of the whiche			

29 James Chester of Bristow merchaunte for his arrerages for one ton of leade yet not payd as before apperethe — 7 – –

⟨William Cole for his arrerages for certen money taken forthe of the churche stocke as before apperethe — 20 –⟩

Richard Hill as in the ryghte of Julyan his wife executrixe of the last will & testament of Gyles Wye for her arrerages as before apperethe — 25 –

Briget Rogers for the lagacie of her late husband John Rogers to be paid 20s the yere for 5 yeres & the firste payment to have begonn at the feaste of Seyncte Michaell in the yere of our Lorde 1564 whiche is alleged by her that Alexander Browne shalde paye — 5 – –

Richard Hareley for the buryall of his mother for his arrerages as apperethe — 6 9

⟨John Butler for his arrerages for the price of certen leade received by hym of Sir Thomas Russell knyghte — 4 10 –⟩

The wife of one Thomas Alen for her arrerages as apperethe — 3 4

Henry Grenewood for the some of £15 by him received of Mr Perte for his arrerages — 10 –

⟨William Coxe for his arrerages for too dayes standing in the churche howse — 16⟩

The sayd churche wardens for theire proper arrerages whiche they have redye to delyver up — 37 11

It is also to be noted that Ellyn Ekynsale wydowe by her last will & testament did geve & bequethe forthe of her too tenementes lyeng at the over ende of the Oldbury Strete one annuall or yerly rent of 12d to be payd to the churchewardens toward the reparyng of the parishe churche of Tewkesbury aforesayd whiche Ellyn died in the yere of our lord 1568

Md Mr Cole hathe in his custodie of the gyfte of Mr Whityngton a chalice of sylver & gylte

30   Md It is agreed by Mr Baylyffes & theire brethern that Edward Deaken shall have the howse that he nowe dwellethe in by lease for the terme of 21 yeres from St Mary Day last & granted at the feast of Easter Anno 11 Elizabeth etc. At the yerely rent of 30s & reparacions to be kepte by the tenante & payd to fyne 2s

⟨Roger Gilberte dothe owe for one seate that he hathe taken in the
      churche   12⟩

Heare followethe the just accounte of Roger Turbell & John Leate churche wardens of the forsayd parishe of Tewkesburie for one whole yeare that is to sey from the 12 daye of Aprill unto the 23ᵗⁱ daye of Apriell then made & geven up in the parishe churche of Tewkesburie unto John Buttler & Alexander Broune then baylyffes of Tewkesburie in the presens of other burgeses & others of the commynalltie of the same towne in the yeare of our lord God ⟨1569⟩ 1570

	£	s	d
Receved one cupe of syllver & parte gylte			
Receved in lead one tune & 6 hundrethe lakkyng 3 pounde			
Recevyd in brase half a hundrethe lakkyng 2 pound			
of Rychard Ekensale for a rome in a seate for hys wyf wythe Mystres Morrey			20
of Roger Gylbart for a rome in a seat for hys wyf			12
of Mr Coale for the buriall of Mr Wylliam Coale		6	8
for the standings in the churche howse		3	6
of Roger Tyrret & hys wyf & Watter Symons & hys wyf for a seat			12
of Mystrys Smythe for the half accar in the Aven Hamm		3	4
of Mr Wyat for the rent of the churche howse		3	–
of Wylliam Dole for his mothers howsys rent			12
of Alexander Driver for the rent of his gardens in the churche yard			4
of Edmun Deken for his huse rent for half a yeare		15	–
of Thomas Pychin for rent			12
for standings in the churche house		2	11
for pichin dunge			4
for a hope of lead asses			6
of Mr Thornbie		6	8
of John Plumer for a rome in a seat for his wyf			20
of Byddell & Harry Tomsons wyf & her mother lawe for the hynmust seat in Seynt Gorgys Chappell			8

31 appears in left margin beside the "of Alexander Driver" line.

Memorandum that all thees partties that is Byddels wyf & Harry Tomsonns wyf & her mother law muste paye 2d a yeare every one wyche is 6d a yeare & Byddell hathe payd 2 yeares rent

of Watter Wakeman for a rome in a seat for hym & his wyf			18
of John Wylkes for a rome in a seate wheare his wyf dyd kneele			16
of Thomas Cleadon for a rome in a ⟨the⟩ seat ⟨that John Wylkes hathe taken⟩ for hys wyffe		2	⟨16⟩

	£	s	d
of Rychard Kinnard for a rome wythe his father in a seat			12
of Wylliam Thornbie for a seat for hym & his wyf		2	4
of John Leyt for a rome in a seat whear the good wyf Russell dothe kneelle for hys wyf			20
⟨for wrytting thys a count			6⟩
of Thomas Bancke & Rychard Cotten for a seate for theyre wyfes		2	–
of Thomas Pychen for rent			[...]
of Edmun Deken for his howse rent		15	–

32   Heare followethe a juste note of all suche somes of money as the forsayd Roger Turbell & John Leat hathe layd owt for the repracyons of the churche & all other matters

	£	s	d
for the weying of lead to Clemens			4
for beesoms			1
delyverid to the clasyar in lead 6 pound & a half		[	]
to Pears for 5 bars of iren for the glas wyndowes			8
for lyme			3
for paper & spent at the vysytacyon at Durhurste			3
to Wylliam Jeines the somner the laste parte of the taske for the half akar in Aven hamm			2½
to Clemens for sweping the gutters			8
to the Curate for making the presentment			12
to the sumner for the carrege of the presentment			4
for mendyng a surples			1
for beesoms			1
for putting in of the presentment to the qweanes commysynars			6
for a horse loade of coles			12
for nayles			1
delyverid to John Coale 3 pound of lead to mend the clocke		[	]
for ⟨gressyng of the bells⟩ greece for the bells			2
for 16 pound of soder		8	–
to 4 men to ryd the dunge owt of the steple for 8 dayes 6d a daye a peace		16	–
for a barrell of lyme			12
to the plumer for a daye worke			10
for a man to serve hym			6
to the pargytter for 2 daye worke			16
to a man to serve hym			12
to the plumer for a dayes worke			10
to a man to serve hym			6
to a pargyter for 2 dayes			16
to a man to serve hym			12
for a barrell of lyme			12
to William Doale for 2 mattes for the churche seatte			9
for makyng of a hearthe for the plumer and nayles			2
to John Cole for mendynge the baldrykes			4
for greace for the belles			2
for besomes			1
to John Cole for ryngynge the bell		6	8
to John Cole for mendynge of the cloke			12
to Clemence for makyng cleane a chapell & settyng up a dore			2
to Clemence for makyng clene the gutteres			8
to Edward Adames for mendyng the thyrd bell whele & tymber and nayles & clapes of ieron		2	9

33

for grece for the belles		1
for besomes		½
to Alexandur Grene for a hyde of whytlether	2	–
Pentycoste mone	3	6
for a nomyly booke		8
to Pearse for a townge for the bawdrycke & nayles to brase the therd bell		3
to John Cole for makyng 4 bawdryckes & brasyng the therd bell & makyng owre presentment		22
for mendyng a surples		1
to thre men to gather the corne for the churche ale		12
for paper to make baggys		1½
for wrytyng this acowntes		6

Md That the foresaid Roger Turbyll & John Leyght have paste theyre acowmtes the 21 day of Maye 1570 & also the newe churchwardennes Richard Ridgdale & Thomas Portar with theyre associates have gayned by the churchale thys presente yere 1570 the juste soomm of £8 16s and so the hole soom that they have receved is   9   12   8

34   Heare after folowithe the trew and juste acommpte of Rychard Ridgdale & Thomas Portare churchwardennes of the parryshe churche of Tewkesburye aforesayd for too hole yeares that is to say from the 10th of day of Maye and in the yeare of owr Lorde God 1571[1] unto the 4 day of May & in the yeare of owr Lord God 1572 Then made & geven upe in the paryshe churche of Tewkysbere unto Thomas Downbell ⟨then⟩ and Hew Slysar baylefes of Tewkysbere and dyvares other of the foresayd parryshe of Tewkysbere

A note of the lead whiche we receved of Mr Baylyffes which was a toonne 700 & 23 pounds and more in sowder 4 pounds & halfe received more in belbrase & copper halfe a hundred lakyng 3 pounds and a quartar

Heare foloethe a note of all shuche of mone whiche the foresaid churchwardens have receved in the tyme of theyre offyse the hole some is with the stoke whiche they receved of Mr Baylyffes and the gaynes of the laste churchale is £18 5s 10d

	£	s	d
35 [Received:]			
in mone of Mr Bayles in stocke		16	8
more of owr gayne by the churchale	8	16	–
of Richard Davys for the buryall of his wyffe in the churche		6	8
of Wylliam Morres for the rente of his shope in the churche howse		2	–
of dyvares parsones for standyng in the churchowse at Bartylmew Fayre		4	–
of Mr Mallard for the buryall of his wyffe in the churche		6	8
of John Band for the buryall of Mr Twyge in the churche and for the belles		10	–
of Thomas Rogeres for the buryall of the goodwyffe Webe his motherinlaw		6	8
of dyvares parsones for standyng in the churchowse at Saynt Mathuse fayre		3	8
of Thomas Doonne for his wyves roume in a seat whyche was Maude Parlares			20
of Harry Lyse for his wyves rowme in the same seate with her			16
of Rychard Rogeres Wylliam Coxe and of Thomas Rogeres for the seate whiche was the good wyffe Webbes		6	8
of Mr Mallard for the rent of too howsis whiche the goodwyff Eckinsole gave to the church			12
of dyvarese parsones for standing in the churchowse at Bartylmew Fayre last		5	–

[1]   *recte* 1570.

of Richard Coxe Edward Baston & of Thomas Bradle for theyre thre romes in a seate whiche was Mrs Cox before	5	–
of Thomas Crumpe for his wyves rome in the same seate		20
of Rychard Stone for the rent of the churchyard for one yeare	4	10
of Roger Gylbarte for his rome in a seate		8
of Alexander Dryvar for the rent of a garden in the churcheyard		4
of Mrs Smythe for the rent of halfe a naker in Aven hame	3	4
of Edmond Deakenes fo [sic] one halfe yeres rent for his howse	15	–
of Wylliam Morrys for the rent of his shope in the churchowse	2	–
of dyvares parsones for theyre standinges in the churchowse at Saynt Mathewse day	2	–
of Mr Bayle Sclysar for the buryall of his wyffe in the churche	6	8
more of hyme for a rome for his wyffe		16
of Georg Frebanke Thomas Frebanke Thomas Shylde Harry Shaw John Collenes Rychard Woode and Edward Adammes for theyre 7 rowmes in a voyde seate one the fur syde of the churche	4	8
of John Ryse for his wyves romme in a seate whiche was her motheres And hathe yeldyd up his other seate the whiche was his ⟨other⟩ to the proffet of the churche		10
of Richard Brokbanke for his wyves rowme in a seate whiche was the good wife Hewse		[...]
of Thomas Jones for his wyves romme in a seate whiche was the goodwyfe Grenes		12
of Rychard Kynnard and of Wylliam Flechar for 2 romes for theyre wyves in a seate whiche was the good wyffe Kynnardes	2	8
of Rychard Rydgdale for a seate whiche was Mrs Arkelles for his wyfe and John Russelles wyfe ⟨and John Nashe⟩ wyfe	2	6
of Richard Ridgdale for a rome with Kellam Cottrell and James Phelpes		12
of Edmond Deakenes fo [sic] one halfe yeares rent of his howse	15	–
of John Leyght for pygeon downg	4	–
of Matson for the rent of a oven		2
of Mrs Smythe for the rent of halfe a nakar in Aven Hame	3	4
of Edmond Deakens for one halfe yeares rent of his howse	15	–
of Humfrey Hurste for pygeon downg		12
of Wylliam Nycolson for a seate in the lower end of the churche		16
of Edmond Deakenes for one halfe yeares rent of his howse	15	–
of my partner Portar for a stone for a boy to sytt		2
of Mr Wyet for one yeares rent of the churchowse	3	4
of John Kennard for his wyves rome in the seate whyche was his motheres		16
of Thomas Bundy for a rome for his wyfe in a seate whiche was Blanche Perce		16
of John Leyght in parte of 10s which he hathe geven to the churche 3 barrells and a halfe of lyme at 12d the barrell		[ ]

36 appears beside the "of Thomas Jones" line.

Sum	18	5	10

Heare after Folowythe a note of all suche somes of mone as the foresayd Rychard Rydgdale and Thomas Portar have layd owght and payd for the reparyng of the foresayd paryshe churche with all other charges to the same belongynge for the tyme binge the whiche soome is £10 19s 9½d so that we have in stoke remaynyng the just soom of £7 6s ½d

[Expenses:]	£	s	d
to John Cole for rynging of the bowbell at Crystmas		6	8
to Clemennes for to helpe the plummer for 3 dayse			21
to John Cole for paving in the churche for 2 dayse			14

	to Water Symonnes for 2 dayse to pave with hyme		14
	to the smythe for mending the cloke		6
	for a baldryke for the third bell		3
	for mending 3 other baldrykes		6
	for a baldryke for the lyttell bell		1
	for lycker for the belles and the cloke and for besommes		5
	for spysyng the bell ropes		4
	for barres for the wyndowse		2
37	for mending 2 bell wheles		3
	for mending 3 baldrykes		6
	for whytlether for the belles		4
	for paving over Mrs Malliard		3
	for besomes		1
	to Clemmenes for clensing of the leades and the gutteres upon the churche after the greate froste and snow		12
	more to him to open the spowtes		4
	to Harry Garner for shuttyng the clapper of the greate bell	4	–
	to Harry Slatter for the makinge up of thre wyndowse with stone for 3 dayse him selfe and his man		4
	for 2 barrelles of lyme		2
	for beasomes at Easter		1
	for the taske of the somner		2½
	for Penticoste mone	3	6
	to the Archdecon at the cowrte		3
	for contynewing the cowrte		4
	to the somner		3
	to Harry Slatter for a dayse worke for him and his man		16
	for a barrell of lyme & halling		14
	for 2 sawteres and the boke of the injunsions at London	3	8
	to Morres for mending the dex		3
	to John Cole for rynging the bell	6	8
	for a prayer sent frome my lorde byshope for the quene		4
	at Gloster for the copy of owre Artycles and the wryting of owr presetntment [sic] with other chargis		18
	to Robart Collenes for glasing of the wyndowse in part of payment	30	–
	the goodman Fleacher for 6 dayse worke hyme selfe & his boye	8	–
	more to him for 13 pounds of sowder and a halfe at 6d the pound	6	9
	more to hyme for nayles a rafter and 4 barrell staves		10
	to Flocke for makyng cleane the churche grate		6
	to John Cole for rynging the bell at Candelmas	6	8
	to a laborar for clensing the gutteres		8
	for the making of a new gate in the churche yard & all stuff	4	8
	for the mendyng a surples		[...]
38	for mending off the dyall	4	4
	for washing of the toweles and the bord clothes and the surplessis at tymes		6
	to Robart Collenes	6	8
	for a tabell sent from my lorde byshopes and the frame to sete him in		10
	to Clemmenes for clensing the gutteres		8
	for nayles		7
	to Thomas Smythe		12
	to to men to helpe to way the lead Wylliam Jansons & Clemenes		8
	for a bundell of lathes		3
	for lath nayles		4
	to Clemmenes for a day & halfe		8
	to Clemmens to help the plummer		8
	to Thomas Grenwod for nayles		6

more for nayles		1
to Clemmenes		4
for a barrell of lyme		11
for nayles		1
to the goodman Fleachar for 8 dayese worke upon the church and for		
3lb of sowder more than owr owne	11	4
the curate for wryting owr presentment		8
Launcastar for caryeng of hyt to Gloster		2
to John Cole for ringinge the bell	6	8
for nayles		1
to Thomas Smythe for making up of 3 wyndowse in the churche		16
to Fynche for ryddyng away the downg from the churchewall		6
the smythe for making barres for 3 wyndowse		16
for bordnayles		4
for a stryke of lyme		3
for a corde delivered to John Cole		10
for a barrell of lyme		14
to Edward Cooke		12
for a barrell of lyme		14
to Edward Cooke for 5 dayse and a halfe whytlymyng	3	8
for a barrell of lyme		15
for a stryke of heare		2
for too barrells of lyme		20
to Edward Cooke for 10 dayse whytlymyng one the churche	7	6
for a barrell of lyme		15
to Edward Cooke for 2 dayse		16
to Robarte Collennes	10	–
to Edward Cooke for 5 dayse more one the churche	3	8
to Edward [...] for wasshing [...]		[...]
for barres for the wyndowse		8
for mendyng the cloke	3	5
for mendyng the dyawll	3	4
to Robart Collennes for the reste of glasyng of 12 score foote and od		
besydes 2 panes of his owne new glasse	20	–
for carryeng owr presentment		2
for a stryke of herlyme		3
for owr chargis at Gloster when we went to the comysynares	3	4
for mendyng of a surples		6
to John Cole for nessesarys abowght the belles and other thynges nedfull	4	4
for a prayer sent frome the Chawncler to be read in the churche		4
for the wryting of this acownte		12

(marginal: 39)

Sum	10	19	9½

And so remaynethe in stocke	7	6	½

Whiche some of £7 6s is delyvered unto John Myllenton & Robert Davis newlye elected churchewardens, the 18th daye of Maye Anno Domino 1571[1] in the presence of Thomas Downebell & Hewe Sklyser bayliffes of Tewkesbury & the rest of theire company & paryshoners of Tewkesbury

(marginal: 40)

[Added]

The Lord doth choose no man worthie, but by chooseing he makes them worthie

He hath choosen us that we should be holly

---

[1]   recte 1572.

41   Here followeth the trwe and juste accompte of **John Myllington & Robert Davys** churche wardens of the parishe church of Tewkesbury aforesayd for two yeeres That is to saye from the 4th daye off Maye & in the yeer of our Lord God 1572 unto the 25 daye of Aprill and in the yeer of our Lord God 1574 Then made & geven up in the parishe churche of Tewxbury foresayd unto **Roger Malliard & Roger Torblle** then being baylyffes of Tewxbwry & to others of the parishe of Tewxbury

First a note off all such things and somm off money as the forsaid John Myllington & Roberte Davis have reseved to the usse of the parishe church of Tewsbury duryng the tyme off theyre offyce as foloweth

	£	s	d
of Mr Baylyffs in stock	7	6	–
in gaynes off owr church alle	9	14	–
of Mr Wyett for the churchhowse soller		6	8
of Mr Baylyff Mallyard for that Elner Powell did geve unto the churche yerly		2	–
off Edmond Dekens for two yers rent	3	–	–
fore the standings in the churchhowsse		7	1
off Katern Morys for her shop a yere		4	–
off Mrs Smythe for two yeres rent for a aker		6	8
off John Plummer for the churchey for on yeere		5	–
fore the lone of the players aperell		3	4
of John Bubb for that Thomas Bryen did geve		5	–
of Gilles Gest for the buryall of his mother		6 [...]	
of Thomas Hitch for his rome & his wyffe in the seat which was Peter Huslocke		17	
of Wm Toney for his rowme & his wyffes in the seat which was Peter Huslocke		18	
of Mr Frebanck for his romc of his seat		18	
of John Davis for his wyffes rome in Mr Frebancke seat		12	
of Robert Davys for his wyffes rome in Mr Frebancke seat		12	
of Gilles Geast for his wyffes rome in the seat which was Mrs Slawters		12	
of Mr Dewey for a rome in the same seatte		12	
of John Myllyngton for his wyffes rome in the same seat		12	
of Mr Allen for his wyffes rome in the same seat		12	
⟨. . .⟩			
of Roger Wilkes for his wyff rome with hur mother		12	
of William Russell for a rome within his mothers good wyffes Kings seat		[...]	
of Mr Baylyff Torblle for his wyff rome in Mrs Ricards seatte		16	
of Mr Hill for his wyffes rome within Mystrys Ricards seat for cosideracion that he is allowed his wyffes former rome [for] his dawghter in lawe		2	–
of Richard Bubb for his wyffes rome wythin good wyff Brockbancke seatte		8	
of John Man for his wyffes rome within good wyff Kings		12	
of Thomas Cooke for his wyffes rome within Mrs Walker seatte		12	
of Symon Barells for his wyffes rome in the same seatte		12	
of William Cooke for his wyffes rome in the same seatte		12	
of good man Sowthern for his wyffes rome in the seate which was Mrs Geast		12	
of Margaret More for a rome in the seat which was John Barckley wyffes		4	
of good wyffe Broockbancke for hur rome in the same seate		[ ]	
of Wyllyam Fild for his rome in the seate which was Humphrey Richards		16	

42 (at left margin beside "of Mr Baylyff Torblle" row)

of Robert Grene for his rome in the sam seat		16
of William Leyght for his wyff rome within Mystrys Smyth		12
of ⟨Wyll⟩ Hary Turnor for his wyffes rome in the same seat		6
of Richard Rogers for his rome within Edward Nutbye		12
of William Masten for his wyffes rome in the seat which was Thomas Taylor wyffes		12
of Hary Shawe & Raffe Bydll for their wyffes rome	2	–
of Peter Bowyer for his wyffes rome wythin good wyff Davys		12
of James Dawnce for his rome within Thomas Cromp		12
of Thomas Knyght for his rome & his wyffes within James Bartlmew wyff	2	4
Sum is	24 –	8

Detts oweng unto the parishe church of Tewxbury which we the said churchmen cowld not gether up

Mr Rycards gave	20	–
John Wakman for his buryall gave	6	8
Humphrey Richards gave	20	–
Mr Morey oweth for his wyffes buryall	6	8
Mr Carricke for the buriall of his wiff in the churche	6	8
Jhon Fyld for the buryall of his mother	4	–

43 Heare after foloweth a just note for all such somes off money as the forsaid John Myllington & Robert Davys have bestowed & laid owt for the repayring of the parysh church of Tewxbury with all other chardges belonging to the same

	£	s	d
John Colle for ringing the bell two yers		26	8
for 8 ells of holland of 20d a nell for the curett surplysse		13	4
for making of the same surplysse		3	–
for a surplysse for William Johnsons		4	–
for making of the same surplysse			4
Robert Collens for the workmanship of 424 fotte of glasse in the chauncell	6	–	–
Richard Barrett for the mending of 4 windowes in the chawncell for the stone worke		46	7
Hary Smyth for mending of the bares to the same windowes			20
Edward Adames for tymber to make the yate & the stylle & the grate		8	4
for bords & nailles to the same yatte		2	–
William Kene for 6 dayes work & halff in making of the yate & the stylle & the timberwork of the grate		4	4
Hary Smyth for mending of the bares of the grate			6
William Wadley for mending of the grate			8
for a hide of whit lether		6	6
the Penticost money for two yere		6	8
for mending off the beares & naylls			16
for a bondell of lathes & naills to mend on of the ylls			4
for clensyng of grate			3
for saweng a pese of timber that mad the yat & the stile			3
the somner for the church lands for two yers			5
John Colle for 5 baldrycks for the bells & the spysyng of the ropes			16
John Leyght for a barell of lyme & the caridg			14
John Colle for making clene the gutters		2	–
for weshing of the surplysses & the towells			8

for besomes		4
for wrytyng of our presentmentes		8
for a bell rope	5	–
for the lytlle bell rope		10
good man Fletcher for sowder and workmanship	3	4
John Sklater for the making up of the churchyard wall & the lyme which went to it	4	[...]
John Coll for making clene of the gutors		12
John Coll for making 4 baldricks		8
good man Whone for taking up of 7 shets of lead & for laiyng them again & nailles	2	8
Hary Smyth for mending of the bolts of the second bell		[...]

44

for making of the men to drynck at the vysytacyon time once at James Daunce & once at Gilles Toney	3	4
for making off two bylles of presentment		9
for a comunyon booke	5	4
William Kene for mending of the seats	2	6
for bord naylles		12
for mending of the second bell & for iron & nails	3	–
for 4 barrells of lyme & for caridg	4	2
for 2 bondell of ston lath		8
for lath nailles		7
good man Whone for 13 dayes and halff work	10	6
for mending of the stocke of the bell & a pesse of timber		20
John Colle for spysing of the ropes		4
for a stock for a bell	2	4
for draweng of the stock unto the church		2
for shyds for a wyndles & for spyck naills		2
for 14 pound of iron		21
for 4 brasys and 2 bowsters for the bell & for shottyng of all the rest of the brases	3	–
for the making of 47 gret nailles		4
for hanging of thre belles	8	–
to make them drinck		3
for speek nailles & bord naills		4
for yron & for the making of the naylls		7
for lycker for the bells		3
for besoms & for 2 shids of wood		2
for a mans hyer		12
for wrytyng of thys accompte		8

Sum	16	3	11

So that by this accompte we the said John Myllinton & Robert Davys have yett remaynyng besyds the detts which be oweng in stock the just somm of £7 17s 9d

Remaining	7	16	9

45   Md that William Leighte & Edward Baston hathe receved at the handes of Roger Malliard & Roger Turble they being baylles the 25th dayes of Aprell anno domino 1574 the juste sum of eight poundes nyne pences

	8	–	9

	£	s	d
I saye [received]			
of Mr Mallarde for rente			12
of Richard Woode for his wyffes rome in a seate with her mother			12

of Richard Nansan for his rome in the seate where his wyff kneleth		16
of John Fidowe for his wyffes rome in a seate with Jone Davis		8
of Richard Barkar for his wiffes rome in a seate which was James Fookes		12
oute of the comon coffer for the towne seale	3	2
of John Compayne & Edmond Deacons for grownd to sett a seate on		20
of Humfferey Davis for his rome in a seate with Thomas Crompe		12
of Harrye Turner for his rome in a seate with Thomas ⟨Croomm⟩ Coocke		10
for standinges in churchehowse on Bartlemew daye	7	3
of Thomas Smythe for his rome & his wyffes in a seate in the lowerend of the churche		16
of Charles Stratforde of William Wackman for two romes for theyr wyffes – the seate that was Mres Wackmans		2
of Charles Stratforde for his rome in a seate with John Leatht		12
of Roger Millard for a lyttle seate for hym & his wyffe		2
of Niccollas Cleveley for his rome in a seate with his wyff		4
of William Johnsons for his wyffes rome in a seate		8
of William Lye for his wyffes rome in a seat with his mother		12
of Mr Bayllyff Geaste for his wyffes rome in a seate with his mother		[...]
of John Barbon for his wiffes rome with Mres Cole		12
of Robarte Kedwarde and John Wyett for theyr wyffes romes in a seate		4
of Edmond Deacons for on yeeres rent for his howsse		30
of John Beysan for his rome and his wyffes in John Fealdes seate		16
for standinges at Saincte Mathewes Fayer	2	–
of John Crompe and William Wodeley for theyr romes in a seate in the eastile	2	–
of Father Millard for a little seat for hym & his wyff		12
of Thomas Driver for a rome for his wyff in a seat that was Mres Bartletes		6
of Edward Tirrottes wyffe for her rome in a seate with Jone Davis for on yeerre 4d & so to paye at Easter yeerlye for the same seate		4
of Edmonde Tallowe for a little seate in the easte ille		6
of Katterine Morris for on yeeres rent for hir shoppe	6	–
of John Wattsson for his rome in a seat		12
of Richard Arkell for his wyffes rome in a seat with her mother		12
And that wheras Thomas Knight hathe paid for two romes for hime and his wyff in a seat with James Bartlemewes wyff as appeareth in the former accompte the afore said James Bartlemew & James Wardens wyff hathe by consent repaide the money so that the right restethe in them		[ ]
of Humffereye Davis for his a rome for his wyff in a seat with Mr Frebancke		16
of James Phellpes for a rome for his wyffe in the seat with Mres Nanssonn		12
of Mres Smithe for the rent of her half accre	3	4
of Mother Bennett for her rome in a seat with William Doles wyff		8
of Mr Poyner for the seate behinde next to Mr Carrickes	3	4
of John Grindle for two romes for him & his wyff in a seat that theye have used to knele		16
of Edwarde Baston for his rome in a seate with his father		8
of William Leight for his rome in a seate with John Hewes		8
of John Plommer for ⟨re⟩ on yeers rent for the churcheyard		5
of Thomas Bradeley for his rome in a seat with Richard Kinard		12
of Harrye Woode for a rome for hym & his wyff in a seat that was James Flowers		12

46

47

of William Hyll for ⟨the⟩ his fathers rome ⟨with Thomas Bradeley⟩   12

The just summ receved is   12   18   10

Herafter Followethe the juste sum that William Leight & Edward [Baston] have bestowed & paid for the use of the churche

	£	s	d
Penticoste moneye		3	4
for the discharge of the bockes at the visitacion			4
for the sidesmens drincking			18
for beosomes			3
for liccor for the beelles			4
to Thomas Grenwode for making a kaye and mending a locke & a making of a hinge			10
for nayles			2
for making clene the gutters			16
to William Keene for a dayes worcke			8
to Flocke for making a stone waulle againste the dore at the vaute			12
for nayles			2
to Thomas Grenewode for making a boulte, a staple & a keye			7
for paper for the regester bocke			4
for making clene the chapell		2	—
for 4 dayes worcke for sclatting to 2 men		5	3
for making of a keye			4
for 7 hundred of lathe nayles			14
for a barell of lyme			11
for 4 dayes worcke to two sclatters		5	4
for 6 dayes worcke to a sclatter		4	8
for 3 hundred of lathe nayles			6
for stoping the watter oute of the churche porche			16
for making a dore & whockes & hinges for him			6
for a rope for the lyttle bell			10
for white lether & making balderickes to John Cole			4
for a barell of lyme			13
to Ades for making to balderickes & letther			8
for making clene the gutters			12
for making 4 balderickes for the belles			8
for wyer for the clocke			2
John Cole for ringing the bell		6	8
for 2 barolles of lyme		2	—
for 2 dayes worck for 2 ⟨men⟩ sclatters		2	8
for naylles			2
to Rieve for worckg in the churche			6
for a boarde			8
to 2 men for sclatting 3 dayes worcke & a half		4	8
for 2 barelles of lyme & for carring to the churche		2	4
for nayles			1
for 1 dayis worck to 2 sclatters			16
for nayles			8
for 2 dayes worck to 2 men		2	10
for making clene gutters			2
for wasshing the clothes			8
for a barell of lyme		10	1
for a bosshell of charcole			3
for weying of leade			6

48

for a barell of lyme		15
for 8 bundell of lathes	2	8
for planckes to laye under the gutters	2	–
for 17 pounds of sowder	11	4
to John Fletcher for 7 dayes worcke for him & his man	8	–
John Cole for ringing of the bell	6	8
William Keane for making of half the great bell wheale		12
for tymber & ironworck		10
to the castle	6	–
for writting this accompte		8

The just sum paid is	5	5	9

So that taking oute £5 5s 9d oute of £12 18s 10d we do rest indebted unto the churche £7 13s 1d The which we have paid & discharged

49   Md that William Fielde and Thomas Mallyarde thelder chosen churchewardens for 29th day of Maye anno 1575 Thomas Perkins and Thomas Geeste beinge then bayliffes received at the said bayliffes handes in stocke for the churche £7 13s 1d

The said churchewardens stand charged uppon diverse accomptes left in arrerages before this time as foloweth: viz. of

James Chester for certen leade	7	–	–
Julian Wye		25	–
Richard Harley		6	8
Alexander Browne for five yeeres arrerages of the bequest of John			
Rogers since anno 1564	5	–	–
Henrie Greene behinde of his receipte in his bayliwielde		10	–
Thomas Allens wife for her formor husbandes bequest		3	4
Alexander Driver for 3 yeeres rent for the garden in the churchyarde			12
Matson for an oven rent 3 yeeres			6
Mr Wyett for the churchowse this last yeere		3	4
Mr Rickardes bequest		20	–
⟨Humfrey Richardes bequest 20s⟩		10	
John Wakemans wife for his buriall		6	8
⟨Mr Carick for the buriall of his wife		6	8⟩

Summ	16	6	6

More there is to bee reced to thuese of the churche that is behinde unpaide thre yere the somes folloinge

of Mistres Poynter for the buriall of her late husbande the some of	6	8
of Master Perkins for the buriall of his late wyffe the some of	6	8
of Thomas Kedwardes that his predcessor Edwarde Fyllippes gave		
to the churche the some of	6	8

Somme totallis in arrerages	17	6	6

The seyde churche wardens haue reced to theuse of the churche as followethe

of William Trigge for the buriall of Willyam Lyee the some of	6	8
of Roberte Jenninges for his roome in a seate in the southe ylle		4
of Humfreye Davis for grounde to builde a sette uppon by Mr		
bayllifes concente the some of	2	–

	£	s	d
of John Ellis for a rome for his wyffe to knele in the seate with Thomas Acleytone the good wyffe Gregg & the goodwyffe Plommer the some of			12
50 of John Leighte for his wyves rome in the seate that was Mr Thornbies		2	–
of John Hawlle the whoper for his wyves rome in a seate where William Baker dyd knele			12
of Mihaell Tailer for his rome in the seate where Allexander Green dyd kneele			12
of the goodwyffe Yeavance for the whole yeres rente of her shoppe in the churche howse		10	–
of William Fyelde for his wyves rome in the seate where hee & Roberte doeth kneele, hee makinge the seate longer of his owne charge			8
of Thomas Allen that came from Westencote for his roome in a seate where Mr Cotterell dyd knele		2	–
of William Orrell for the seate where William Fyeldes wyfe & Thomas Malliardes wyfe Ninor did knele		2	–
of Doritie Richardes for that hir late husbande gave to the churche the some of		10	–
of Thomas Malliarde for his wyves rome in the seate with John Wyetes wyffe & John Leightes wyffe the some of			20
of Thomas Rogers for the buriales of Mr Carique & his wyfe the some of		13	4
of Misteris Colle for the buriall of her sonne Richard Lyee the some of		6	8
of Thomas Malliard thelder for grounde to builde a seate upon for him & his wyfe nexte beneathe the pulpytt on the southe side he payenge the charges thereof him selfe the some			8
of Edmonde Deacone for this yeres rente of his howse		30	–
for standinges in the churche howse at Barthelmewe tide laste			14
⟨Some totallis reced is juste	12	5	3⟩
of Mrs Smythe for rente of the halfe accre that she holdethe		3	4
of the good wiffe Yevans for a quarters ⟨for⟩ rente her shope in the churche howsse		2	6
Somme totallis received is jowste	12	11	1

Hereafter folloeth the juste some that the seyde William Fyelde & Thomas Malliarde hathe bestowed and payde to theuse of the churche in the yere beinge wardens as followethe

	£	s	d
to Mr Poynter by thapoyntemente of Mr Bayllif for the quittance of ⟨myese⟩ of Boure of Glocester towchinge myese & rates the some of		10	–
for paper to make a small regester boke			1
for the drinkinge of the sworne men at Mr Hilles the daye they were sworne			16
to Persone Bankes for Penticoste moneye the some		3	–
for our drinkinge and the reste of the sworne mene at suche tyme wee mett aboute a presentmente			3
to the Regester at the deliveringe upp oure presentemente			6
for beesesomes			1
to Thomas Grenewod for lockes & keyes			17

	for naylles to sett one the lockes		1 ½
	for mendinge the churche yarde grate		1
	for weshinge the curates surplices		2
51	for whitleather		2
	to John Fleycher for worke hee dyd uppon the churche before tyme & unpaid by other vid.	4	–
	to John Fleycher for two dayes worke for him & his mane thre dayes	4	4
	mor to John Fleycher for sowder		20
	to John Colle for takinge a note of the seates		4
	to John Colle for makinge of bawdrickes for the belles & gresinge of them & for whit leather		8
	to Thomas Grenewod for 3 keyes & mendinge the cheste in the chauncell		11
	for naylles to sett one the same lockes		1
	for whitt leather to Richard Fielde		8
	to Corse for makinge the newe seate for Mr Bayllifes the summe	6	8
	for playnkes to leye in the bottome the newe seate		15
	for naylles to naylle them		1
	for beessomes		1
	for weysshinge the surples		2
	for a matt to the newe seate		14
	for mendinge the newe seate beinge brokene downe at a playe		2
	for naylles to doo the same		1
	to two men that carried the armure ⟨th⟩ by thapoyntemente of Mr Bayllyffes to the churche		2
	to Humfreye Addys & Flucke for pavinge in the churche the some of		12
	to Corse for mendinge the churche yarde gate toward the streate & puttinge in of a boorde		4
	for oure expences at Winchecome the some of	2	6
	for weysshinge the surples		2
	for a boorde to make a beynche in the seate when yt was broken downe		6
	to Corse for doinge the same & for naylles		5
	to John Colle for makinge of a booke of weddinges christeninges & burialles by commaundemente of Master Chancellor the some of		20
	to the Regester at the deliveringe upp the same booke		6
	to John Colle for lyckeringe the belles 3d for mendinge of bawdrickes 6d & for mendinge of bell ropes 3d some		12
	to John Colle for ringinge of the bell	13	4
	to Dyxsone for mendinge the tresselles of the greate bell		4
	to Thomas Grenewode for makinge a keye to the coffer John Colle hathe to putt in his bookes and other necessaries & for naylles to naille the locke		3 ½
	for wyer John Colle had to mende the cloke		½
	for wesshinge of clothes & surplices againste Easter		8
	for a barrell of lyme & carriage of the same to the churche		13
	for two whitlether mailles to make baulderickes for the belles the some of	2	4
	to Thomas Grenewod for the makinge of a staple to the bare of the churche dore		1
52	to Barrett the massone for worke in windoes	4	10
	to Nichollas Wyett for makinge a forme & fotinge another		14
	for two newe bellropes & there bringinge from Worcester	12	6
	for a communion booke	7	6
	to the cloke maker of Worcester for mendinge of the cloke the some of	26	8
	to John Colle for makinge another regester booke of weddinges christeninges & burialles		20

to John Colle for makinge of 2 bawderickes & mendinge of bawderickes & licoure		16
for lycker for the clocke when yt was newe mendyd the some of		8
to Roberte Collins for 12 fote glase at 7d the fote the some of	7	–
to Roberte Collyns for makinge of 7 fote of olde glase the some of	2	4
to Roberte Collyns for payntinge the dyall in the churche		20
for beesomes		2
for whitlyme		1
for wasshinge of clothes		6
for owre charges & other sworne men at the Archedeacons vicitacion at Winchecombe	4	–
for Penticoste moneye	3	–
to John Fleycher for takinge upp the lead in the southe yell & layenge thereof againe & for sowder & mendinge the leades over the chancell	23	7
for mendinge of Mr Bayllifes seate		3
to Nichollas Smethine highe constable for the dyscharge of the parishe for the castelle for the which wee have an acquittance vid.	17	4
for writinge this accounte		8

Summe totallis payee is juste	9	2	10½

Soo that takinge oute the seide some of £9 2s 10½d from the seide some of £12 5s 3d the seide churche wardens do remaine indebted unto the churche over & above the arrerages afore seide in the juste some of £3 ⟨2s 3d⟩ 8s 2½d

The which seide some of £3 ⟨2s 3d⟩ 8s 2½d is by the seyde Willyam Fyelde & Thomas Malliard in the daye of the yeldinge upp this their accoumpte by them full paide & discharged

More there is in arrerages to bee reced and too bee charged to the churche wardens nexte elected over & above that afore specifeid as followethe

of Mr Malliard for the rente out of his house		12
of Mr Morrye for the buriall of his late wyfe in the churche	6	8
for a seatte sett to Byddells wyfe Harrye Thompsons wyffe & her mother in lawe theye owe for 5 yeres 2d a yere for everie of them savinge that Byddells wyffe paid two yeres rente before hand	2	2
Jhon Plomer owethe for the laste yerres and thesse yerres rente come Seynt Marry daye next in Lente	10	–

53

Md that Charles Stretford & Wyllyam Johnsons were chosen churchewardens the 8th daye off Julye in anno 1576 Nycholas Greenewood & Kennellm ⟨being⟩ Cotterell being Baylyffes the sayed churchewardes rech [received] at the bayliffes handes in stock for the churche the sum of £3 8s 2½d

The sayed churchwardens stand chargyd upon dyverse accomptes left in arerreges before this tyme as appereth partycularlye as folowithe

James Chester for certeyne lead	7	–	–
Julyan Wye		25	–
Rychard Harleye		7	8
Alixander Browne for 5 yeeres arrerages of the bequast of John Smith alias Rogers since anno 1564	5	–	–
Henrye Greene behind of his receipt in his baylywyke		10	–

Thomas Allens wife for the bequest of hir former husbandes	3	4
Alixander Dryver for 3 yeres rent for the garden in the church yard		12
⟨Matson for 3 ovens rent for 2 yeres		6⟩
Mr Wyet oweth for the rent of the churchowse for one yeere	3	4
Mr Riccardes bequest	20	–
Humfreye Davis for John Wakemans buryall	6	8
Mr Baston for the buryall of Mr Poyner	6	8
Mr Perkins for the buryall of hys late wyffe	6	8
Thomas Kedwardes that hys predicessor Edward Philippe gave to the church	6	8
of Mr Maliard for the rent of his howse		12
of Mr Morrye for the buryall of his wife	6	8
for a seate sett to Byddles wife Harrye Thomsons wife & hir mother in lawe they owe for 5 yeeres 2d a yere for every of them saving Biddeles wife paid 2 yeres rent before hand		2 [...]
John Plommer owith for 2 yeres rent for [...] churchyard cum Saint Mary Daye in Lent		[...]
Sum of the hole arereges is	17	16 [...]

54 Rech [received] of Wylliam Fyld & Thomas Malliard in leade the sum of 26 hundred pounds & a half & 13lb

⟨Rd [received] of Alixander Dryver for a pece of cloth		6⟩
⟨Rd [received] of Mr Walker for scrapes	3	–⟩

It is ordered by the bayliffes that where Mr Poyner hath paidd for the seate next behinde the seate that was Mr Carickes The same shall be & remayne to John Barston. And further that the seate before it which was Mr Carickes shall for certen resunable consideracions by his sones to be perfourmed uppon talke had with the bayliffes remayne & be to the use of Richard Carique & Harry Carrique when they shall come & be inhabiting with in that town. And in the meane season John Barston to have the use thereof & Thomas Rogers the use of his seate next to the same

The true and just accompt of Charls Stratford & William Johnsons churche wardens for on yeare that is from the 8th daye of Julye anno 1576 unto the 16th daye of June anno 1577 made unto William Hyll & Thomas Crompe baylyffes of Tewxburye & other of the parishe

First a note of all suche somes of money as the said churchwardens have receved to the use of the churche

of Nicholas Grenewood & Kenelme Cottrell then beying baylyffes as is affore said	3	8	2½
of that which was left in areregis of Mr Morye		6	8
of Mr Perkyns of his areregis		6	7
of John Barston of his areregis		6	8
of Thomas Kedwardes of his areregis		6	8
of Mr Wyett of his areregis ⟨2s 4d⟩ that he owed for on yers rent of the churchouse		3	4
of Alixander Dryver of his areregis for the rent of a garden in the churchey			12
of Mr Malliard of his areregis			12
of John Plomer for the last 2 yers rent		10	–
of John Parsons for his wyves seat			12
55 of Mr Baylyffe Hyll for old vestmentes sold to hym		16	–
of Mr Walker for smale peces of a vestment sold to hym		3	–

of Alixander Dryver for on smale pece of a vestment sold to hym		6
⟨of Charls Stratford for a pece of imagerye sold to hym	10	–⟩
of Thomas Parker of Longdon for the old Byble sold to hym	10	–
for the hyer of players gere	3	8
of John Cole for 7 stepes of steyer sold to hym		8
of Edmond Decons for rent of his howse	15	–
of Thomas Hilley for half yeares rent of the same howse that was Decons	15	–
of William Moris for 3 quarters rent of his shop in the churchowse	7	6
of Mrs Smythe for the rent of the half acre for on yeare	3	4
of Alixander Dryver for rent of a garden in the churchey for on yeare		4
of Mr Malliard for on yeares rent		12
of Thomas Rogers for the seate next behynd Mr Baylyffes seate for Richard Carique & Harie Carique	20	–
of Rychard Cotten for his rome in the sete with Rychard Grege		12
of George Morye for his rome in the the same seate		12
of Robart Hawle for his wyffes rome in the seate with Hawles wyffe		12
of Rychard Cruse for his rome in the seate with John Baston senior		12
of Thomas Hilley for his rome in the seate that was Edmond Decons		12
of John Sorman for his rome in the seate with Michael Tayler		12
of William Johnsons for his rome in the seate with Wyllyam Hyll		12
of Thomas Kenersley for his rome in the seat wythe John Watson		12
of Harrye Arned ell for his wyffes rome in the seate that was her mothers		12
of Anne Davis her syster for her rome in the same seate		12
of Rychard Smythe trowman for his wyffes rome in a seate with Rowland Lancasters wyfe		8
of Harye Moore for his wyffes rome in the seate that was Humfrey Brushes wyffe		12
of Nicholas Allen for his wyffes rome in the same seate with Harye Morris wyffe		12
of John Hale for his wyffes rome in the seate ⟨that⟩ withe Harrye Shawes wyffe		12
of Thomas Kenersley for his wyffes rome in a seate		12
of William Aunton for his wyffes rome in the seat that was Peter Huslockes wyffe		14
of Richard Cox for his rome in the formost new seate	3	4
Thomas Wigon for his rome in the same sete & his wyffes rome in the other new sete	6	8
of Henrye Dowll for his rome in the same seate & his wyffes rome in next seate to that 3s & hathe yelded up to the use of the churche his rome which he had in the next seate before that & also a seate which he had taken before for his wyffe	3	–
of John Shaw for his rome that was Henrye Dowlls	2	–
of Edward Baston for his rome in the same seate with Rychard Cox 12d & hathe yeldyd up his other rome to the use of the churche		12
of Thomas Pomffrey for his rome in the place that was Edward Bastons	2	6
of Mr Baylye Crompe for his wyffes rome in in the myddelmost newe seate 20d & hathe yeldyd up her other rome to the use of the churche		20
of Mr Grene for his wyffes rome in the same seate	3	4
of Wylliam Johnsons for his wyffes rome in the same seate 2s & hathe yeldyd up her other rome to the use of the churche	2	–
of Mr Leyght for his wyffes rome in the other new seate	3	4
of Mr Sclycer for his wyffes rome in the same seat 2s & hathe yeldyd up her other rome that she had to the use of the churche	2	–

56

of John Ryse for his wyffes rome in the same seate 2s & hathe yeldyd up her other rome that she had to the use of the churche	2	–
of Richard Simons for his rome & his wyffes in in the romes that was John Ryse wyffe & Wylliam Johnsons wyffe	3	–
of Mystris Rycarkes for a rome for hir dauther with John Hoges		12
of Giles Geast for his rome in the new seat next before William Fylde Seate 12d & hath yeldyd up his other rome to the use of the churche		12
⟨of Mystris Rycardes for a rome for hir⟩		[ ]
of John Myllinton for his rome in the same sete	2	6
of Richard Fild for his rome in the same seate	2	6
of James Grene for his rome & his wyffes rome in the next new seate	5	–
of Barnard Farmer for a rome in the same seate with Jame Grene	2	6
⟨of Harrye More Thomas Churchey & John Hodges for the litle formost new seate on the north syde	4	–⟩
of John Hodges for his wyfes rome in the seate with Harrye Moores wyffe		12
of Wylliam Phyllypes for his wyffes rome in the seate that was Mrs Sclycers		18
of Rychard Lapyngtom for his wyffes rome in the same seate		16
of Thomas Kedward for his rome in the seate that was Mr Baylyffe Crompe		20
of Thomas Dryver for his rome in the seate that was Giles Geastes		[ ]
of Harrye Morris & Ralfe Bidell for the littel formoste newe seate on the north side	4	–

57 (margin, left of Giles Geast line)

The whole some that we have receved is just	14	11	10½

The churchwardens continued ⟨in⟩ theyr accompt untyll [ ]

Further the said churchwardens have sett to Mr Copley the rome in the seate for his wyffe that was Mrs Baylyffes Crompes & receved for it	2	6
⟨To John Butler & Rychard Butler for theyre two romes in the seate where Gilles Geast his rome was⟩		
Also Mrs Tratman that was Mrs Dewye hathe agreed to paye 6d a yeare for to have her rome at suche tyme she come to towne & hathe paid for on year		6
of William Tanner for his wyfes rome in the seate that was Thomas Taylers		10
of Thomas Wheler for hier of the players geare	4	–
of William Moris the last quarters rent		⟨...⟩
of Roger Tirett for his rome & his wifes rome in the place that was Rychard Williams rome & Thomas Mundy hathe yeldyd up his rome ther		16
of Thomas Harvard for his wyffes rome in the seate with John Hawles wyffe		12
of Thomas Churchey & Thomas Goodman for theyre 2 romes in the seate that was Gyles Geast	5	–

58 A note of all such somes of money as the said churchwardens hathe bestowen and paid ⟨for⟩ in the said yeare as followeth

for wayeng of lead	8
at the recevyng of our othe at the Archebushopes visitacion	4
for a book of Articles	6
for the drinckyng of the sydmen	18
for the puttyng up of our presentment	8
to the somner	8

	£	s	d
in charges at Gloucester		2	6
to Thomas Frebanck for wryting our presentment			8
to Thomas Frebanck for that the last churchwardens dyd owe hym			8
for a communion cupp gilt with a cover & also a nother communion cupp ungilt & without cover more then the chalis was sold for		23	6
for a Bible of the largest volumn	2	6	–
to Thomas Coles wyffe for making the pristes surples		3	–
John Cole for makyng four baldrickes			12
to Harye Lyes for makyng a tablecloth			12
for besoms			1
to John Cole for lycor for the bells			1
to a laborer for makyng clene the gutters			10
to John Flacher for castyng of a 100 & half a hunderth of lead to mend the places that was stelen aweye the other yeare by the boyes		2	8
to Nodley for makyng the deyce for the Bible that standes at the pulpett		2	–
for a litle lock for the weddyng church dore			4
to Harrye Dowll for nayles that Flecher bestowed in mendyng the lead			2
at a nother tyme at Gloucester to the Archbushopes officers & our charges		7	6
to Adis for pavyng the chapell wher the collectors of the poore do sytt		2	8
to Adis for pavyng & other work which he dyd in the churche			12
for taske for the half acre			2¼
to John Cole for ringyng of the bell		13	4
for besoms			1
to John Cole for makyng 3 baldrickes			7
to John Cole for licor for the bells			3
to John Cole for licor & smale cord that he laid out for mendyng of the clock			3

59

	£	s	d
to Nicholas Smythend for the discharge of the towne & parishe for the castell		17	4
to Adis for clensing of the grat			8
in chargis at Winchomb at the Archdecons visitacion		5	–
for Pentecost money to Parson Banckes		3	–
to Mr Doffe for that he laid out at Winchomb for us about the colleccion for Thomas Browne			12
for wrytyng of our presentment			8
to the somner			8
to John Cole for makyng the register booke of christonyng weddyng & buryeng for the register of Gloucester			10
to a labrer for makyng clene gutters in the iles & other work that he dyd			12
for 2 barrelles of lyme		2	–
to Harye Rycardes for halyng it to church			2
for 2 bushell of hear to Hary Dowll			6
more for lyme			6
to the parjeter for plasteryng and whytyng the walles and wyndowes in the churche		4	–
⟨to Adis ⟨...⟩ for makyng clene the gutters⟩			
to Adis to help John Cole to mend the clock			1
for Packthryd to spyce the rope of the greate weyght			½
for nayles at Wylliam Fyldes			5
to the swayeres for sawyng the tymber for the seates			18
to Wylliam Kene for 10 days worke		9	2
to Edward Adams for his mans work for the seates & other formes 11 days		9	2
to Tomsons for his work in the churche 7 dayes about the seates & other things		5	10

to John Smythen for plancke & for bordes for the seates		12	2
to John Smethen ⟨for⟩ for a dayes worke thate Flecher dyd before he			
died in settyng up the lead wher it was stolen awey the year before			10
to Giles Toney for 2 shydes			1
to John Cole for besoms			2
to Harye Doull for 200 of bord nayle			12
for a hunderth of hach nayle			5
to Harye Dowll paid for 10 peny nayle			8
for a hundred of bord nayle			6
for bord nayle & other smale nayle			4
for hynges for 3 dores for the setes		2	–
to Hale the laborer for makyng clene the gutters in the steple & for			
makyng clene the chapels behyng [sic] the chaunsell			14
to Robart Kedwardes hyghe constable for the discharge of the			
bowroughe & parishe to the castell for the last half year		17	4
for wrytyng of this accompt			12

The just some that we have laid out is   10   15   10¾

So remayneth in our handes £3 5s lackyng a farthyng

Further we have loned out some players geare to Thomas & John Wheler the note wherof we received by theyr hand wrytyng & they most paye for hyer of it on mydsomer yeve & then delyver it agayne 4s

Areregis there is dwe to be received & to be chargyd to the next churchwardens as followeth

James Chester for certen lead	7	–	–
Julian Wye		25	–
Rychard Harley		6	8
Mrs Browne of the bequest of John Smyth alias Rogers	5	–	–
Henry Grene		5	–
Thomas Allens wyffe		3	4
Mrs Rycardes		20	–
Humfrey Davis		6	8
Mr Grenewood for 2 curtens		13	–
Mr Morye for a pece of velvet		18	–
Mr Cottrell for fryng & whyt sylke		9	8
Mr Grenewood & Mr Cottrell for that they received of Mr Reade	3	–	–
⟨Thomas & John Wheler		4	–⟩
Mrs Buttler for the buriall of Mr Browne		6	8

The said churchwardens continued in theyre accompt untyll the 3 daye of September & have paid out as foloweth

for a matt that is in the chaunsell			6
for our absolucion & the somners fee & our charges & the certificatt at			
Gloucester		5	6
to Barrett for 7 dayes worke & half a daye		6	10
to Rychard Barrett for 28lb of sowder for sowder for the leades		18	4
to Wylliam Heyns for his worke 3 day & half		2	5
to John James for on days worke			8
to Harrye Dowll for nayles to fasten the lead that was sonck over the			
bodye of the churche		2	8
to Thomas Pomfrey for coles to heate the irens for sowderyng			8

to the somner for his fee for cytyng us to appere ⟨to⟩ before the deane
   to be swore to certen articles apoynted by the Quenes Majesty   6
to Adis for pavyng Mr Browns grave and other places & for lyme to
   ley the same   5
to a workman for mendyng the dore at the clocke and nayles   2

The some is   38   2

Also the said churchwardens bestowed upon the necessarye reparacions of the leades fyrst 100 & a half which Flacher sett up

Also John Leytt receved at 3 tymes from the free scole on a hundred fortye & three pound

& he receved at a nother tyme 10lb

Also Rychard Barrett ⟨bestow⟩ receved towards the reparacions of the leades half a hundred and 6 pounds

62   The true accompte of Charles Stratford & William Johnsons churchwardens anno domino 1576 & yelded up 3 September 1577 to John Bubbe & Richard Field elected for that yeere folowinge. So that in stock ye[lded] to the newe churche wardens 44s 2d And thereuppon the newe churchwardens by order are appointed to geve accomptes at Easter next folowinge & then others to be chosen. William Hill & Thomas Crumpe bayliffes.

The charges of the newe churchwardens John Bubbe & Richard Field anno 1577

First yeld to them in lead twentie three hundred poundes
in brasse half hundred lacking 2lb
five corslettes furnished tenn calivers sixteene murrens fower pickes
in yron one barr one highe candlestick one casement 2 chaynes
one riche coape five players gownes 4 jackettes 4 beardes twoo heades
tenn towelles 7 albes 5 surplisses & 11 other pieces of lynnen
2 curtyans received at the handes of Mr Greenewood by Richard Field &
   John Bubbe then churchewardens

63   **The just and true accompte of John Bubbe & Richard Fyeld churchewardens in anno domino 1577 And the same by them yelded upp in Maye in anno 1578 to Master Pace & Mr Wakeman bayllif and other the parishoners. Richarde Rogers and Thomas Donne ellected then for the yere followinge:** ⟨So that the saide churchwardens⟩

   of Mistres Ricardes in parte of payemente of 20s the which her husbande
     gave by will to the churche the some of 6s 8d and for the rest there
     is order takene shee to paye ytt yerelie 6s 8d reced   6   8
of Thomas Morris for the loppe of the ashe   12
of Edwarde Tyrrettes wyef for her rome in the goodwyfe Davies seatt   2   –
of Roberte Jonsons dowghters for their fathers seatt   12
of Richarde Nestes wyffe for a rome in the same   10
of Richarde Donne for the hyer of the players apparell   3   4
of Willyam Morris for his quarters rent due at Chrismas for his shope
   in the C/howse   2   6

of Lennorde Tornar for the seatte in the churche the whiche was his wyves	3	4
of John Colle for the hollowe elme in the churcheyeard	5	–
for the lopp of the two elmes	4	–
of Willyam Kynne & Thomas Morris for tholde parte of the u tree in the churchyerde	2	–
of William Morris for a quarters rente	2	6
of Thomas Hylle for halfe a yeres rente	15	–
of Allexander Dryver for the rente of a gardene in the churchyearde		12
of Richard Arckell for his rome in a seatt		12
of Roger Malliarde for rente due to the church		12
of Mistres Smythe for the yeres rente of the halfe acre in the Avone hamm	3	4
of Kennelme Cotterell for fringe etc	9	8
of the goodwyf Perkes the goodwyf ⟨Wuall⟩ Waull & the goodwyef Parsons for their romes in the seate that was Mr Butlers the some of	2	6
of John Plomer for the rente of the C yearde	5	–
of Connande Parsons for the buriall of his father	6	8
more over wee have received in gaynes to the churche by the churche alle all thinges cleerlye accoumpted and the charges borne that wee wer at the some	9 10	–
of Thomas Hylle for halfe yeres rente due in the feaste of Thannunciacion the some of	15	–
of Mr Grenewood & Mr Cotterell	40	–

Some totallis of all that which wee have received in moneye as afore is specified and the 44s 2d the which wee received at owre firste enteraunce is just	18	8 [...]

64   The particulers the which the same churche wardens have paide & leyd owte as followeth

to three menn for weyinge of lead		12
for oylle for the clocke		1
for the carrienge in & owt of the harntz & makinge of ytt cleane		3
to Robert Kedwardes for the castell money	17	8
to Humfreye Addis for clensinge the gutters aboute the churche		8
for whipp corde to mende the corde of the clok		2
to Richarde Barrett for sowder & workemanshipp aboute the churche the some of	13	6
to a workman to helpe Barrett		8
for colles & rassine		6
to one of Worcester for a roppe for the fore bell	4	8
unto John Colle halfe a hyde of white leather	2	–
unto John Colle for makinge of 3 balldrides		8
for sope & gresse for the belles		2
for makinge of the staple & for a horsse locke for the whome bridge		12
for wesshinge of the sirpleces & other clothes		4
unto a clocke maker for mendinge of the clocke	16	–
to the same mann for hangenge of the thirde bell	3	4
for mendinge the hamber & the weyers and for the makinge of a backe springe	2	–
to Willyam Fyelde for wyer		2
to Willyam Woodley for naylles		2
for greesse for the belles		1

to John Colle for ringenge the bowbell at Saincte Thomas Daye	6	8
to Humfreye Addys for makinge the newe steepes goinge downe into the churche porche & for takinge upp of a frame & bringinge yn of yearthe to make the same leavelle	2	10
for two barrelles of lyme	2	–
to Richard Barrett for mendinge of the leades and ruffe castinge a syde of wawll		21
to his workman		10
to Richarde Barrett for 10lb of sowder bestowed apon the churche & workmanshipp	7	6
to John Colle for ringgenge the bowble at Saincte Mathewes Daye	6	8
for a roppe to hange the greate peayce of the clocke weyenge 38 pounds at 3d a pound	9	6
for naylles to mende the churche yate		1
for soppe for the belles		1
for owre charges at Winchecombe	2	–
Penticost moneye	3	6
to the goodmann Jordyne the highe constable for the castell moneye	17	4
for a drynkinge for the seide menn		9
to Humfreye Addis for mendinge the bawldrycke of the lyttell bell		1½
to Mr Doffyllde for wrytinge owre presentmente made to tharchedeacone		4
to Thomas Freebanke for wrytinge of these accoumpte		12

65 (in margin beside "for a drynkinge for the seide menn")

⟨Some totallis by us paide is juste the some of	6	7	9⟩

⟨Soo that wee are to paye to theuse of the churche deductinge the seide some of £6 7s 9d oute of thaforeseide some of £18 8s 6d (by us received) the just some of	10	–	9⟩

Tharerages that is due to be reced: And to bee charged to the nexte churche wardens as followeth

to James Chester for certene lead	7	–	–
to Julyan Wyee		25	–
to Richarde Harleye		6	8
of the heiers of Allexander Broune for the bequest of John Smyeth alias Rogers	5	–	–
of Henrye Green		10	–
of Thomas Allens wyef		3	4
of Mistres Ricardes that doeth remayne unpaid of the gyfte of her latte husbande 13s 4d the which shee is to paye the same by 6s 8d yerelye		13	4
⟨Humfreye Davies oweth⟩		6	8
of Mr Grenewood for two curtens		13	–
of Mr Morrye for a pece of vellett		18	–
of ⟨Mr Grenewood⟩ & Mr Cotterell for ⟨that⟩ that they owe parcell of that they received of Mr Read	⟨3⟩ 20		–
of Mr Butler for the buriall of Mr Broune		6	8

Some totallis arerages is just	20	2	8

More that is by us paide unto those whose names are under writen for the players geare as followethe

to Roberte Collens for payntinge	4	6
to Roger Mylwarde for makinge of garmentes	4	8

to Richard Westone for makinge a jerkine			13
for 6 sheepe skynns for Christes garmentes		3	–
to William Fyelde for buckerine for capes			8
for two kippe skines for the thunder heade			6

The whole some by us paid is	7	3	–

So that deductinge the seide some by us reced oute of the seide some of £18 8s & 6d there rest by us to paye the just some of £11 5s [...]

more paid to Richard Coxe the some of	46	4

So that wee the seide C wardens have paid to the bayllyfes & other their bretherne £8 15 [...]

66   Md That Richarde Fyelde & John Bubbe deliviered upp their accoumpte to Richard Pace & William Wakeman bayllives & other their bretherne & parishoners the 13th daye of July 1578 And the seide bayllffes delivered in the seide daye to Thomas Donne & Richard Rogers the churche wardens for the yere followinge the full some of £8 10s 8d

Md That Mr Butler hathe in his securitie & safe kepinge to the use of the churche a silver cuppe

Here followethe the trew and juste accounte of Thomas Donne and Richarde Rogers churchwardens of the parishe churche of Tewxburye afor sayde for two yeares that is to saye frome the 13th daye of July 1578 and in the year of oure lorde 15⟨7⟩80 then mad & geve up in the parishe churche of Tewxburye afore sayde unto Hew Slyser and Richarde Rudgdale then baylis of the same towne and also to other theyer brethern and burgesis with commanalte of the same town there present

First a trew and perfit account of all somes of money as the above named Thomas Donne & Richarde Rogers have received to the use of the parishe churche of Tewxburye during the time of theyr office

of the churche stocke in redy money	8	10	8
of Jhon Donn for a seatt ⟨of⟩ on the east side and he repayringe the same			10
for the hyer of the players apparell		6	8
of Elnor Shilde for a rome in the seatt that was Richarde Rudgdalle wifes			8
of Jhon Westerman for a rome in the same seatte			12
of Ales Perkines for a rome with Jhon Fildes wife			12
of Roger Wiette for the hire of the players apparell		3	–
of Ann Dounton for a rome in the seatt with Thomas Donnes wife			12
that Roger Wiette yeldede up a seatt on the weste side and we have plased his wif with Mother Bennett in the rome that was Walles wifes		[	]
of Richarde Clarke for his rome in the seatte that was Richard Rudgdalles		2	6
of Richarde Clarke for his wiffes romme in the seatt with Jams Greme wiffe		2	6
of Henrye Jeninges for a rome that was Richarde Gregges			12
of Goody Chaunler for her rome in the sett [which] is Goody Hoggis			6
⟨of Jhon Mane for his roms in the seatt that was Roger Miller wiffes⟩			
of Nicholas Seple for a rome in the seate with hes wiffe			12
of Rowlande Rightes wiff for a rome in the same seatte			12
of Richarde Feller for a seatt that was Roger Millards wiffe			16

67

of William Yeavens for the rentt of his shope	10	–
of Hille for the rentt of his housse	30	–
of William Dewye for the buriall of his mother	6	8
of Thomas Frebanke for the sete that his wife dothe knele in	3	–
of Thomas Merychepe for his wiffes rome in the seatt with Goody Hews	2	–
of Richarde Filde for his wiffes rome in the same seatt and he yelding up a nother rome to the use of church		12
of Jhon Filde for his wiffes rom in the seatt that was Richarde Fildes wiffes		10
of Thomas Merychep for a rome for hime selfe in the seatt with Jhon Coxe		12
of Thomas Pitte for his wiffes rome in the ⟨same⟩ seatt with Jhon Fildes wiffe		10
of Richard More for his wifes rome in the seatt that was Roger Jhonsons		10
of Jhon Hiett for the buriall of his wiffe	6	8
of Mistris Smithe for the rent of her acre	3	4
of Jhon Plommer for rentt of the churchyard	5	–
of Mistris Ricardes for her arerages	13	4
of Allexander Driver		12
of Hwe Windowe for his wiffes rome in Richard Cottens seatt		10
of Hille for Mihellmas rentt	15	–
of Williame Yeaves for halfe yers rent	5	–
of Petter Barrett for the seat that was William Hilles	12	–
of Hille for Saynte Marye rentt	15	–
of William Yeaves for a quarters rent	2	–
of Jhon Plommer for rentt	6	–
of Mistres Smith for rent	3	4
of Thomas Smith of Waulton for castell money		⟨...⟩
of Master Hill for the buriall of his sonne	6	8
for the buriall of a man of Mr Rodes	6	8
of Richarde Bube for his rom in the seate with Brockbankes wiffe		12
of Allexander Driver		12
of Androwe Bothane for the buriall of his child		[...]
of Thomas Perkins for a rom in Mihell Tayllers seatt		[...]
of William Fild for Robart Greans rom		[...]
of Thomas Smith for castod money		[...]

Sum   17 10 10

68   Tharerages that is due to be received and to be charged to the next churchwardens as heare after followethe

to James Cheaster for sertayne lead	7	–	–
to Julian Wye	25	–
to Richarde Harley	6	8
to the heires of Allexander Broune for the bequest of John Smyth alias Rogers	5	–	–
of Henry Greane	10	–
of Thomas Allens wiffe	3	4
to Humfrey Davis	6	8
of Mr Greanwoode for two curtens	13	–
of Mr Morcy for a peace of velvett	18	–
of Mr Greanwoode & Mr Cottrell for that they owe for a partte of that they rechd of Mr Read	20	–
of Mr Butler for the buriall of Mr Broune	6	8
of John Baston for the buryall of his wyffe	6	8

of the executors of Mr Malliar for his buriall & a stonn as was layd
over him   10   –
of Mr Gest for the buriall of his mother   6   8
of William Cox for the buriall of his wiffe   6   8
of Jhon Hiett for the buriall of his daughter   6   8
to Richard Ekinsoull for his areragis   2   –

Hear after followeth a note of all such somes of money as the forsayd Thomas Donn and Richarde Rogers have paide & layde forthe for the nescessary reparation of the parishe church of Tewxbury as foloweth

for makinge of a bill and deliveringe of the same   8
spent at Gilles Tones on the side men   16
spent at Glocester   12
to the regester   6
to Jhon Jorden for castell money   17   8
to Richarde Barrite and his man   19
to a nother man to help Barit   8
for a hundred of nayles   6
to Humfrey Addis for a baldricke for the great bell   6
for a loke for the church gatte   10
for mendinge of the bear & iron   4
for bringing prossus for the curat at the apoyntment of Mr Bayllis   4
to James Phelpes for too bagges to mak balwrikes   2   –
for thre bundell of lath   15
for a barell of lime   14
for licker for the belles   2
to Savige & his man for waggis   7   4
for a leven bundell of lathe   4   7
for half a barell of lime   7
for licker for the belles   2
to Jhon Colle for ringing of the bell   3   4
at the meting of the side men   5
to the puritor for the deliverng of the presentment   4
to Henry Smith for mending the gret bell clapper   10   –
to Jhon Coll for ringing the bell   3   4
for a lodd of scaitt   6   –
to Richarde Filde for souder   18
for iron to make the claper   6   –
to Jhon Daston for castell money   17   8
spent at Glocester   22
for beasomes   1
spent on the side men at Giles Tones   15
to Gorge Richards by the apoyntment of Mr Baylis to fech Frith   2   –
to the paritor for deliveringe of the presentment   4
for whetlether to make balwrickes   4
to James Phelpes for a hevey malle   12
to Addis for makinge a ballwricke for the great bell   4
for iron and workmanship for the seconde bell clapper   8 [...]
for repayring the gatt at the church grat   2   –
for a loke for the yatt   12
for a kay for the heather yat   4
for a loade of sklat   5   4
for 9 bundell of lath   3   9
for fouer barell of lime   4   –
to Richard Barret for souder & workmanship   17   6

69

	for nayles		2
	to Merichep for year		9
	for mending a dore be hind the fant		1½
	to Jhon Daston for castell money	17	8
	to Jhon Coll for ringing the bell	6	8
	⟨to Jhon Coll for ring the bell	6	8⟩
	to Robart Sklifer for castell money		[...]
70	for a barrell of lime		10
	to Savige for workmanshipe		10
	for hear to Merrichep		3
	to Addis fo [sic] makinge of two balwrickes		8
	to Thomas Greanwoode for a buckell for a balwrike		2
	spent on the sidemen at ther metinge		4
	for making a bill		4
	spent at Derhust at visitation		14
	spent on the sidmen at the bull		8
	for beasomes		1
	for licker for the belles		2
	to the glasier	19	8
	to the parritor for fouer bookes	2	–
	to Harry Doulle for nayles to make the scaffoulde		1i
	to the parritor		6
	for colles and rasson		7
	for a caldron that was spoyled		12
	for nayles to mend the leads		4
	for a bundell of lathe		4
	for makinge clean of the gutters		8
	for licker to the belles		1
	to Richard Barrett for souder & workmanshipe	16	4
	to Nicolas Wiett for mending a whell		3
	unto two sclaters	3	1
	for 8 hundreth of lath nayls		15
	more over to the sclaters for workmanship	5	4
	for 7 hundreth of lath nayles		12½
	for ringine of the bell	3	4
	for mending of the surples		4
	a Addis for whepping dogges		4
	spent on the sidmen at another meting		4
	to two workmen to help Henry Smith	5	1
	for the ringine of the bell	3	4
	to Jhon Colle for makinge a book		22
	to Jhon Colle for making two balwrickes		8
	to Flocke for layinge two stones in the upper end of the church		3
	at the metting of the sidemen		4
	at Winchcombe fo [sic] Penticost money	3	6
	at the vissitacion of the sidmen spent	2	4
	to the parritor at Winchcom		4
	to William Kenn for mending the nether gatte		3
	to Jhon Fildd for half a hide of whetlether		20
71	to Jhon Colle for making of thre balwrickes & mending two other		12
	for licker to the belles		1
	to Addis for making two balwrickes		6
	for carrag of the sklatt		4
	to Jhon Coll for ringine of the bell	6	8
	to Savig for seven dayes worke	4	8
	to Haynes for thre dayes worke		21

to Haynes for fouer dayes worke	2	–
to a man to helpe them		21
for beassomes		1
to Addis for a balwrick for the therd bell	3	–
to Savige for sixt dayes worke	4	–
to a man too helpe hime	2	8
to Haynes for 5 dayes worke	2	7
for a busshell of colles		3
for borde nayles		5
for 12 hundreth of lath nayles	2	–
for rasson		2
to Savige for on dayes worke		8
to a man to helpe hime		6
for a corde for the saunce bell		8
for iron & workmanship for the clock		6
to Jhon Colle for mendinge to ballwrickes		4
to Thomas Grenwood for mending a buckell for a balwricke		1
for beasomes		1
for fouer bares of iron for on of the windows		8
to the glasier	8	5
at Winchombe for Penticost money	3	6
to Thomas Myllechep for herlyme		9
to the paritor		6
for makinge of the bille		4
spent on the sidmen at Winchcombe		4
to Thomas Greanwood for maknek a pine for a balwricke		1
⟨to th⟩ for a whop of lime		1
spente on the sidmen at the bull		8
for nayles to mende a dore		2
to Addis for mendinge the same		1
to Richard Fild for half a hid of whetlether		22
for writinge this booke		12
for a rope for the third bell	10	3
for a balwrick for the second bell		[...]

72   These churchwardens were discharged uppon this their accompt & paid the arrerages remaynynge in their hands to the next churche wardens chosen 20s

73   **The trewe accoumpte of George Freebancke and Thomas Myllichep churchwardens by them geven and yelded upp unto Thomas Crumpe & Richard Clarck baylyfes and to theire bretherne and other the parishoners the 7th daye of Apryll anno (1583) as followethe**

	£	s	d
of the last churchewardens the 14th daye of June (1579)	20	–	
of William Yevans for rente		2	6
of Allen Wilson for a seat			10
of Mr Morrye for velvet the some of		18	–
of him for the buriall of his sone		6	8
of Richard Egingtone for a seate		2	6
of Richard Rogers		11	8
of Richard ⟨Sadler⟩ Eckinsall for rent		2	–
of William Yeavans for rente		2	6
of Richard Wood		6	8
of Anne Hassarde ⟨for a seate⟩			12
of Mr Chambers ⟨for a seate⟩		20	⟨3 4⟩

of Nicholas Smysend ⟨for a seate⟩		20
of the goodwyef Drynkwater ⟨for a seate⟩		12
of William Yeavans for rent	2	6
of George Morrye ⟨for a seate⟩		6
of Bowlande Wright ⟨for a buryall⟩	6	8
for the goodwyef Allens ⟨buryall⟩	6	8
of Richard Wood for rent	3	4
of Thomas Hyllie for rent	15	–
of William Yeavans for rent	2	6
of Allexander Dryver ⟨rent⟩		12
of Edwarde Braforde ⟨seat⟩		6
of Anne Cotsall ⟨seat⟩		12
of Thomas Edwardes ⟨seat⟩		20
for John Braforde his wyeives buriall	6	8
of Thomas Hyllie for rent	15	–
of Richard Sclycer for a seat	2	–
of Thomas Hyllie for his wyeves seat		12
of Allexander Dryver for rent		12
of Wylliam Yeavans for rent	2	6
of Mr Hyll for his wyeves buriall	6	8
of Richard Gregg for his wyves seat		12
of Robert Hewez for his wyves seat	2	–
of John But for his wyves seat		12
of William Fooke for his wyves seat		20
of Thomas Leaper for a seat		18
of John Compayne for his wyves seat		12
of John Itheridge for a rome in a seat		12
of Margerie Springe for a rome		6
of Mrs Baskerville for a roome		6
of Robert Mynse for his wyves roome		10
of Sir Dufr his wifes rent		12
of George Whytledge seat		12
of George Freebancke for a rome in his wyves seat for Ellizabet his dawghter		12
74 of Weedowe Fyelde for a stonne	2	–
for the roomes of George Rygg & his wyef		10
of the goodwyf Shigeltone for a roome		4
of William Yeavans for his rent	2	6
of Richard Wood for a roome		12
of Richard Wood for his wyves & daughters rome	2	–
of Weedowe Tyrret for her husbandes buriall	6	8
of Richard Feller for his wyves buriall	6	8
of Thomas Heynes for a roome		12
of William Yeavans for rent	2	6
of Thomas Hyllie for rent	15	–
of Mr Hyll for a stonne layd uppon for Mr Wytherstone	10	–
of Luke Hurst for hyer of players apparelle	2	7
of Wedowe Lyngie for a roome		6
of Allice Wakeman for a roome		12
of the goodwyef Braforde for a roome		12
of John Plommer churchard rent	5	–
of William Setterforde for a roome for his wyef		12
of Robert Gynes for a roome		12
of John Rayer for a roome for his wyef		12
of William Yeavans for rent	2	6
for the hyer of the players beardes		6

of Richard Moore for a roome in a seat		16
of William Leight rent at St Mary Day 1582	4	–
of William Yeavans for rent	2	6
of Thomas Sclycer for a roome	2	–
of Richard Masone for his rome & his wyves	2	–
for the boordes		4
for brasse	14	6
of Richard Gregg his fathers gifte	3	4
of Mr Baskerville & Robert Astone for a seate	3	7
of Thomas Freebancke senior for a rome in a seat for his dowghter Margerie		12
of Mr Hill the some of	16	–
of Weedowe Fyelde her husbandes gifte the some of	10	–
of Richard Sclycer for his wyves seat	2	–
of John Bustone junior his wyves buriall	6	8
of Mrs Perkins buriall	10	–
of Richard Waters for a seat	2	–
of Richard Butler & John Butler for a seat		12
of Thomas Hyllie	15	–
of John Watsone for a seate		10
of Rabye of the Mieth ⟨seate⟩		12
of Mr Geast ⟨buryall⟩	6	8
⟨of the goodwyef Phelpes⟩		⟨16⟩
of William Mountayne seat	4	8
of Androwe Bawghan ⟨buryall⟩	3	4
of Weedowe James for a roome		12
for the buriall of Mr Seeborne	10	–
of Anne Snowe & her dawghter for 2 romes	2	–
of Androwe Bawghan for his childes buriall	3	4
of [ ] Foxe of Waltone for his seat		12
for the buryall of Charles Stratforde	6	8
of Thomas Hylle	15	–
for the players capes		6
of Edythe Plomer for a roome		12
of the goodwyef Hawker for a seat		18
of William Crosse for a seat		18
of Catherine Morgaine for a roome		12
for a seate for Thomas Myllechepe and Thomas Freebancke junior		12
of Richard Wood for the buriall of Mrs Smyth	6	8
of Pert & for his wyef and for Rychardes and his wyef for a seat	3 barrelles lyem	
of John Shawe for his wyves rome		12
of William Horcote for his wyeves rome		12
of Ellizabet Freebancke the dowghter of William Freebancke for a roome in seat		12
of Marye Thompsons for a roome		6
of John Sthevens for his wyves rome		6
of Henrye Dowlle for the buryall of his wyef	6	8
of James Felpes for the change of a rome in a seate for his wyef and that James Green ys to have a rome with James Felpes the some received is		16
of William Wood for a rome in the munckes seate on the west side the churche		14
for the change of a seate of John Hassarde to bee placed in Thomas Pumfreis seat		8
of Mr Colle for a rome in a seat with Richard Barker for his wyef		8

75

of William Leight for halfe yeres rente		4	–
of John Plomer for a yeres rent for the churcheyerd		5	–
of Richard Eckinsoll for rente			12
of William Evans for aquarters rent		2	6
of Thomas Hille for halfe yeres rent		15	–
of John Warner for his roome with Thomas Cooke & his wyefes roome with her mother		2	–
of John Coolle for his wyves roome with her mother			12
Some totalis received is	22	17	8
Wereof is payed the some of	21	6	2
Rest just to be payed the some of		31	6

76 The payementes made bye the seide churche wardens as followith

to Humfreye Addyes for weyenge of leade			4
for the emptynge the grate			9
for the clensinge of the gutters			8
for halfe a hyed of whytleather		2	–
to Raphe Byddell for mendinge a locke			11
to the lawnderer			2
for hatche naylles			7
for lycor			2
for two hogges heades of lyem		3	8
for makinge peges for the belles			4
to Thomas Smythe & to Thomas Heaynes		10	8
for a shide of wood to Christofer Canner			1
for 7 busshells & a halfe of hear		2	–
to Edwarde Gregsone for worke		5	–
to Thomas Grenwod for worke			6
to Nicholas Myllorde			4
that wee spent ⟨&⟩ at Mr Morries			3
to Smythende for boordes			14
to the glasyer		34	–
to Nicholas Myllorde		2	6
to Addyes & Flucke		2	4
for boordes lycor & a small corde			17
to Addys for his quarters wages			4
to Thomas Heynes for sclattinge		2	8
to John Colle for ringinge the belle		13	4
to John Colle for makinge the balrudges			16
to the Castelle Gloucester		17	4
at the visitacion at Derehurst		7	11
for wesshinge of the clothes			14
for her lyme		4	–
for the hanginge of the great belle		3	6
for mendinge of the clocke		2	6
for mendinge of the bell wheele		2	6
for lycor & wesshinge the clothes			4
for 4 busshelles of here lyem			12
for waysshinge the surplyces			4
to the Castell		8	5
for halfe ahyde of whytleather			18
for bysomes			1

to Heaynes for parjettinge	3	4
to Mopp for carringe of lyme		16
to Nicholas Mylwarde for makinge alettyr		16
to William Sawtherne for hallinge of lyme		3
for 8 stryck of heer	2	–
for tuckinge the third bell	3	8
to John Colle for ringinge the belle	6	8

77   Payementes as followeth

for lycoure		4
for bysomes		1
for carryenge of lyem		2
to Thomas Freebancke junior for ahoges heed of lyeme		20
to Heaynes for worke done		16
to Mopp for carridge of lyme		8
for clensinge the gutter & for alad payele		6
for whytleather		2
to Henrye Smythe for makinge barres of iron		6
to the glasyer	28	7
to Mother Dod		1
for wasshinge the surplyces		3
for Fluck & Addys for digenge of stones		6
for whitleather & lycor		6
for 2 busshelles of here lyme		6
to Addys & Flucke for takinge downe the clapper		6
to Henrye Smyth for mendinge the clappers		18
to Addys for clensinge the gutters & pavinge the graves		4
for arope for the lyttell bell		16
for 2 busshelles of heer lyme		6
for Mrs Dowles seat a busshell & halfe heare		4
to John Colle for the ringinge of the great bell	6	8
for abusshell of here lyme		3
to Addys for a ballrudge		6
to the glasier	20	–
to William Wodley for mendinge the clapper	7	8
for wesshinge the surplices & bysomes		4
for lycor & naylles		4
for wasshinge		3
for leather & makinge a ballwryck		7
to the glasier at two tymes	22	–
to Heaynes & for 2 busshells here lyme		14
to Mrs Colle for iron for the bell clapper	5	7
for mendinge of the clocke		3
for wasshinge the surplices & for licor		5
for hear lyme for Mr Stratfordes buriall		3
to Kyen for mendinge the beare		4
for whyt leather & lycour		4
to Fluck for mendinge the lead		4
for balwryckes		18
for wesshinge		2
for abusshelle of here lyme		3
for the staple for the churche yatt		5
to Addis for his quarters wages		4
for ahundred of boorde naylles		3
for makinge of two surplices		3

78   More payed as followeth

to Nicholas Mylward for makinge seates	3	4
for the side mens dynner	3	–
to Willliam Hytche for hallinge of lyme		2
at the Bull for charges		18
unto Smyeth & Heaynes	4	–
for abarrelle of lyme		12
unto Edward Gregsone	2	–
unto Heayns	2	2
unto Symons for delivery of the lettre		10
unto William Wyllies for the yaet	3	7
unto Grenewood for makinge of barres		6
for abell rope	5	–
for halfe a hundred boorde nayles		5
for lathes & laeth nayles	2	4
unto Heaynes for workmanshipe	2	3
to Grenwood		2
to Symons for delivery of the byll		4
for wasshinge the surplices and clothes		6
John Colle for paper & balwrycke		6
for buckells for the belles		6
for mendinge the surplices		6
to the castell	8	6
for clensing the gutter & hallinge of lyme		6
for abusshell of stonne lyme		4
to John Colle for ringinge of the gret bell	4	5
to the castell	8	5
to Addys & Flucke for layenge the stonne		16
to Wodlers menn in dryncke for the makinge of the clapper		7
for abusshell of lyme & weshinge the surplices		7
at Gloucester	3	–
for nayles		1
at the vycitacion at Derehurst	2	4
for the mendinge of the bell clapper	5	–
for wasshinge the surplices & abusshell of lyme		7
for lycoure & anewe hallier		5
to Kinges for hanginge the churche yaet		4
to Henrye Smythe for makinge the clapper	4	–
for wasshinge the surplices		2
to the glasier	26	–
to the castell	17	4
⟨for arome for Thomas Frebancke⟩		⟨12⟩
penticost money	3	6
to the archedeacone		12
for wasshinge the surplices		4
to the parriter		4

79   More paid as followeth

for abooke	6
for charges with the sidemen	12
for carrienge the byll to Gloucester	16
for mendinge of alocke	1
for naylles	1

		£	s	d
at Gloucester			2	–
⟨at Derehurst⟩			⟨2	4⟩
for the ⟨mend⟩ wasshinge the surplices				4
for nayles				1
for lycor for the belles				2
to William Willies for a yate			5	–
for wasshinge the surplices				4
for the stuffinge achusshinge				6
for nayles				2
for lycor				2
unto John Colle for ringinge of the bell			6	8
for 2 barrelles of lyme			2	–
for nayles				6
for 3 bundelles of lathe				12
to Savidge for worke				12
for makinge clene the gutters				6
to Mrs Colle for irone			2	10
to John Colle for makinge the cusshinge & for makinge bawlrickes				18
to the wrighter for makinge the accounpt [sic]			2	6
to the glasier			6	8
Some payed is		21	6	2

The arrerages that is to be received

	£	s	d
Mrs Downebell		10	–
of Henrye Dowll for astone		3	4
for the buriall of Mr Freebanck receved		6	8
of John Myllingtone for 3 hundred weight of lead		[ ]	
of Gylles Tonye for 35 pounds of lead		[ ]	
of Richard Mathewe & Salsburie for the hyer of the players geere		3	4
of Thomas Hatle for aroome in the monckes seat abarrell of lyme		[ ]	
of William Wodley by his owne report		6	8

80 **The trwe acounpte of Thomas Hylley and John Mon churchewardens by them geven and yelded uppe unto Nycolys Grenewood and John Rysse baylyffes and to theyer bretherne and other the parysshesyeners apon the 24 daye of Maye anno domino a.m.v.r 84**

	£	s	d
as folowethe			
in money of Gorge Frebancke and Thomas Mylychepe the laste churchewardens		31	5
of John Wyet for the buryall of hys chylde		3	4
of Hary Dowle for a stonne to laye over hys wyffe in the churche		3	4
of Thomas Kedwardes of Wautun for the Castell		3	4
of Jarvyce Batten for hys wyffys seatte with the goodwyffe Kynges			12
of the same Jarvyce for the grownd before Umfery Davyce to bylde hym a seatte apon			6
of Wyllyam Evance for mydsommer rent		2	6
of Masterys Downebell for her hussbandes buryall in the churche		10	–
of Thomas Hylley for Myghellmas rent		15	–
of Master Wyllys for hys chyles buryall		3	4
of John Mattewys wyfe for her seatte with Andrewe Bowthans wyfe			11
of Thomas Leylond for a seatt for hys wyfe with the goodwyfe Syverne			12
of Wyllyam Evance for Myghellmas rent		2	6

of John Kyngys for a seate for hym & hys wyfe		6
of Hary Wakege for a seat for hys wyff with hys mother		8
of John Hardyng for a seat behynd Thomas Hunderhylles seatte		9
of Wyllyam Salsbery & Rychard Mathaws for the hyer of the players rament	3	4
of Wyllyam Leyt for the rent of the halfe acard	4	–
of Wyllyam Evance for rent for Chrystmas quarter	2	6
of Thomas Campyne for a seate for hys wyfe in the goodwyfe Dowdys place		18
of John Raby for a seatt for hys wyfe with the goodwyfe Wollrege		12
of Thomas Alyne for a place in a seatt for hym selfe		12
of Thomas Alyne for a seatte for hys wyfe with Thomas Gestes wyffe	2	6
of Edward Lye for hys partt in a seatte		18
of Larance Mond for hys partt in the same seat with Edward Lye		18

<table>
<tr><td>81</td><td>of John Fylde for hys seatt with Edward Lye</td><td>2</td><td>–</td></tr>
</table>

of John Wyllyams for hys seat with Edward Lie		12
of Thomas Perkyns for hys wyff and John Taylers wyfe hys dawghter		16
of Wyllyam Cornell for a sette for hyme selfe and hys wyfe next unto Thomas Perkyns seatte	2	–
of John Hawle for a seat for hys wyfe wythe Wyllyam Cornell		10
of Gyllys Downbell for a seat with Robard Asson		18
of Wyllyam Wallford and hys wyfe for a seat that was Alexander Dryvers		22
of Thomas Sclysser for a seat for hys wyfe wythe John Kynardes wyfe		12
of Wyllyam Wyllys for grownd to sett hys seat on		3
of Elzabethe Frebanke for her fathers buryall in the churche	4	4
of Thomas Rogers for a seat for hys wyfe with Thomas Perkyns wyfe		9
John Wyllyams for the churche ayrde	5	–
Wyllyam Leyt for the rent of the halfe acar	4	–
of Wyllyam Evance for Sent Mary quarter	2	6
of Wyllyam Hyett for a seat for hys wyfe with John Hyett		12
of Thomas Campyne for hys seat with Umfery Davyce		18
of Masterys Downebell for her seatte for her foure chylderne / Anne Asson / Elnar / Mary / and Alyce Downebell ⟨for theyr lyves⟩	5	–
of Wyllyam Phelpys for a seat with John Davyce wyfe	2	–
of Thomas Knyghtys wyff for a seat with John Fyldys wyfe		12
of Thomas Hylley for hys rent for Sent Mary	15	–
of John Boote for a seat with Thomas Alyne		16
Wyllyam Wadley by cause he refused to be waye mon gave unto the churche	6	8
of the goodwyfe Leper for a seat with the goodwyfe Coke		16
of the goodwyfe Wollrege for her seate with Jonne Persons		12
of Chryster Canner for a seat for hys wyfe with John Shallys wyfe		12
of Nycolys Cleveley for the byryall of hys wyfe	6	8
of Nycolys Clevely for the chargys of the carte att the tolseying	2	4
for the lonne of the reparell at Chrystymas	8	2
of Rychard Wood & John Harlyey of Mathen for the hyer of the reparell	5	–
of Gyllys Tony for lead	3	5
⟨of John Mon for hys seatt Wyllyam Wyllyam [sic] Leyt & John Hewys		12⟩

<table>
<tr><td>82</td><td>The totall som of the reseatys that the churchewardens have resevyd for the yere ys</td><td>9</td><td>7</td><td>2</td></tr>
</table>

The paymentes made by the sayd churche wardens unto the baylyffes as folowethe

at Wynchecum at the vysytacyon ther for pentycost money	3	6
in exspencys at the same tyme	5	6
for the wayeng of the leade that remayne in the churche		4

Item	£	s	d
for a halyer for the for belle rope			4
for lycare for the bellys			1
for whessyng of the lynyne clothes			4
for wrytyng when we furst entred for the goodys in the vestery			4
for whesshyng of all the surplesys			4
for a honey bage to make bawlryges			8
for one bawlryge & mendyng of a nother			4
unto the Castell apon the 27 daye of Maye		34	–
at the vysytacyon that was kepe in Cheltnam		3	5
unto Umfery Addysse for maykyng of bawlrycke and lycar a yerne pyne & besoms			6
at Dowrest at the archedecuns cortte			14
to the plommer for mendyng of the gotters behynd the hyghe aultter and for sowder		9	6
for wood & collys & clensyng of the gotter			8
for to halyars for the thurd bell & for lycar			5
for whessyng of all the lynnyne clothes			8
unto Jamys Phellpes for to hony bages		20	–
unto Umfery Addysse for maykyng & mendyng of bawlrygys for the bellys			16
for halyars for the secand bell rope			4
for maykyng of the bowsters for to of the bellys			4
for nayllys & lycar for the bellys			2
for ryngyng of the daye bell at Chrstymas		6	8
at the Chaunselors courtte at Glossytur		2	10
for lyme and pavyng of the churche		3	2
for wyer & lycar & mendyng of the clocke			4
for whasshng of the surplesys agaynst Chrystmas			3
for a rope for the lyttyll belle and a hallyayre for the gratte bell			13
unto Umfery for maykyng of a bawlryge for the gratt bell			4
for maykyng of the curates surples			12
for a loke & a stapull unto Hary Smythe			13
for wasshyng of 4 surplesys			3
for ryngyne of the daye bell		6	8
at Glossytur at the vysytosyun ther			10
at Cheltnam at the vysytacyun ther			17
for lycer for the bellys			1
for to barelles of lyme & hawlyng			12
unto Thomas Heynes for stopyng the wyndow and mendyng the walle under the same wyndow		2	3
unto the smythe for mendyng the bares			4
unto the glasyer for glasyng of the wyndow in the ylle by the cloke		31	2
unto Thomas Heynes for swypyng of the wyndowes in the churche			4
at the archedecons cortte to the ordenary in the paryshe churche		2	4
unto the deane for pentycoste		3	6
for exspensys at the Boole		3	2
for wasshyng of the surplesys			3
for besoms and leker			2
to the glacyer for glasyng the other wyndows in the churche		10	–
to the sarchand for sommonyng Nycolys Cleveley to the court			2
for chargys of courtt for Nycollys Cleveley		2	8
unto the glasyer for glassyng the lytell weste wyndow and 3 other wyndow on the hether syd of the churche		13	4
unto the clare for wrytyng and maykyne of the boke			20
The totall some of the paymetes that the churchewardens have payd for the eyre	8	4	7

83

There ys to be resevyd of Alexander Dryvers wyff for her howsbandys
    byryall in the churche   6   8

We have ordeyned to be churchewardens Wyllyam Tony and Larance Mone

[one blank page numbered 84]

85   Md That William Tonye and Lawrence Moone receyved those thinges which belongeth
    unto the church of John Man and Thomas Hilley the 13th of June 1584

86   **The accompte of William Tony and Laurence Moone churchewardens of the
    parrishe churche of Tewkesburie for one whole yere that is to saie from the 24th
    daie of Maye 1584 unto the third daye of Maye 1585. Then made and geven upp in
    the parrishe churche of Tewkisburie aforesaid unto William Hyll and William
    Wyllys then bayliffes of the said towne of Tewkesbury and also to other of the
    burgesses and comynaltie of the said towne then present**

First the said chuchwardens do charge them selfes with these sommes of money here
under written by them receavid within the tyme of this accompte, as by the perticulers
of the same following may appeare

	£	s	d
of the olde churchwardens John Manne and Thomas Hilley	25	3	
of John Tommes for his owne place within Mr Lyez and Mr Felde		18	
of goodwife Evans for midsomer rent 1584		2	6
of Richard Sellar for his own roome where Mr Stratford did knele		18	
of certen men of Mathon for the use of the pleyers apparrell		5	–
of John Shild for his owne place with Henry Moones wife		12	
of Thomas Hylley for Michelmas rent 1584		15	–
of William Leight for Michelmas rent 1584		4	–
of Richard Maskall for his wyves roome in the place of olde goodwife Braford		12	
of John Smithesend for 2 roomes in the seate where Nestes wife in the kay lane knelith		2	–
of Nicholas Felde for the hole seate that his mother had		3	4
of him for a stonne to lay upon his mothers grave		[...]	
for the buryall of Alexander Dryver		6	8
of the person of Hyllchurche for the use of the plaiers apparrell at Cristmas last		3	6
of goodwife Evans for Michelmas rent 1584		2	6
of Thomas Dekyns for his roome where Roger Myllward knelithe		12	
of Lewis Brusshe for his roome in the same seate with Roger Myllwarde		12	
of goodwife Evans for Christmas rent 1584		2	6
of Thomas Hylley for his halfe yeres rent due at Sainct Mary Day last 1583		15	–
of goodwife Evans for Sainct Mary Day rent 1584		2	6
of John Hassard junior for his wives roome in the old goodwife Gregges place		12	
of Richard Lepper for his owne roome in the seate where old Nutbye is		16	
of Edwarde Alye for his wyves roome in his mothers seate		12	
of John Clarke for his owne roome and his wyves in the hie seate at the south side of the churche below the pulpitt		20	
of Andrew Boughan for the buryall of his child in the church		3	4
of William Leight for St Mary Day rent 1585		4	–

87   The same churchwardens do praye allowaunce of the somes of money hereafter mencionyd by them paid for the reparing of the church of Tewkisbury and other thinges to the same church appertaynyng during the tyme of their office as by the perticulers thereof ensuyng may appeare

	£	s	d
Richard Feld for lether			20
Addys for mending the bawdryckes			4
for mending twoo wyndowes and for lyme			8
for besoms			1
for mending the eye of the thyrd bell clapper		3	–
for iron for the same		2	2
Addys for mending the bawdrickes			4
for clensing the church grate			8
for staples for the same			8
for a pece of tymber to laye the same grate apon and workmanshipp			3
for mending the stocke of the sanctes bell			3
for wasshing and mending the communyon clothe			3
for mending under the clock in tymber worke			2
for a roope for the second bell		4	4
at Gloucester to the chauncellor & other officers		2	8
of lycour for the bells			1
for coles and candles for the plomer			6
to Thomas Grenewode for nayles & a grete hoocke			15
for 47 pounds sowder at 8d the pounde		31	4
for woodd and coles			9
for mending the kaye of the church doore and mending the locke & putting in the staple in the churchgate			7
for rydding the gutters 2 dayes			16
the plommer for taking upp the sheetes of ledd and other worckmanshipp which he did		30	–
Raif Byddle for nayles			10
for a ⟨mayl⟩ male to make bawdrickes			12
for making 3 bawdrickes			10
for wasshing the surplesses			3
for a hallyer for the litle bell			3
for wasshing against Christmas			2
for a barrell of lyme and for lycour			12
Addys for making and mending bawdrickes			7
for wasshing the church clothes against Easter			4
Wodley for mending the bell claper		2	6
for mending the church clocke		7	–
for wyre and whipcord			3
to men to helpe up with the peyses and for besoms			3
Addys for mending the bawdrickes			4
for receiving in the last presentment			4
The some totall of the paymentes comethe unto	4	19	4
The which being deducted out of the receptes there remayneth due unto the churche		11	1

The which some of 11s 1d was by the same accomptauntes deliverid unto

John Filde and   Churchewardens allectid
George Morrey   4 Maij 1585

A note of certaine goodes of the churche deliverid to the said John Felde and George Morrey the said 4 Maij 1585

the best coope of tynsell with redd roses
the best pawll for the comunyon boorde
one other pawll of redd and grene satten with a fringe
one other of checker worcke
a table clothe with a frynge of golde
a blacke pawll of velvytt
one greate cwosshyn
one cwosshin of gold and redd velvitt
three redd satten cwosshins
2 curtens of yallowe and greene satten
7 table clothes
10 towells
2 fonte clothes
3 awbes of lynnen
88   a curten of white callycow cloth
one amyce this being a litle lynnen cloth
one bell and a dexte of iron

players apparrell – 8 gownes and clokes
            – 7 jirkyns
            – 4 cappes of greene sylke
            – 8 heades of heare for the apostles and 10 beardes
            – a face or vysor for the devyll

In peces of leadd remaynyng in the vestrye wayed the said 4 Maij 1585 1210 pounds

Memo^rd There is owing by John Myllington for 300 wcight of leadd

Also there is owing by Thomas Hall for 210 pounds of leadd lent him by Laurence Moone and William Tony the last churchwardens

Lykewise there is owing for the rent of the churchyard for a yere endid at Saincte Mary Day 1585 to wit 2s 6d by Edith Plomer and Laurence Moone for half a yere endid at Michelmas last & 3s 4d by Richard Arkill for a nother halfe yere endid at St. Mary Day last.

1585	Churchewardens	John Field
	elected 1585	George Morrey

The accompt of Johon Field & George Morrey churchewardens for one yeere begininge 3rd dae Maij 1585 & endinge 15 Maij anno 1586 George Morrey & Thomas Geast then bayliffes with many other burgesses & parishoners present

Receiptes	£	s	d
of the last churchewardens Laurence Moone & William Tonye in stock	11	1	
of Mrs Crumpe geven by her husband		20	–
of Mr Arkell for rent of the churchyard for one whole yeere		6	7
of Margery Bundy geven by her mother		6	7
of Thomas Hilley for one yeeres rent of his howse		30	–
of goodwife Evans for one yeeres rent of her shoppe in the market howse		10	–
of William Leight for one yeeres rent of his acre in Avonham		8	–
of Mr Hill for his childes buryall		3	4

	£	s	d
of John Baylie for 2 roomes for him & his wife in a seate with Nicholas Cleveley		2	–
of Anne Parker for a rome in the same seate with Nicholas Cleveley			12
of Thomas Cowles for a rome in a seate with Humfry Davies & James Davice		2	–
of Richard Waters for his wifes rome with Mrs Morrey & goodwife Nutbye		2	–
of John Webley for 2 romes for him & his wife where Mr Mauson kneled		3	–
of Margery Bundy for 2 romes for her & her brother Nicholas where her mother kneled		2	–
of Peter Barret for his wifes rome with Margery Bundye			12
of John Hardinge for his wifes rome with Roger Gilbtes wife			12
of Mr Boche for his rome with Edward Barston & Richard Cockes		2	6
of Mr Arkell for the churchyard to be received at Michaelmas next 1586		5	–
Sum Tote	5	17	3

89 Laid out by the churchewardens for that yere

Expenses	£	s	d
Addes for caryinge up weyghtes when we first receaved the accompt of lead			3
at the visitacion for a booke of articles			7
for the somoners fee			4
for the registers fee			4
for receavinge next our presentment			4
for pentecost money		3	6
for the sides men dynner		4	5
for 15 pounds of yron to mend the 3d bell clapper			20
Wodley for woorcking it		3	–
the plumer for 11 pounds of soder		7	4
him for woorcking it			11
for coles at that tyme			2
Addes & 2 men for seamige 20 shetes of lead		3	4
for nayles to the same			2
for a mayle			14
for a presentment put in to the registeres office			4
for a bill of recusantes wryting at the sessions			6
Addes for makinge & mendinge baldrickes for one whole yeere		2	2
for expenses at Gloucester sessions			6
for makinge a sirples			3
for a presentment at Michaelmas sessions			4
for 8 pounds 3 yardes of yron to mend the bolt of the 3d bell clapper			13
for woorckmanship		4	–
Addes for caryinge up the same			2
for 6 halliers for the belropes			18
Charles Hewes for 10 footes of glasse a barr of yron & nayles		5	1
the clarck for a yeers wages		13	4
for Savage for half a dayes worck			4
for casting 6 hundred & half of lead		15	2
for wood & coles then			14
for laying the ledden gutters			6
Addes for poynting the stone gutter			2
for simoing the same gutter			12

for taking downe glasse in the scholehowse		2
for turninge the eye of the 2 bell clapper		4
for licor		1
for 2 plates & nayles for the chauncell doore		2
for 3 lockes keyes & boltes about the same	3	–
Heynes for 2 dayes woorck		16
at Gloucester to the register, sumoner our expences & wryting a register for 3 yeeres	4	7
for 13 pounds of soder & woorckmanship about the tower	10	–
for taking up & newe seaming 36 shetes of lead	8	–
of 2 hundred of nayles to nayle the same	2	–
for charkcole used at the tower topp		5
for washing surplesses & churche clotes for the whole yeere		8
for a barrell & bushell of lyme & a bushell & half of heare	2	–
Heynes for 2 dayes sklatting	10	1
for sklatt pines		1

90

for souderinge the gutter over Sir Beardes chamber		8
for coles used ther		2
for white leather		18
for a presentment a Gloucester		4
for white leather		20
for beesoms		1
for lycor for the belles		3
for clensing the gutters		6
for a key for the clockhowse doore		4
Savage for a dayes woorck		9
for nayles for the leades		2
for 2 crestes		2
for a bill of presentment		4
Addes for mending the gutter		4
Savage for woorck		6
for a bushell of heare lyme		4
for a key & mendinge the churchard locke		4
for a strickles		2
for 8 pounds of yron to make hoockes & hinges for the churchyard gat & woorke		21
for mendinge the beare		3
at at [sic] Gloucester sessions for a presentment		4
for expenses there		6
for paper & wrytinge this accompt		20

Suma totalis in expenses	6	3	7

So that uppon this accoumpt remaynethe due to be paied to the churchewardens as laid out more then they have receaved	6	4

Arrerages due to the churche they finde for this yeere

by Mrs Mylton for her husbandes buriall	6	8
⟨by Mr Pacies gift⟩	⟨10	–⟩
for Mr Pacies buriall	6	8
to the churche to be awnswered by the churchewardens 108 pounds of leadd	[	]

1586	Churchwardens	John Field
	still remayning for this yeer 1586	George Morrey

The accompt of John Field & George Morrey continuinge churchewardens for their accompt yelded 15 dai Maij 1586 unto the 28 of Maye 1587 then geven up to William Wakeman & Roberte Mylton bayliffes and others present

Receiptes	£	s	d
of Wedowe Sklicer for her husbandes Richard Skliceres buriall		6	8
of Mrs Pacie for her husbandes gift		10	–
of Thomas Hilley for Michaelmas rent		15	–
of William Leight Michaelmas rent		4	–
for Mr Fitzhewes buriall		6	8
of Mothers Evans for Midsomer rent for her shopp in the markett howse		2	6
of William Wodley for his wifes buriall		6	8
of James Greene for the belles according to an order late agreed uppon			12
of John Man for his wifes buriall		6	8
for the belles for William Thomas		2	–
for Nicholas Clevely his gift		10	–
for a stone to laye over Mr Perkins grave		2	–
for Roger Burtones buriall		6	8
of Thomas Rudgdales for St Mary Day rent		15	–
of William Leight for St Mary Day rent		4	–
for buriall of Mr Willis childe		3	4
for Richard Maskalles wifes buriall & belles		8	4
for goodwife Tirrettes buriall		4	8
for the belles then		2	–
of Nicholas Field for rent of the churchyarde the next yeere		6	8
of William Fooke for a roome in a seatt		2	4
of Walter Weaver for a room in a seate		2	6
of Richard Hewes & Georges Rogers for a seate for them & their wives		3	4
for a George Peytons wifes roome		10	1
for Roger Tapsters wifes rome			12
for William Persons wifes rome		2	–
of James Habbock for 2 roomes for him & his wife		2	–
for Giles Downbelles wifes rome		2	–
of Walter Hopkes for a rome			6
of John Tayler for a rome			12
of William Turbell for a rome		2	–
of John Braford for his rome his wifes & Wedowe Cheringtons in a seate with Richard Rogers wife		5	–
for Thomas Androwes wifes rome			12
in exchange for 2 romes from John Wodley & his wife to John Hodges & his wife			12
of Dorothe Frebancke for her rome		2	6
of John Bowghan for a rome		2	–
of Thomas Dixon for recording his rome & his wifes a seate wee bilt			6
of John Trigge for his wifes rome			12
of John Leight for a roome		2	3
of Whone for his wifes rome			12
of John Whooper for his wifes rome			6
of Richard Hyett for 2 romes for him & his wife		4	–
of Richard Tyrrett for a seate which was his fathers for him & his wife		3	4
of George Frewen & Alexander Greene for their wives romes		2	–
of John Mann for his rome		2	–
of Thomas Tippenge for his rome		2	–
Summa totalis receaved for this yeer	8	14	4

91

92   Laid out by the churchewardens this yere

Expenses	£	s	d
at the visitacion pentecost money		3	6
for a bill of presentment			4
to the register			4
to the somoner			4
for the sworne mens dynner		6	6
for a hide of white leather		4	4
for 31 pounds of yron for 2 clappers for the forebell & great bell		4	8
Harry Smithe for the clappers		11	8
to a man to helpe him			8
for 5 halliers for the belles			17
for mending the clocke		12	–
for seaming 12 sheetes of lead		2	–
for 2 hevy males		2	8
for makinge & mendinge 7 baldrickes			22
for a presentment			4
for a key to the greate chest			4
for carying the clappers up & downe			3
for wyer for the clock			6
for 4 barrelles of lyme		4	–
for a quarter of a hundred of yron		3	6
for mendinge the greate bell clapper		7	8
for carying up the clapper			2
for 2 halliers			6
the clarckes yeeres wages		13	4
Heynes for woorck about the tower & chancell		6	–
for an yron pynn for the baldrick of the greate bell			2
for half a hide of white leather		2	2
back againe the rent of the churchyard receaved the last yeere		5	–
for makinge & mending baldrickes			16
Addes for mending diverse places in the churche			12
for spicing a rope			2
for nayles faboute lead & lathe			4
Heynes for poyntinge the iles and clensing the gutters		2	9
for 4 crestes			4
for 4 bushelles of heare			12
for halfe hundred of yron abating 20 pounds		4	6
for mendinge the great bell clapper		4	8
for Smithes coles			18
for carying up the clapper			1
for wasshing surplesses & clothes all one yeere			12
for mending a surples			3
for 9 foote of newe glasse & 10 foote of old in the wyndowe next the pulpet		7	4
for castinge two hundred & half of lead & wood		7	–
for woorking the same about the chancell		3	–
for licor & besomes the whole yeer			10
for 3 halliers			6
for mending certen plaices			6
for 6 pounds in quarters of rope for the grete paise			20
for placing it up			2
for mending the lock & key of the gret chest			4
for a bushell of choles to heate the stoning gutters over the yles			4
for simoning the same gutter		3	6

for a plate & nayles for the 2 bell			8
for nayling about the belles			4
93 Addes for keepinge dogges out of the churche			6
for 9 of soder		6	–
for woorckmanship			16
for 15 pounds & half of sheete lead			23
for coles			4
for a lock & key to the churcheard gate			6
for mending the gate			6
at the archdeacons visitacion pentcost mony		3	6
to the register			4
to the somner			4
for the bill of presentment			4
for the side mens dyner		5	6
for 2 doores to the chappell		2	6
for 2 lockes keyes hackes & hinges		2	6
for nayles			2
remayning due to the churchwardens uppon the last yeeres accompt		6	1
for paper			2
for 2 halliers for the bell ropes			6
for articles delivered by the pariter			12

Summa tote 8 15 4

So that by this accompt remayneth due to the churchwardens lade out above their receiptes 12

Arrerages due to the churche this yeere

of Mr Greenewood for the buriall of Hyett of Walton & the belles	8	8
for the rent of the churcheyard	5	–
of John Myllington owing of old	300 pounds of lead	

Md The lead charged of old uppon Lawrence Moone was receaved by us whereof we delivered to Mr Willis 100 & the other hundred is in store

Churchewardens yet remayning for this   John Field
yeer 1587 and the next yeer 1588   George Morrey

1587
1588

This accompyt of John Field & George Morrey continuing churchewardes from 27 Maij 1587 unto the 20 of Maye 1589 for 2 whole yeeres geven up then to Kenelm Cottrell & Richard Cotton bailiffes & others present

Receiptes	£	s	d
for Mres Downbelles buriall		6	8
for Mr Sklicers buriall & belles		8	8
for Richard Woode his buriall		6	8
for the belles at John Smythsendes buriall		2	–
for goodwife Brafordes buriall		6	8
for Mary Coles buriall & belles		8	8
for Mres Allens buriall		6	8
for the belles at Robert Jeynes buriall		2	–
for Mres Clarckes buriall		6	8

	for Mr Wakemans buriall & belles	8	8
	for burialles of William Walford & his wife	13	4
	for buriall of Mres Pacie	5	9
	for Richard Waters buriall	6	8
	for Thomas Dun his wifes buriall	6	8
94	for Mr Leightes buriall	6	8
	for Robert Ashtons buriall	6	8
	for Thomas Porters wifes buriall	6	8
	for Mres Yerworths buriall	6	8
	for Thomas Underhills gift & belles	5	4
	for Thomas Rudgdale Michaelmas rent	15	–
	of goodwife Leight Michaelmas rent	4	–
	of Bryne for the churchard 1588	2	8
	of Thomas Ridgdale St Mary Day rent	15	–
	of wedowe Leight rent then due	4	–
	of William Hewes for his wifes rome in seate with John Coles wife		12
	of William Knight for a rome in seate with his wife		12
	of William Hill for his rome with William Johnsons	2	–
	for George Lydes wifes rome in seate with Myllichepes wife	2	–
	of William Dun for his wifes rome & Julian Pacies rome in the seate which was their mothers	4	–
	of Morgan Pacies wifes rome in the same seate	2	–
	for Thomas Greenow his wifes rome in seate with John Baughans wife	2	–
	of Mr Stephens for a rome with Robert Jeynes	2	–
	of Roberte Younge for a rome in seate with John Butt	2	–
	of Roberte Younge for his wifes rome in seat with wedowe Shild		12
	of Richard Brooke for his rome & his wifes in seate with Richard Bubbe	2	–
	of John Tonnes for his wifes rome in seate with John Bawghans wife which rome John Hodges hath exchaunged for a rome in seate with Lawrence Moone		20
	of Edward Crondall for a rome in seate with Roberte Younge		16
	of Edward Crondall for his wifes rome with Roberte Younges wife		12
	of Thomas Walford for his fathers seate for himself George Walford & Mary Walford	2	6
	for John Leightes wifes rome in the seate with wedowe Leight besides yelding up her other rome		12
	for belles for Thomas Leaper		22
	of James Greene in exchange of his seate to kneele with his wife		12
	of Wedowe Leight Michaelmas rent	4	–
	of Thomas Rudgdale Michaelmas rent 1588	15	–
	of John Barston thelder to exchange his rome into William Fookes seate		4
	of Richard Arkell for his wifes rome in seate with Besant		8
	of Mr Clarck for his sones buriall	3	4
95	of Thomas Dounton for exchaunge of 2 romes for himself in seate with John Hasard & his wife with William Huses wife	2	–
	of Thomas Smithe for romes for himself his wife & Alice his dawghter in Downtons seate that was	3	–
	of Nicholas Field for 2 elmes	10	–
	for lopp of an asshe		4
	of Thomas Plevie for his rome in seate with John Hasard	2	–
	of Thomas Gibsons for his wifes rome in seate with Richard Brooke		12
	of Peter Reve for his wifes rome in seate with John Fild his wife		12
	of Thomas Ridgdale rent for St Mary Day 1589	15	–
	of Wedowe Leight rent then due	4	–
	of John Myllington for rent of the churcheyard 1589	3	4
	for Mr Wyattes buriall	6	8

	£	s	d
for John Wyattes sones buriall		3	4
of William Cleveley for a rome in seate with Thomas Dowles			20
for the gift of Mr Morreye		20	–
for Mr Cottons wifes rome in seate with John Buttes wife		2	–
of Edward Mann for his wifes roome in seate with Hawkes wife			12

| Summ total | 14 | 19 | 5 |

Laid out by the churchewardens in these 2 yeeres to be allowed them

Expenses	£	s	d
for mendinge the church doore lock			3
for a bourde & nayles for the clock howse			4
for a piece of whitleather			16
for half a hide of whitleather		2	4
for taking downe the little bell			4
for a rope for the small peyse			18
for mending the pall			6
for a staple for the stock of the great bell			6
for careng the little bell to the key & hanging the peise			3
for caring the little bell to Worcester			6
for caring the bell into the tower			2
for nayles & plates for the little bell			22
for stocking the bell			4
for mendinge a lock			2
for a bill of presentment			4
for mending a beare			3
for casting the little bell		23	–
for a barrell of lyme & cariage of it to the churche			13
for a hide of white leather		4	6
for a peece of a rope			4
for spicinge the 3 bell rope			3
for wyer for the clocke			4
for mending the stayers			4
for besoms			2
for half a hide of white leather		2	8
for mending William Brafordes seate			6
for clensing the gutters			10
for taking downe the rayles			12
for 7 elles & quarter of clothe 18d ell		10	10½
for making a surples			18
for mending in the clock howse			3
for a ladder caringe to churche & 2 mens hier to help the glasier			8
for setting up a pane of glasse			6
for 27 pounds of rope for a bell rope		6	6
the clarcks wages for a yeer		8	4
for plates for the 3 bell			8
for mending the bell whele			8
for wyer for the clock			3
for paper to Mr Masson			4
for stretching a bell rope			2
for a bill of presentment			4
for castle money & Chepstowe bridge		21	–
for a man to help aboute the wyndowes			12
for a barrell of lyme & cariage			13
for mending the clock & wyer			11

96

for clensing & new making the chappell flower at the church doore	2	8
for plates for the churche dore etc.		11
for mending diverse holes		8
for a sute aganst John Underhill		3
for mending the chauncell doore		10
at Wynchecombe at the busshoppes visitacion for pentecost money etc.	10	6
for 34 pounds of yron to amend 2 bell clappers	4	2
for woorckmanshipp	8	6
Addes for cariage up of them		4
for nayles to mend the leades		3
for a peece of a rope		7
for clensing the churche grate & mending the grate		16
for a lock & key to the gate		6
for a presentment		4
for charges at Gloucester for deliverye of a presentment for the bishopes visitacion	2	2
for 9 foote of glasse by the clock howse & 9 foote in the chauncell	9	–
for 26 dosen of quarrell glasse about the chauncell & by the clock howse at 10d a dosen	21	8
for seaming 10 sheetes of lead over the chauncell	2	6
2 men to helpe the plumer		16
for 44 pounds of soder about the chauncell coles & woorck	20	6
for seaming 7 sheetes of lead uppon the ile next the abbey		21
for 7 pounds of soder coles & woorck	5	7
for 26 pounds of rope for the great peyse	6	6
for nayles & hanging the peyse		6
for seaming 14 shetes of lead	3	6
for mending the greate bell whele		6
for 3 pounds of soder coles & woorck	2	6
for making cleane the gutters		10
for spicing & mending 3 ropes		6
for a hide of white leather	4	8
for a rope for the ⟨great⟩ sanctes bell	2	6
for a service booke for the curate	4	4
for mending a ladder		3
for bolstring 3 belles & taking out the brasses		18
for 2 rowlers wier shides & nayles		9
for woorck aboute the belles	16	2
for half a hide of white leather	2	4
for mending the 3 bell clapper	4	6
for 18 pounds of iron	2	3
for carying the clapper up & downe		2
for exchaunge of 60 pounds of brasse	10	–
for 12 pounds of newe brasse	6	–
for mending the gudgeons & plates of the greate bell	3	4
for mending & making plates & nayles for 2 belles	2	8
for mending holes in the churche		6
for spicing a rope		2
for besoms & a bourd		2
for removing 2 seates		8
for mending the churchard gates & wall hinges & nayles	2	11
for led nayles & mending a key		8
for oyle for the clock, licor for the belles & baldrickes 2 yeeres	2	6
for newe baldrickes & mending of baldrickes for 2 yeeres past	7	9
for halliers for the belles for 2 yeeres past	4	7
for washing & mendinge the churche clothes for 2 yeers past	5	6

97

for a service booke for the clarck	4	4
the clarck for half yeer wags	6	8
due uppon the last accompt		12
for paper		3
for taking downe the railes		6

Summa totalis	16	6	10

So remayneth due to the churchewardens uppon this accompte laid out
above their receiptes   27   5

98	1589	Churchewardens	James Greene
		elected for this yeere	Thomas Cowles

The accompt of James Greene and Thomas Cowles churchewardens begining 20 Maij 1589 unto the 14 of June 1590 and then yelded upp before John Barston and William Fooke bayliffes & others present

Memorandum No stock in money delivered to these churchewardens
for that the churche was left indebted to the last churchewardens as
appeareth by their accompt   27   5

Memorandum That the inventorie appearing in this booke ⟨and⟩ of churche goodes delivered to John Field & George Morrey in their first yeere was found good & delivered to these churchewardens except certen defectes viz. one towell & 2 lynen albes wantinge

Moreover the accompt of lead then weyed & due to these churchewardens was two hundred pounds saving 8 pounds

More John Myllington then remayned owing to the churche 300 weight of lead

More whereas 12d a yeerely rent was geven out & allwayes paid out of Mr Eckinsalles tenementes in the highe streete, the same appeareth to be owed over sithence George Frebanck & Thomas Myllichep did accompt anno 1583

More then remayning in the vestrye in barres of yron for wyndowes 14 longe barres & 9 short

Receiptes	£	s	d
for Mr Wyattes gift to the churche		10	–
for Mr Wakemans gifte to the churche		20	–
for William Turbelles sones buriall		3	4
of Wedowe Phelpes for the belles		2	–
for Mr Stephens wifes buriall		6	8
of Thomas Wawford for Giles Downbelles sone his buriall		3	–
of Mr Greenewod for Hyettes buriall of Walton		6	8
of Mr Willis for the belles		4	–
of Thomas Ridgdale for a yeeres rent		30	–
of Clement Potter for a yeeres rent of the churchyarde		5	–
of Wedowe Leight for half yeeres rent		4	–
of Leonard Turner for buriall of Mr Blomers child		4	4
of George Whitlech for a rome in a seate			12
of William Phelpes for a rome			18
of Fraunces Pace for his wifes rome		2	–
of Mrs Woode for a seate for her and her daughters		5	–

	of John Smithe for his wifes rome		12
	of Jone Leight for a rome	2	–
	of Thomas Cole for his rome	2	–
99	of Thomas Cole for his wifes rome	2	–
	of Christofer Kannar for a rome	2	6
	of Richard Orrell for his wifes rome	2	–
	of John Skullye for his wifes rome	2	–
	of George Lyde for a rome	2	–
	of James Greene for chaunge of his rome & his wifes into one of the newe seates before the desk	5	–
	of Richard Greene for a rome in one of the newe seates	3	4
	of Richard Hewes for a rome in them	3	4
	of John Shawe for a rome in them	3	4
	of Richard Greene for his wifes rome	2	6
	of Richard Hewes for his wifes rome	2	6
	of Thomas Hawker for a rome	2	–
	of John Shawe for exchaunge of a rome for his wife		6
	of Alexander Baughe for 2 romes for him & his wife in one seate	2	–
	of Thomas Walker for 2 romes for him and his wife	2	–
	of John Field for his rome	2	–
	of William Wodley for a rome	2	–
	of John Underhill for a rome	2	–
	of Michaell Tayler for his wifes rome		12
	of John Hasard thelder for exchang of a seate		6
	of John Hasard the younger for his rome	2	–
	of Thomas Sklicer for exchange of his rome into one of the new seates		16
	of Mr Creswell for a newe seate	10	–
	of John Skulley for a rome	2	–
	of William Guilberte for a rome in one of the newe seates	3	4
	of Mr Willis for his wifes seate	2	6
	of Thomas Hale for his wifes rome	2	–
	of Richard Bradford for his wifes rome	2	–
	of John Fissher for his wifes rome		16
	of Thomas Dyer for his wifes rome		12
	of Mrs Wakemann for a rome in her seate for her children	2	–
	of Thomas Plevie for exchaunge of his rome into a newe seate		16
	of William Kedward for a rome	2	–
	of Thomas Jones for to build for him & his wife		16
	of Richard Orrell for half yeeres rent of the meadowe in Avon Ham	4	–

Md That Thomas Budd is licenced to make him a seate ⟨5⟩ by the pulpitt & paid nothing

Summa tot   9 18 2

100   Layd out by these churchewardens to be allowed them

Expenses	£	s	d
at the visitacion pentecost money & other charges		5	6
for mending a bell clapper		9	4
for mendinge the spindel of the clock			6
for making a sawc pitt			8
for sawinge the greate tymber into planckes & carying into the churche		13	8
for a bell rope		4	4
for licor for the belles			4
for a barrell of lyme			11

to Addes for pavinge		12
for mending a bell clapper	6	–
Dicksun for making a bell whele	9	8
for mending the band of that whele		9
the clarck for his yeeres wages	13	4
for white leather	3	–
for balderickes		6
for clensing gutters & nayling lead		18
for nayles & mending the clock		6
for the clarckes seate	10	–
for 2 lockes for the churchyard		8
for removinge seates	4	8
Addes then for his woorck at them	2	4
for nayles to the seates		14
for fillinge the sawe pitt		6
at an other visitacion	6	–
for floring the bell lofte	26	7
for casting lead laying it & sowder	28	10
Addes for helping 2 dayes		16
Walker for helping the plumer 2 dayes		18
for nayles		2
for a bell rope	3	–
for woorck on the tower		12

Summa tote	7	19	4

So restethe in the churchewardens handes in stock above all theire
charge laid oute   38   10

Md Delivered to the newe churchwardens then chosen William
Cleveley and Thomas Sklicer in stocke   38   10

More to gather up of William Turbell for his wifes buriall	6	8
More of Mrs Rise for her husbandes buriall	6	8
Paid more of Mr Bradley for his seate	10	–
More arrerages of Mr Eckinsalls rent	8	–
More of Mr Myllington	300 of lead	

Md The churche yet oweth to John Field uppon his accompt the sum of   27   5

101   1590

Churchwardens elected	William Clevely
for this yeere	Thomas Sklicer

The accompt of William Cleveley & Thomas Sklicer elected churchewardens 14 of June 1590 for that yeere followinge & geven uppe the 9ᵗʰ daye of Aprill 1592 ⟨to John Myllington & John Manne then bailiffes and other being present⟩ to William Willis and John ⟨Manne⟩ Hasard then bailiffes for that these churchewardens without accompt ⟨the⟩ remained twoo yeeres ⟨unto 1592⟩ in that office

Receiptes	£	s	d
of the late churchewardens in stock remayning		38	10
of Thomas Rogers for a sete			12
of James Wargent for a rome			18
of William Thornbury for a rome for his wyfe			12

of William Cornwall for the bells ringinge			12
of Robert Jeines for a rome for his wyfe			12
of ould Jeines of Suthwyck for him & his wyfe		2	10
of Thomas Rudgdall for halfe yere rent		15	–
for the belles ringinge for Jone Parsones			12
of Jhon Jenes of Suthwyck for him & his wyfe for 2 romes			20
of Nycholes Floxley for the sete to him & his wyfe			12
of William Heiet for him selfe			12
of Jhon Abesone for a rome for him			12
of Richard Hues for a rome for his wyfe			18
of Jhon Plevey for a rome for his wyfe			12
of Jhon Griyne for a sete for his wyfe			12
on Easter Day was a yere delivered devocion of well desposed peple		6	5
of William Dune Thomas Decons Gyls Fyld for rome to byld a set upon			12
of Elsbeth Trindall for a rome			10
of Thomas Rudgdall for halfe yers rent		15	–
of Phillip Chaundler for a rome for his wyfe			20
of the wydow Gibs for a rome for selfe			12
of Joarge Peyton for a rome for him selfe		2	–
of Mr Bradley for his sete		10	–
for the buriall of Mr Clarke in the church		7	–
of Richard Rogers for the buriall of his wife in the church		5	–
for somethinges here omitted set downe in the end of this accompt [added]		[	]
of Richard Orell for the halfe aker		8	–
of Frances Pacy for a rome for his wyfe		2	–
of Mrs Wakman for a rome in her set that is voyd		2	–
of Mr Fouke for the exchainge ⟨for⟩ of a rome his wyfe			18
of Raphe Barthelamew for a rome for his wyfe			16
of Richard Paine for a rome for his wyfe			18
⟨of Richard Rogers for the buriall of his wyfe in the church is before accompted [added]		5	–⟩
102 Joarge Frewen for a rome for his wyfe		2	–
of Richard Grene for the buriall of his father in the church		6	9
of William Rushall for a rome for himselfe			20
for the churchyeard		5	–
of Richard Jeins of Suthwyck for the ringing of the bels			18
of Richard Hasson for ringinge the bels			12
for the buriall of Mr Turbill		6	8
of Richard Fisher for a rome for him & his wyfe		2	–
of William Cleveley for the exchaunge of a set ⟨rome⟩ for his wyfe			12
of Richard Flecher for a rome for his wyfe			12
of Mr Cotterell for a rome which was voyd in his wyfs set		2	–
of Thomas Grene of Waulten for a rome for his wyfe			16
of Mr Kedwoldes for a rome for himselfe		3	–
Sum is	10	16	11

The juste sume payd by William Cleveley & Thomas Sklyser churchwardens payd unto Charles Hues for the moving of 16 shets of led att 8d the shet		10	8
Payd him more for 38 pounds of sowder att 9d the pound		28	10

	£	s	d
for coiles for this worke			16
unto Mr Rudgdall for haliors & besoms			7
unto Adice for ⟨makinge & mendinge⟩ besoms			4
for the mendinge of the clocke			6
for a booke of artikells			12
of the sydesmens diner & our oune		2	4
for the ringinge of the bell		6	8
to Adyes for makinge & mendinge the bawdricks against the quens holyday			16
for mendinge the gret bell irons			12
for 2 males for white lether		2	–
to Mrs Cole for 18 pounds iron			18
unto William Wodley for mendinge the grete bell claper		3	8
unto Jhon Sanders for mendinge the gret bell irons			4
for clensinge the gutters			12
unto the clark for ringing of the bell		6	8
for lycer for the belles			1
for unto Jhon Saunders for iron & for shotinge the gret bell claper		3	8
Jhon Saunders for shotinge the second bell irons			8
Jhon Ingland for helpinge Jhon Saunders with the gret bell claper			6
to Mrs Cole for iron		4	10
unto Jhon Crowley for 9 dayes worke		4	2
unto goodman Haines for 10 dayes worke		8	4
for pynes & sklat			6
for 7 bundelles of lathe		2	11
for 7 hundred lath nayles			14
unto Philipe Wyet for 1 dayes worke			6
⟨un⟩ for 8 barelles halfe lime		7	–
unto Adyes for mendinge the pavement			3
⟨unto⟩ att the vycitation for 1 boke of artykells			6
for pentycosse mony		3	6
for the sydesmenes diner & our oune		2	4
to the regester			12
to Thomas Halle for the exchainge of the gret bell claper		20	–
for 7 bushell of here		2	4
unto Adyes for the clansinge of the grat			8
unto Charls Hues for the makinge of 26 foote of ould glasse att 3d		6	2
for four foote of new glasse		2	–
for 8 pounds 3 quarter sowder att 8d the pound		3	10
for coles			4
the clarke for ringinge the bell		6	8
for makinge clene the gutters			6
for the caringe up of the gret bell claper			2
for four haliors			12
for 1 new brope [sic] for the second bell		4	4
to Adyes for makinge & mendinge of the baldricke			16
for a male to make badricks			20
to Jhon Fyld for halfe 1 hyde lether			20
more to Cherls Hues for glasse		3	4
unto Adyes for mendinge the badrickes			6
unto Saunders for mendinge the churchard yeattes locke			4
to the clarke for ringinge the bell		6	8
for nayles			1
unto Adyes for pavinge the church			12
for 1 barell of lime			10
for licor & a halior			3

103

for the deliveringe of a presentment to Gloster		10
for halfe 1 hyde of white lether		18
for four haliors		12

Sum payd is	8	19	10

Resteth to the church	37	1

A note of mony owinge to the church at the time of deliveringe up this acount

for buriall of Mr Allen	6	8
for the buriall of Leonard Freuen	7	8
Charles Hues	fyfty pounds led	
Thomas Rudgdall halfe yeres rent	15	–
Richard Orell halfe yeres rent	4	–

The 9th Aprill 1592 was paid by Mr Rudgdall for the somers ringinge	6	8

for makinge clene the church and sum besoms delivered just to William Phelps	2	1

104   An acount mad by William Phelps church warden the 26th May 1594

	£	s	d
in mony of the churchs		26	1
of Mrs Lancaster for the buriall of her child in the church		3	4
of the wydow Doughte for the buriall of her husband & ringing the bels		7	8
of Jhon Style for a rome for him & his wyfe		3	6
of Thomas Rudgedale for rent		15	–
of Jhon Henbury for pygins dong		4	6
of Jhon Smyth for a rome for him selfe		2	6
of Thomas Hale for a rome for him selfe		2	6
of Robert Smyth for a rome for his wyfe			20
of Goody Turner for exchainge of her set		2	–

⟨In the formor accompt of William Cleveley and Thomas Sklicer it appeareth that they charge themselves to have receveth £10 16s 2d which is mistaken their receiptes being but £8 14s 6d⟩

⟨So that the churchwardens overcharge themselves 42s 5d⟩

⟨In the same their formor accompt it appeareth that they charge the churche in expenses £8 19s 10d which is mistaken their expenses being £9 4s 4d

⟨So that the churchwardens undercharge themselves 4s 6d⟩

⟨Md in the said receiptes that acknowledge but 2 half yeeres rent receaved of Thomas Ridgdale and they do charge one half yere to be collected by the next churchewardens so as appereth to be concealed in this accompt one half yeer rent – 15s⟩

⟨Also they acknowledge but one yeres rent receaved of Richard Orrell and they do charge one half ycre to bc collected by the next churchwardens so as appeareth to be concealed in this accompt one half yeere – 4s⟩

⟨Also they acknowledge but one half yeeres rent receaved for the churchyard so as one yeere rent is concealed – 5s⟩

⟨Nevertheles it seemeth that the churche is indebted to the churche wardens 26s 11d of which in this accompt they pray no allowance⟩

All this is mistaken by perusing theyre accompt in some omissions, viz. receaved of John Gubbins for his wifes rome 16d Thomas Grinner his wifes rome 2s Hugh Ashleworth his wifes rome 12d John Ryde his rome 12d Walter Jeynes 12d William Phillipes & his wife 2s 8d Widow Phelpes 3s 4d John Shild his rome 2s 6d Mr Balthrop 3s John Dewet his wife 18d Thomas Rudgedale rent 15s Mr Langston 2 romes for him & his wife 5s

1592	Churchwardens elected	William Phelpes
	for this yeere 1592	William Dun

The accompt of William Phelpes elected churchewarden with William Dun the 9th of Aprill 1592 and geven up by him alone William Dun being deceassed before Kedwards Alye and John Bubbe being bayliffes taken the 26th of Maye 1594 for twoo whole yeeres then ended

Receiptes	£	s	d
in stock of the last wardens		27	1
of Mrs Lancaster for her childes buryall		3	4
of Wedowe Downton for buriall of her husband in the churche and			
ringing of the belles		7	8
of John Stile for 2 roumes for him & his wife		3	6
of Thomas Ridgdale for rent		15	–
of John Henbury for pigeon dunge		4	6
of John Smithe for his owne rome		2	6
of Thomas Hale for his owne rome		2	6
of Roberte Smithe for his wifes rome			20
of wedowe Turner for exchainge of her seat		2	–
of William Guilbert for buriall of his wife in the churche		6	8
of Mrs Bubbe for exchaing of her seate		2	–
of William Sowtherne for his wifes rome			18
of Thomas Maunsel for his owne rome		2	6
of Thomas Ridgedale for rent		23	4
of Richard Orrell for a yeeres rent of the half acre		8	–
of Mighell Ratcliff for his owne rome		2	6
of George Frewen for exchainge of a seate		2	–
of John Hawker for his owne rome		3	–
of Mrs Hasard for exchaunge of her seate		3	–
of Mrs Cole for exchaunge of her seate		3	4
of Mr Lye for his mothers rome for Margery & Elizabeth his			
daughters		3	4
of Thomas Ridgdale for rent		23	4
of Thomas Phelpes for 2 romes for him & his wife		6	8
of George Walker for his wifes rome		2	6
for Alice Phelpes a rome		2	6
of James Sowtherne for earnest for 2 romes for him and his wife			12
of Wittinge for 2 romes for him & his wife		2	6
of Thomas Ridgdale for rent		23	4
of John Underhill for his wifes rome		2	4
of Henry Hopkins for buriall of his wife		6	8
of Thomas Deacons for his wifes rome		2	6
of Fraunces Kinges for his ⟨wifes⟩ owne rome		4	–
of Thomas Maunsell in earnest for the half acre			12
of George Frewen for exchaunge of his seat		2	–

105

of Thomas Plevie for his wifes rome	2	6
of Mr Wyatt for a seate for him self	3	4

Summa totalis	10	17	1

Expenses

Layed out by these churchewardens to be allowed them uppon this acccompt as followeth

	£	s	d
to Mr Field for making the seate booke			12
to Saunders for mending the churche dore lock			4
for licor to the belles			2
to Addes for sweping the church one yeere		3	4
for the 3rd bell rope		4	8
to Mr Ridgdale & Addes for ringing		6	8
for a horse hide		4	2
for spickes for 2 belles iron and hanginge of the second bell		2	3
Addes for wasshinge the belles			12
Addes for clensing the gutters			12
Saunders for makinge the greate bell clapper & newe bowlinge the other 3 & a newe eye for the second bell clapper		20	–
Addes more for the bell ringinge		6	8
Addes for making baldrickes			12
Saunders for making the great bell clapper		8	–
Rabye to helpe him			12
Addis for licor			2
for longe nayles			6
for iron for the bell clappers		15	10
Clowes for clensing the gutters			12
Clowes for making 2 newe baldrickes and mendinge 2 olde			16
for washing & mending the churche clothes			20
for licor			1
Charles Hewes for mending & drawing up of 20 sheetes of lead		13	6
for nayles for that worck			10
for a newe stock amending the churche dore lock & the dore next the vestrye			16
for a preching place in churchyard			3
for a rope for the greate bell		5	4
Charles Hewes for mending the chauncell yle		12	6
for lycoringe the belles			3
Saunders for woorck at the 3rd bell			16
then to Pharao also			6
for mending the vestry dore			8
to William Guilbert for his wifes rome			16
for whitlether to make bawdrickes		2	8
for makinge a sute of bawdrickes		2	–
Sawnders for 2 newe eyes for baldrickes			4
for sinage money		3	5
for a booke then to the chauncelor			6
for makinge the quarter clock & amendinge the greate clock		30	–
Nuttinge to helpe Sampson in the same		35	–
Reve for a frame & other thinges there unto		12	–
for iron & steale for the same		6	6
for wyer for bothe clockes		6	6
for 2 ropes for the quarter clock		4	–

106

for nayles			6
Charles Hewes for drawinge shetes & about the top of the tower		7	–
Nuttinge for nayles for his woorck			9
Mathewes for oyle			6
Mathewes for clensinge the gutters			12
for wasshing the belles			6
Summa	11	17	6

Arrerages by this accompt

Mr Allen his buriall	6	8
Leonard Turnor his buriall which William Phelpes acknowledgeth to be receved by William Dun	7	8
Thomas Rudgdale halfe yeeres rent charged by the last churchewardens which William Phelpes chargeth uppon William Dun	15	–
Richard Orrell for halfe yeres rent of the half acre charged by the last churchwardens and yet resteth by Richard Orrell unpaid	4	–
one ⟨half⟩ whole yeeres rent for the half acre unaccompted by these churchewardens which William Phelpes accompteth by him owing	8	–[1]

M⟨d⟩ Whereas Mr Ridgdale demandeth for ringinge the bell ⟨for⟩ & church sweeping for these 2 yeeres which is allowed 46s 8d It is in discharg thereof awnswered that Mr Ridgedale oweth for the churchyard for one yeere in Thomas Sklycer his tyme & 2 yeeres in these churchwardens tyme 15s & it appeareth he & Addes receaved 16s 8d & Parret received of Mr Cotton 6s 10d in all 39s 6d so as then is owing ⟨to⟩ then to him with allowance 6s 10d for a newe yate 14s which was paid in the next accompt

Charles Hewes for fiftie pounds of lead

Mrs Myllington for three hundred of lead

These parcelles of lead receaved by the next accompt following

107   22 October anno 1595

It was then agreed by common consent in the chamber that allowaunce be made for keping of the clock a yeerly pension 26s 8d

That allowance be geven for ringinge the bell morning & evening wynter & somer – 20s

It was then also declared the auncient custome of the towne that no taker of any seate or roume in the churche shall have partie to challenge the same after one yeere ended from the tyme of his or her departure out of the towne

That uppon decease of any wife in the towne it shalbe in the churchewardens by consent of the bailiffes (if need so requier) to place any other woman in the same rome uppon a quarterly rent to the churche until the husband of the decessed woman shall mary againe And then she to take suche place as in meane tyme no husband to challenge the place

That none be placed in any of the masters sixe seates nor in the myddle rowe above the clarckes pewe nor within 4 seates of the pulpitt belowe & so upon & on bothe sides in the bodye of the churche without consent of the bailiffes

---

[1]   Discharged [in margin]

Anno 1594 et 1595

William Guilberte Churchwardens
John Skullowe

Thaccompt of William Guilberte and John Skullow elected churchewardens Maii 26 anno domino 1594 And by them geven upp in the chamber October 12 before Richard Cotton & Thomas Hilley then bailiffes and other the burgesses for all the tyme they had continued in the said office viz. 2 whole yeeres and more unto Michaelmas last ended anno 1596

	£	s	d
for buriall of Mr Hasard & belles		8	8
of George Frewen for exchange of his seat			20
of Phillip Chaundeler for a rome in the 5th seate of the 3 rowe		3	–
of Nicholas Wever for the 8 seate of the 7 rowe		5	3
of Kenelum Chaundeler for a rome in the 6th seate of the 3 rowe		3	–
of Edward Lea for a rome for his wife in the 10th seate of the 2 rome		3	–
of Thomas Hawkins for a rome for his wife in the 15 seate of the 4 rowe		2	6
of John Severne for his wifes rome in the 17 seate of the 3 rowe		3	–
108 of Giles Harmer for his owne rome in seate 12 rowe 1			16
for 40 pounds of old yron		3	8
of Thomas Jeynes of the abbey for his wifes rome seate 10 row 2		3	–
of Thomas Rudgedale for Michaelmas rent due for his howse anno 1594		23	4
of Mr Awdrye for the bequest of George [*sic*] Tonye geven to the churche		20	–
of John Myllington Junior for his owne rome seate 7 rowe 3 and his wifes rome seate 15 rowe 4		5	6
of Henry Marshall for his owne roume seate 2 rowe 3 and his wifes rome seate 10 and in the same rowe 3		6	4
of Richard Wever Bryan Tayler & Richard Bradford for ground to build on in the body of the church		2	–
of Thomas Hawker for exchaunge of his wifes roume into seate 19 rowe 4			16
of William Wrenford for the first seate in the 2 rowe		3	4
of Roberte Jorden for his owne rome seate 1 and rowe 4		3	7
of Henry Marshall for the belles		2	–
of Henry Williams for his owne rome & his wifes seate 9 rowe 2		5	6
of Christofer Cannar in exchainge of his wifes rome seate 8 rowe 6			16
of Thomas Dixon for his owne rome seate 5 and rowe 3		3	4
for pigeon donge at Easter 1595		3	–
of Griffithe Thomas in exchang of 2 romes into the 21 & 22 seates of the 5 rowe			18
of Richard Leight for his wifes rome into seat 20 rowe 5		2	6
of Richard Guildinge for his wifes rome in the same seate		2	6
of John Slawghter for a rome for him self seate 2 rowe 3		2	6
of John Holtham for his wifes rome seate 22 rowe 3		3	6
of Thomas Rudgdale rent at St Mary Daye due anno 1595		23	4
of Mr Kedwardes buriall & belles		8	6
of Thomas Churchey for his sone in lawes buriall & belles		8	6
of Bryan Tayler for his wifes rome in seat [...] rowe 3		3	–
of John Stile for exchaunge of his rome into seate 9 rowe 4		3	–
109 of Thomas Rudgedale for rent due at Michaelmas anno domino 1595		23	4
for one yeres rent of the half acre		10	–
of John Skullowe for exchaunge into the 9th seate of the 4 rowe			4

of Ricard Wever for his wifes rome in the 7 seate of the 5 rowe	2	6
of John Jorden for his owne rome seate 11 rowe 2 & his wifes rome seate 19 rowe 3	6	–
of John Rayer for his wifes rome in the 17 seate of the 5 rowe	2	6
for William Dun his legacie to the churche	20	–
of Richard Tyrrett for exchang of his seate into the whole 10 seate rowe 4	16	–
of Mr Carr for his rome in the 6 seate of the 5 rowe	6	–
of William Phelpes for the first yeeres rent of the half acre & Orrelles 8s uppon him charged	17	5
of Thomas Ridgdale for rent due at St Mary Daye anno 1596	23	4
of Mr Myllington for lead due unto the churche longe sithence by him borrowed	18	–
of Roger Wyatt for his owne rome in the 6 seate of the 6 rowe	3	8
of John Severne for his rome exchanged into the same seate	2	6
of John Jones for his owne rome & his wifes seate 8 rowe 2	5	8
of Thomas Stile for his owne rome & his wifes seate 10 rowe 2	5	–
of Thomas Rogers for exchange of a rome into the 11 seate of the 4 rowe	2	6
of Hughe Tunckes for his wifes rome seate 11 rowe 2	2	6
of Henry Tonye for his owne rome seate 6 rowe 6 & his wifes seate 15 rowe 4	6	8
of George Whitleche for exchange of his wifes rome seate 7 rowe 6	2	–
of John Braford for his fathers buriall	6	8
of Richard Smithe for his wifes rome seate 24 and rowe 3		12
of Richard Gildinge for his rome in the 11 seate of the 4 rowe	5	–
of William Gilberte Senior for exchang into the 16 seate of the 5 rowe	5	–
of Mr Parker for his rome in the 6 seate of the 5 rowe	5	–
of William Guilberte Junior for his owne rome seat 2 rowe 3 & his wife seate 8 rowe 6	5	–
of James Braford for his wifes rome in the 12 seate of the 2 rowe	2	6

_110_

of Mrs Cole for her gifte to the churche to be the buriel after her deceasse		20	–
of William Turbell for Mr Davies buryall in the church and the belles		8	8
of Roger Wyatt for the belles		2	–
of those summes of money which were imposed uppon the parishe for coveringe the longe roufe over the body of the church which amounteth to a farr greater summ to be bestowed uppon needfull further reparacions as the same may be gathered	13	8	2
of Charles Hewes for 600 of lead of that was taken of the roufe		53	7
for buriall of Peter Cottrell		6	8
of Mr Cottrell for his daughters Elizabeth rome seate 12 rowe 3		3	4
for buriall of Nicolas Foxe		6	8
for Mr Vaughans buriall & the belles		8	8
of William Muttinge of his imposicion as aforesaid			12
of William Turbell for his wifes rome in the 3 seate of the 6 rowe		3	4
for two hundred & half of the rent bourdes bought to cover the roufe until it was finished with leade		8	4
of Roberte Hope for his wifes rome seate 24 rowe 4		2	6
of Roberte Mynce for a yeeres rent for the half acre rented at [ ]		10	–
of William Kegeley for his owne rome seat 5 rowe 4 & his wifes seat 17 rowe 3		10	–
of Barnard Cartwright for his owne rome seate 2 rowe 7			18

M^d Which in the tyme of these churchwardens accompt the Mrs seates were translated next to the bailiffes seate and then were these persons, viz. John Feield Thomas Phelpes

John Thonnes Thomas Cowles & William Russhall before admitted in the upper seates & William Johnsons in the place of Henry Turnor by them exchaunged were placed next behind the masters seates & William Dole removed into the first seate of the 4 rowe. Also in respect that Mr Barstons seate was then altered being next behind the bailiffes seate his wife is by consent removed to the seate next unto the masters seates and Mr Cottons wife receaving the place of Mr Foakes wif in the 3 rowe Mrs Foooke is appointed with Mrs Barston.

Some of receiptes   39   15   –

It appereth no rent awnswered for the churchyard by all the tyme of these churchewardens

111   Expenses laid out by the said churchewardens duringe the tyme of their office to be allowed out of theire said receiptes

	£	s	d
for clensing the yles			12
for pentecost money		3	6
Nutinge for mendinge the clock		2	6
for a hundred of bourde to lathe the church roufe		6	–
for a booke of injunctions			6
for returning our presentment			16
Hanbage for 6 dayes woorck		5	–
Sawnders for 1700 nayles		19	3
for cariage of leade into the plume howse			22
for halling wood to churche			6
for cariage of sand & water			14
for Hanbage for 8 dayes woorck		4	2
for ryddinge gutters			12
for caryinge upp lead		3	–
2 men for a dayes woorck			14
3 men for helping with bourdes			18
for sand from Twyninge			8
for layinge bourdes on the churche		2	–
2 men for 2 dayes			16
for a pound of waxe			12
at the visitacion			16
for hawlinge bourdes			6
for 6 balrickes making		2	–
for makinge 3 eyes			9
for 2 bell ropes		10	6
for mending the grate		3	–
for mending the pulpett			6
Savage for woorck & lime			20
Nuttinge for his half yeres wages ended at [ ] for kepinge the clocke		13	4
Byrt for altering seates		6	4
Kynges to helpe him			12
for carying out dust there			12
more for 3 newe seates		4	2
for pullinge up lead			4
for pavinge & lyme		2	–
Charles Hewes for laying 80 shetes of lead 9s 16d	5	6	8
for paving them 1d a sheete		13	4
him for 20 pounds of soder & working it		20	–
at the visitacion			12

Nutting for half yeres wages ended at [ ]			
for the clock		13	4
Saunders for nayles			20
Saunders for bell nayles & a baldrick pyn			14
Saunders to trusse the belles			18
him for 3 keyes for the register cheste			13
for a register booke			12
for paving 2 graves & lyme			18
for licour at sundry tymes			7
Mr Rudgdale for wages assigned him to receave due at the last church accompt		15	–
for taking up a lead pipe in the churchyard		2	–
for mending the braces of the grete bell		2	6
at sundry tymes for wasshing & mendyng the clothes			8
William Phelpes and by his accompt demanded		20	8
Mr Rudgdale for bel ringing for a whole yeere ended at [ ]		20	–
Bradbury for half yeeres wages		6	8
to men of Cheltnham for a debt about their lead		3	–
Thomas Tayler for nayles			3
to Mylwright sumer to discharge our apparaunce			12
goodwife Maliard for her right in a seate		2	6
at Derhurst at a visitacion		4	–
for candles 1 pound & half			6
for a hundred of wood		4	–
Hanbage for 6 dayes worck		4	6
at sundry tymes for weying of lead & carying the same upp the stayers		4	8
for bourd to make the pan			15
for a pound of talowe & licoure			6
for wynding lead up the tower			6
Mydlewright the somner			12
Mr Curtes to go to Winchcombe			16
Saunders for 3 dayes		2	6
Charles Hewes for laying 18 shetes on thile		18	–
him for laying lead from Cheltnham		22	9
him for castinge 2 tones & half & 200 of lead at 16d a hundred	3	9	4
him for casting 600 of lead at 18d		9	9
him for nayles			3
him for laying one shete			16
him for soder & working it		6	–
Nutting for a quarter ended at [ ]		6	8
to supply raffle money		5	–
Byrt for 3 dayes		2	–
for whitlether to mald buldrickes		6	–
for making 6		2	3
for nayles soder & charcole		2	–
for a bell rope		5	10
for a deske in the pulpett		2	10
at Gloucester			16
to Nuttinge for keping the clock half yeer ended at [ ]		13	4
for rydding the gutters			12
Kene for woorck		2	–
Bradbury for paving		2	–
him for ridding gutters			11
him for 3 dayes woorck & mending one of the baldrickes			20
Saunders for mending brasses of the greate bell		2	6
expenses twise at Winchecombe		2	4

_112_

Kinges for woorck	3	4
Mr Cottrell for lead	10 –	–
him for bourdes		36
Nutting for half yeer ended [ ]	13	6
for sinage money	4	–
for 300 & 24 pounds of lead 14s per hundred	45	–
for exchange of 70 pounds of lead ½ per pound	2	9
Some expended	43 –	20

113 M^d September 1 anno 1596 to supplie the negligences of the said churchewardens the roufe over the plume howse being fallen downe by tempeste Mr Bailiff Morrey tooke in hand to repayer the same and laide out of the money before by him collected for armors & other services imposed uppon the towne for & about the said reparacions as followethe

	£	s	d
for a peece of tymber to John Hardinge		6	–
for sawinge the same & halling to the churche			12
Mr Cottrell for powles 3		[	]
Willis for 4 dayes woorck		4	–
his man for 5 dayes woorck		4	2
Kinges for 5 dayes worck		5	–
Willis for use of his tackle		2	6
geven them & others to drinck that help them			6
for 15 bundles of stone lathe		7	9
for lathe nailes & speek nayles		5	6
for iron plates			9
for 3 lodes of sklatt		18	–
for 5 barrelles of lyme		5	–
for 3 barrelles of heare			12
for 7 cresses			7
Savage for 25 dayes		25	–
Fraunces to serve him		12	6
Summa	5	–	5

M^d He also paid Thomas Dickson owinge to him for his woorck uppon the seates in the churche 2 yeeres past – 20s

Also he acknowlegeth to receave for Thomas Jeynes buriall in the churche October 20 6s 8d so as it is allowed him in accompt for a half yeeres wages paid to Fraunces the sexten

Paid also for lether to make baldrickes – 2s

Received hereof George Frebanck for a rome in the seate with Mrs Davies – 3s 4d – So Mr Morrey acquited

Uppon these accomptes appeareth that William Guilberte and John Skullowe the last churchewardens have laide out in expenses above their receiptes – £3 6s 8d

114 Anno 1596 et 1597 et 1598

Robert Jeynes   Churchewardens
John Tommes

Thaccompte of Robert Jeynes and John Tommes elected churchwardens the second daye of November 1596 regno Elizabeth 38 And by them geven up in the chamber November 7 anno 1598 before Edmund Balthrop & Henry Tonye the bailiffes and other the burgesses for all the tyme they had continued in the said office viz. 2 whole yeeres then ended

	£	s	d
Receiptes			
receaved in stocke		nothinge	
of Thomas Ridgdale Michaelmas rent for his howse		23	4
for pigeon donge		2	–
of Mrs Kedwardes for her rome 17 seate: 3 rowe		3	6
of Mr Sellers for his wifes roume 10 seate: 3 rowe			5
of William Shene for his wifes rome 18 seate: 4 rowe		4	–
of Mr Lye for a yeeres rent for the churcharde ended at St Mary Day 1598		11	–
of Ann Wyat for her rome 13 seate: 3 rowe		5	–
of Mr Hilley for exchange of his wifes rome to 17 seate: 4 rowe		2	–
of Mr Lancaster for his & his daughter by the 7 seate: 2 rowe		2	–
of John Vicaries for Thomas Rogers rome 8 seate: mydlerowe		6	8
of Barnard Cartwright his wifes rome [ ] seate 6 rowe			18
of William Parsons for his rome 6 seat 2 rowe	4s in tymber		
of Kedward Chaundler for his wifes rome 5 seate: 2 rowe		3	4
of Thomas Dixon for his wifes rome 11 seate: 2 rowe		2	–
of Johane Bryan and Katharin Bryan for the little seate by the 8 seate in 2 rowe			12
of John Porter & Thomas White for a seate set up for morners & they to geve place at funeralles		4	–
of Richard Blancket for his rome 9 seate: 3 rowe		4	–
of Stephen Downbell for his rome 3 seate: 3 rowe		2	–
of John Parker for his wifes rome 5 seate: 2 rowe		3	4
of William Britten for his wifes rome 13 seate: 6 rowe			20
of John Stile for his wifes rome 14 seate: 4 rowe		4	4
of William Hyett Junior for his rome 4 seate: 2 rowe		3	–
of wedowe Gilbert & her daughter George Tustians wife for their 2 romes 14 seate: 4 rowe		3	–
of William Yates for his rome 2 seate 3 rowe			18
of Henry Morison for his wifes rome 19 seate: 3 rowe		3	–
of Stephen Downbell for his wifes rome 14 seate: 4 rowe		6	–
of Mr Parker for his wifes buriall in the churche & belles		8	8
of Harry Morison for his mother in lawes buriall		6	8
for 2 silke curtens in the vestrie		6	8
of Mrs Cole for a stone to lay over the ground for her buriall		5	–
of Mr Lye for his wifes buriall in the churche & 2 stones to laye over her & himself hereafter		20	–
of Thomas Sanders for the belles at his wifes buriall		2	–
of Mr Pearte for his wifes buriall & belles		9	–
of William Orrell for his wifes buriall in the churche		6	8
of Thomas Ridgdale St Mary Day rente		23	4
of Mr Chambers for his rome & his wifes & in their absence for John Baughe & his wife		12	4
of John Vicaries for his wifes rome 7 seate: 5 rowe		4	–
of William Turbell for his childes buriall in the churche		2	4
of wedowe Hale for her husbandes buriall & belles		8	6
for Mr Thomas Woodwardes buriall in the churche and a stone to lay over him		11	8

115

	£	s	d
for a stone to lay over John Hale		4	–
of James Mason for his rome 4 seate: 2 rowe		2	6
in Julye for a yeres rent of half acre in Avonham 1597		9	–
of Thomas Ridgdale Michaelmas rent 1597		23	4
for the best rope till this tyme unsolde	4	6	8
of William Turbell for his daughter Maries rome with Mrs Davies		2	–
of Nicholas Field for his childens romes Kellam & Anne in their fathers seate		2	–
of Edward Davies for his rome by the clarckes seate		4	–
of William Byttle for his wifes rome 18 seate: 4 rowe		4	–
of Nicholas Wever for exchaunge of his wifes rome into the 14 seate: 4 rowe		3	–
of Thomas Saunders for his wifes rome 16 Seate: 6 rowe			18
of Thomas Mayde for his rome 8 seate: 6 rowe			18
for a stone to laye over Thomas Jeynes of Sowthwick		5	–
of Thomas Jenninges for his wifes rome 4 seate: 6 rowe			18
of Richard Grene for his mothers buriall in the churche		6	8
of Thomas Porter for his sones buriall		6	8
for William Russhalles buriall in the churche		6	8
of John Shawe for his rome 13 seate: 6 rowe			18
of Mr Hodges for his wifes buriall in the churche		6	8
of John Orrell for his wifes rome 14 seate: 6 rowe			18
of Thomas Hale for his rome 6 seate: 3 rowe		2	–
of wedowe Jeynes of Sowthwick for her rome 18 seate: 3 rowe		4	–
of Thomas Rudgdale St Mary Day rent 1598		23	4
for John Myllingtons buriall in the churche		6	8
of George Tustian for his rome 4 seate: 13 rowe			18
of Mr Pearte for his rome & his wifes in Mr Chambers seate		13	–
of Roberte Dennys for his rome 7 seate: 3 rowe			18
of Mrs Collins for her rome 18 Seate: 3 rowc		4	–
of Mr Lye for one whole yeeres rent of the churchyard ended at St Mary Day 1599		11	–
for one yeeres rent of the half acre in Avonham 1598		9	–
of William Turbell for his childes buriall in the churche		3	4
of John Sklicer for his rome 8 seate: myddle rowe		6	–
of John Sklicer for his wifes rome 9 seate: 2 rowe		2	–
of old Mrs Smithe for her rome in Mrs Lyes place		5	–
of Lawrence Moone for his wifes buriall in the churche		5	6
of Roberte Jeynes to exchang his rome into 2 seate: myddle rowe			12
of John Smithe for his wifes rome 18 seate: 3 rowe		5	–
of Mrs Kennett for a rome 6 seate: 4 rowe		6	8
of Thomas Grenowe for his rome 2 seate: myddle rowe		6	–
of Mr Lye for the churchyarde		11	–
of Thomas Ridgdale for Michaelmas rent 1598		23	4
of Richard Bradford for his wifes rome 16 seate: 4 rowe		3	–
of John Vickaries for his daughters buriall & belles		7	8
for Mrs Butlers buriall in the churche		6	8
of diverse persons the summes taxed uppon them by a booke longe before assessed for reparacions of the church as by a note of their names is paid the sum of	10	–	17
Summa totalis of all the receiptes to the day of this accompt geven up	39	8	7

115 bis Expenses laid out by the said churchewardens duringe the tyme of their said office, which they prayen out of the said receiptes charged uppon them to be deducted and allowed as in these particulers may appeare

In November 1596

	£	s	d
for beetinge the iles behind the chauncell & for nayles		5	1
to men that did help to lay downe the leades of the sowthe ile blowen up with the wynde		3	–
Charles Hewes for seaminge those leades		11	–
Saunders for nayles made to fasten them		2	–
the mason to stopp the wyndowe in that ile			18
for whitelether to make balrigges			4
Bradbury for making 2 balrigges			8
Charles Hewes for seming & sodringe ledes over the clock		14	6
Savage & Lawton for 5 dayes woorck		3	4
for a hundred of lathe nayles			2
for a bundell of lathe			6
for a busshell of heare			3
Kinges for mending the grete bell wheele			6
for hatche nayles for the same			1
Saunders for a plate of yron & nayles for the same			12
him for a wedge of yron to reare up the brasse of the greate bell & a little iron plate			6
him for a crampe of iron for the 3 bell			6
for a pound of licor for the belles			4

December

	£	s	d
Lawton for 2 dayes woorck & 2 men to cary rubble into churchyard		2	2
Bradbury for 2 dayes to pull up the leades over the quier			12
for exchange of the greate bell clapper weying 21 pounds more		23	3
for pecing & shutting the 3 bell clapper			20
Jeynes for 4 dayes in peecing sheetes		3	4
for nayles for the same			8
Bradbury for Christmas quarter		5	10
Thomas Rogers to leave his seate with John Stile		4	–
for Kinges woorck & oyle four the clock			4

Januarie

	£	s	d
for carying earthe to fill graves sunck in the churche		2	–
Bradbury for 4 dayes woorck		2	–
for brick to wall parte of the wyndowe over the clock		2	6
for 4 barrelles of lyme & 10 busshelles of heare		7	4
Savage for 2 dayes worck at the wyndowe			12
Charles Hewes for soder		6	2
for a longe ladder		5	–
for 12 pounds of iron for barres in the wyndowe over the clock			18
the mason to laye the graves that sonck with quarrell		4	6

Februarie

	£	s	d
the plummer for 5 dayes woorcke on the side next the porche		6	8
him for 10 dayes on the other side the porche		13	4
Bradbury for 6 dayes to help him		3	–
for bourde nayles to nayle the lathes			8
for nayles to nayle the leades		3	6
the plummer for soder & woorck next the porche & on the northe ile & over the body of the churche		22	–
Bradbury 2 dayes to help him			12

Marche 1597

the pariter to returne a bill for recusantes & his fee		16
wedowe Bridgwood to leave her rome in a seate	4	–
Thomas Hale for 10 barrelles of lyme	8	8
Bradbury for St Mary Daye quarter	5	10
for wasshing churche lynen		8
Sanders for nayles to set up glasse over the clocke		21
him for newe yron barres & shuttinge the olde in the same wyndowe	15	9
for pointing the churche walles	12	–

116   Aprill

Reve for a newe close beere	8	–
for nayles, hinges & greate nayles made for the same	3	7
at Gloucester for fees & Mr Davies & our charges	5	7
for 6 busshell of heare	2	–

Maye

the plummer for 20 pounds of soder laid on the body of the churche	10	6
him for 2 dayes in seaminge the leades	2	8
for oyle for the clocke and belles		8
Saunders for mending the iron strappes of the belles		12
for half a hide of white lether	2	6
for making 2 baldriggs		8

June

for a springe for the quarter clock		12
at the visitacion at Derehurst pentecost money	3	4
for making our bill & a booke of articles		22
for returne of a bill		4
for our charges curate & sidemen ther	2	10
Bradbury mydsomer wages	5	10

August

for a booke of prayer for the fleete at sea		4
for stocking the 2 bell iron nayles & wages	6	1
for iron to mend the 3 bell clapper & wages	13	4
for a presentement at Gloucester		4
for sute againste Thomas Cowles & Hue Baughan there	2	8
Bradbury for making 3 baldrickes		12
for brick for the greate wyndowe & others	8	–
for halling them thither, sand & cariage in	3	4

October

Bradbury Michaelmas quarter wages	5	10
for a newe bell rope	5	4
for 4 halliers for the belles		8
for caringe the coape to London		12
for 2 barrelles of lyme & 4 bushels of heare	3	4
2 men to cary gravell into the churchyard		7

November

for 3 dosen barres prooader & colouring for the grete windoe		15
for iron & worcke for new & olde barres there	7	3
the mason to amend the pillars there	12	–
Poynter for glasinge the said wyndowe	5 2	2
him for 11 wyndowes next the churchyarde	4 –	–
for barres there		2
for 11 barrelles of lyme & cariage	10	2
the mason for poynting aboute the steeple & iles	5	6

December

for 3 halters for the cradle to set up glasse		12
bestowed on Mr Perry our proctor		16
at Gloucester in sute against Parker & Cartwright		12
Bradbury Christmas quarter wages	5	10
for plates for the 2 bell		14
for oiles for the clock & belles		6

March & Aprill 1598

for young elmes to set in the churchyard		9
for an ewe tree		6
for half a hide of whitelether	2	6
for makinge 2 baldrickes		8
for wasshenge churche lynen		8
in expenses at Winchcombe appearing about the statute made for the poore		16
Bradbury for St Mary Daye quarter	5	10

Maye

at Gloucester when we received the register bookes	3	–
for glasing 2 panes in the chauncell & barres	3	2
for mending the 3 bell clapper	6	8
for articles in the churche & a table		21
for pavinge in the churche	2	8

117   June

for oyle for the clock		1
Leland for whitelether		12
for making a baldrick		4
for iron and mendinge the greate bell clapper	20	–
for wasshing a surples		2
Bradbury mydsomer quarters wages	5	10
at Wynchecomb at visitacion pentecost money & fees	4	6
for our charges	2	–

September & October

in sute againste William Lyttle	5	9
in sute againste againste John Lowe	14	5
for making ⟨of⟩ up the scholehowse wall	2	8
for oyle for the clock & licor for the belles		6
for paving over Mrs Butlers buriall		2

for half a hide of whitlether	4	–
for making 5 baldrickes		20
for mending the clock		2
for iron & makinge the 3 bell clapper	20	8
Bradbury for Michaelmas quarter wages	5	10
for registering & casting this accompt	2	–

Laid out for rayling the churchyard

for tymber	42	3
for halling to the pitt & sawinge	4	–
at tymes to make the worckmen drinck	2	3
for entring the postes & raming them	3	4
for wood to make rammers levers & pinnes		12
Jeynes the carpenter for wages	33	–
for 2 pair of hinges for the yates	3	9
for 200 of speek nayles		20
for elmes to set in the churchyard		6
more for sawing	23	4

Summa	5	15	1

Of which receaved by liberalitie of certen persons to be out of this sum deducted 7s

So resteth in the whole	5	8	1

Summa totalis of the whole expenses	39	8	1

And then these churchwardens owen to the churche this £39 8s 1d deducted out of £39 8s 7d

In stock remaining in the sed accomptes handes		6

M^d Those accomptantes at the yelding up of this accompt do remember them to have mistaken in charginge them selves with 6s ⟨for⟩ rent for the churchyarde more then was received with 6s beinge deducted the receiptes appeare £38 17s 1d

This allowance of 11s mistaken in the accompt deducted out of the receiptes it appeareth then in stocke nothinge because the churche owethe unto these wardens 10s 6d

The churche in debte 10s 6d

118 **The aforesaid churchewardens yet continuinge their office from the said 7 of November 1598 unto the 15th of Aprill 1599 because none other were nominated untill that daye do accompte further before the said bailiffes and the whole parishe as here followethe**

Receiptes	£	s	d
of Andrewe Baughan for his wifes buriall & belles		8	–
of Thomas Heynes for his wifes roume seate 6 rowe 6			12
of Thomas Jeffres for a rome seate 3 rowe 3			18
of Thomas Orrell for 2 rowmes him self & his wife seate 15 rowe 6		2	–
of Thomas Rudgdales howse showing by rent 1599		23	4
for Mr Wyattes buriall & belles		8	8

Summa		44	6

M^d These churchewardens did not let the half acre in Avonham for the somer folowinge their accompt which is anno 1599 and therefore muste be charged uppon the next churchewardens

Expenses	£	s	d
for exhibeting a presentment			4
Bradbury for Christmas wages 1598		5	10
for hallyers for the belles			18
for baldrickes mendinge			6
for mendinge the hinges of the churchyard yate			6
for nayles & mending a springe of the clock			4
for barres for the wyndowe on the abbey side glased by 20s geven by			
Alice Clarcke			12
for wasshing lynen			8
for paper & oyle			4
Bradbury St Mary Day wages 1599		5	10
for parchement for the newe register booke		4	8
for 7 pounde of yron for the 3 bell clapper			10
Summa		22	4

It appeareth that these churchwardens did make a perfect accompt for that they had receaved and paied unto the 15 daye of Aprill 1599 so as there then remayned in their handes in stocke to the churche 9s 8d which they paied over to the newe elected churchewardens and therefore are acquited

119   Anno 1599 1600 1602

John Coocke   Churchwardens
Thomas Deacons

The accompte of John Coocke and Thomas Deacons elected churchwardens the 15th daye of Aprill anno domino 1599 regno Elizabeth 42 continuinge in their office untill the 6th daye of Aprill anno 1602 regno 44 and then made and yelded up that daye in the church before George Morrey and John Braford bailiffes and their coburgesses and many others of the parishe accomptinge for all 3 yeeres together.

Receiptes	£	s	d
in stocke of the last churchewardens		9	8
of Richard Bradford for Thomas Donnes buriall in the churche & belles		7	8
of Mr Butler for his mothers buriall in the churche		10	–
of Mr Lye for one yeeres rent of the churchyarde ended at St Mary			
Daye 1600		20	–
for Mr Fowkes buriall and his childe in the churche and 2 stones to			
laye over them		23	4
for Thomas Myllichepes gifte to the churche and for 2 stones laid over			
him and his wife in the churchyarde		13	4
of Thomas Ridgdale for one yeeres rent of his howse ended at			
St Mary Day 1600		46	8[1]
of John Orrell for one yeares rent of the halfe acre of meadowe then			
ended		12	–[2]

---

[1]   Rent for 1600 [*in the margin*]
[2]   Rent for 1600 [*in the margin*]

M^d In lent 1600 the parishe was taxed for reparacions of the churche the booke amountinge aboutes £25

of this taxacion by the churchewardens gathered	20	10	8
of Mr Bailiff Cowles out of Sowthwick for this purpose collected		12	–
of the gift of Richard Barnard of Hardwicke to the churche		6	8
for Mrs Grenewoodes buriall in the churche		6	8
for Thomas Beastes buriall in the churche		6	8
of Mr Lye for one yeeres rent of the churchyarde at St Mary Day 1601		20	–
of Thomas Rudgdale for one yeres rent then ended		46	8
of John Orrell for one yeres rent of the halfe acre then ended		12	–
for the belles at Christofer Kannars buriall		2	–
for the belles of Thomas Kewardes		2	–
for Mr Willis buriall in the churche		6	8
for Mrs Wyattes buriall		6	8

120 (margin, left of "for Mrs Grenewoodes buriall")

M^d Aboute St Mary Daye 1601 the parishe was taxed for reparacions of the walles & windowes fallen on the northeside of the churche the booke amounting aboutes £7 and delivered to the bailiffes to be gathered and paied over to the churchewardens

of this taxation at 2 sundry tymes	4	–	–
more of Mr Baylif Turbervile of this taxacion		56	10
of Mr Baylif Lye		13	–
of Mr Hilley for a bell rope		5	–
for Giles Geest buriall in the churche and belles		8	8
of John Wood for a broken clapper		5	–
of Thomas Ridgdale for his rent one yeere ended St Mary Day 1602		46	8

M^d In June 1601 an other taxacion was levied to supplie the want in the former being too short, and for amending the sowth side & walles of the churche decayed which booke accompted aboutes £24 and was delivered to the churchewardens to be gathered

of this taxacion	17	12	10
of Mr Handfordes man Mrs Wyatt John Vicarage & William Hitche for lead taken of the sowthe side of the church being sklatted	5	18	–
of John Coocke for 7 gutter stones and a piece of yron		2	2
of Richard Bradford for rubble stone left of the church walles		14	–
for the belles for Mr Woodes childe		2	2

121 (margin, left of "of John Coocke")

Seates

of Margaret Smithe for her rome in a seate		20
of Thomas Allen for his rome in a seate	2	–
of Nicholas Allen for his rome in the seate	2	–
of Ralfe Bartelmewe for his rome seate	2	–
for exchaunge of John Hawles wife with her mother		12
of Roberte Edwardes for a rome seate	2	–
of Morgan Jenkins for 2 romes for him & his wife seate	3	–
of Giles Harmar for his rome seate	4	6
of John Rawlinges for his rome seate	3	4
of John Tyrrett for his rome seate	3	4
of Mr Rogers wife for her rome seate	2	–
of William Hyett for his wifes rome seate	2	–
of Leonard Ellis wife for exchanging seate		16
of John Sicelles wife for her rome seate	2	–
of Henry Marshalles wife Alice Higges & Ann Higges in the chappell before the bedemen	2	6

of Roberte Jeninges for his rome seate	2	–
of John Sicell for his rome seate	2	–
of George Morrey for his rome seate	3	–
of William Cowles for his rome seate	3	–
of William Whitlech for his rome seate	4	6
of Thomas Deacons for his rome seate	3	8
of John Leighte for his rome seate	3	–
122 of Nicholas Wever for exchaunge seate	3	–
of John Shawe for his rome seate	3	–
of William Hitche for his rome seate	3	–
of John Bradford for his rome in the same	4	6
of Mrs Cowles for her rome seate	4	–
of Richard Butlers wife for her rome seate	3	–
of John Leightes wife for her rome seate	3	–
of Elianor Leight for her rome seate	3	–
of Alexander Baughes wife for her rome seate	5	–
of Margaret Fletcher for exchange seate	2	8
of Mrs Arkell for Mrs Tonyes rome seate	5	–
Mrs Toney exchange seate	[ ]	
of Mrs Lancaster for her rome seate	4	6
Ralfe Biddles wife exchange	[ ]	
of John Wodleyes wife for her rome seate		12
of Richard Smithe & widowe Rogers seate		lyme
of Richard Underhilles wife for her rome seate		20
for Blomers newe seate	10	–
of Mrs Wyat for her self Ann Wyatt Elizabeth and John her children seate	10	–
of Thomas Porter for his rome seate	5	–
of John Coock and his wife exchange seate	2	–
of John Raye for his rome seate	3	–
of Edwarde Myllichep for his rome seate	4	–
of John Bradfordes wife for a rome seate	4	6
of Thomas Deacons wife for her rome seate	4	6
of Henry Hasardes wife for her rome seate	4	6
123 of Edward Mannes wife for her rome seate	4	–
of Henry Little for a rome seat	4	6
of William Cottrell for a rome seat	4	–
of Thomas Rogers and John Pomfrey and their wifes seate	10	–
of Mr Poole	2	6
John Vicarage exchanged	[ ]	
of John Smithe for a rome seate	6	8
of Mrs Poole & John Tonnes wife for exchange seate	2	6
of Giles Harmars wife for exchange seate	3	–
of Thomas Reve for a rome seate	2	6
of George Morreyes wife for exchange seate	2	6
of John Shawes wife exchange seat	3	–
of John Parker for a rome seate	4	–
of John Slawghters wife for a rome seat	4	6
of Richard Mathewes wife for a rome seate	4	–
of Edward Myllicheps wife for a rome seat	4	–
of William Thornebyes wife for a rome seate		lyme
of Thomas Jenninges for a rome seate		8
of Nicholas Allens wife for a rome seat	2	–
of William Dixon & his wife for romes seate	3	4
of George Cottesold & his wife for romes seate	3	4
of Peter Wharton & his wife for romes seate	4	–
of Thomas Maunselles wife for a rome seate	3	–
John Mathewes wife exchange seate	[ ]	

of Thomas Rogers for a rome seat	2	–
124 of Thomas Jeffries & his wife for romes seate	2	8
of Mighell Wood & his wife for romes seate	2	–
of Thomas Dowers wife for a rome seate		lyme
of Ciprian Rawlyns for a rome seate		12
of Mighel Leight & his wife for romes seat	5	–
Fraunces Kinges wife exchanged seate		[ ]

The whole receiptes totted ⟨by⟩ in the churchwardens papers is
£81 8s but appeareth to be just   81   6   6

125 Expenses laid out by the said churche wardens duringe all the tyme of their said office
to be allowed and deducted out of their said formor receiptes in particular followinge

	£	s	d
for newe makinge of the churchgrate		16	3
for makinge the gutter and lead in the yles over the cloister		12	6
for makinge the greate bell clapper Jun 10 anno 1599		33	4
for glasinge the sowthside		32	–
to Bradbury for his laboure		2	–
for charges at the visitacion and presentment		16	–
for 2 belropes		11	–
for fetchinge a clapper at Aschurche			6
for 2 clockropes		12	4
for mendinge the 2 clockes		13	4
for whitlether for the belles		4	–
for visitacion at Gloucester when the side men were sworne		13	–
for pentecost mony then		3	6
for 2 bokes of articles and injunctions			14
for the pariters fee			8
for going with presentmentes to Gloucester twise		10	–
for makinge the greate bell clapper againe being broken		9	–
for mending the pulpet & a matt		2	10
for washinge surpleses twise			2
for mendinge the belles & licor		2	–
to Mr Curtes for the register booke		6	8
Heynes for takinge up the pentise behind the chauncell in October		7	–
to him for lathe			20
for nayles to Tayler			2
Mappe to serve the sklatter			18
for mendinge the greate clock		2	–
for oyle for bothe clockes			4
for a newe polley for the clock			12
for a whele for the quarter clock		2	–
for 4 baldrickes for the belles			20

126 Laid out aboute the chancell over the cloister

	£	s	d
to Charles for makinge 4 newe pipe gutters, lead & solder in December	7	3	–
for takinge up the gutter rome aboute the chauncell & 50 pound of solder		32	8
Bradbury for 17 dayes woorck there aboutes with the plummer		8	6
for charckole waxe & candles		5	4
to the carpenters for makinge the pentise there		4	–

Over the bodie of the churche for the longe roufe

	£	s	d
for lead to capp all alonge the rowfe for woorck & solder	7	19	3
for Bradburies woorck 6 dayes		3	–
to Saunders for nayles for the same & irons for the pipes over the chauncell		9	6
to Charles Hewes & Bradbury for 2 dayes hisinge up the sheetes		4	–
for hoysing up sheetes over the broken yle		2	–
for feching & carying a clapper at Bredon			8
for wasshing table clothes against Easter			18

Aboute the yles at Mr Beardes chamber

	£	s	d
for sklattinge there and makinge the batt⟨lement⟩ paid Grundye		33	6
for 4 lodes of sklatt		25	4
for two hundred of wood to beete the rafters		2	6
for lathe to Thomas Hale		10	–
for nayles there		3	4
for glasinge aboute the chauncell		6	8
for visitacion at Derehurst presentment & sides mens charges		7	2
for pentecost money		3	6
for makinge the fore bell clapper		7	–
to Mearinge for hanginge the belles and a barr to the churchedore		3	6
for newe braces & nayles for the belles			18
for licor for belles & oyle for the clocke			6
for the churchdore key & a locke			15
127 Bradbury Piper and Barker for pavinge in the churche		8	3
for Bradburyes wages 2 yeeres 1600 & 1601		52	–
for 2 buckles & a pyn for the badlrickes			12
Mr Penny the proctor for sutes against some that paied not their taxacion		4	–
for 2 citacions of quorum nomina		5	–
to Myddlewrighte to go with us 6 dayes		6	–
to Davies for the lyke		2	–
the paritors yeeres fee			8
for bryringe trees 2 yeeres			12
to Skriven for one dayes woorck			6
for whitlether to Mighel Wood against the Quenes holy daye		4	6
to Bradbury for 6 baldrickes		2	–
for a belrope		5	6
for mending the belles & licor at that tyme			10
for a newe brace to the greate bell			12
for oyle of the clockes			3
for Bradburyes yeeres wages 1602		26	–
for visitacion at Derehurst presentment & charges of side men		7	4
for pentecost money 1601		3	6
for the paritors yeeres fee			8
for whitlether to make baldrickes		2	–
for one belrope		5	6
for wasshinge surples & clothes			12
Richard Fletcher for makinge 3 seates in the body of the churche		4	–
then for nayles			8
Reve to enlarge 2 seates			20

128   Laid out for newe makinge the church wall fallen downe over the northeside repaired in June 1602

for fetchinge poles to make the skaffold & settinge them up		5	–
for wood for braggettes & for makinge them		2	6
for nayles then		2	4
to 4 men for fetching wood bourdes & ladders		2	8
for wyde wood to make skaffold poles			18
for wickeringe ropes			18
for wood to make the wynde & whele & to Dixon for making it & gugeons		5	2
for Bradburyes charges to the quarter			10
bought from the quare 240 foote of stone to make munnelles vases tables & longe buildinge stones	4	–	–
for 30 barrelles of lyme		30	–
for 11 bote lodinge of sand		5	6
to Tyler for cariage of lyme & sand		4	2
for 100 & half of bourdes to make skaffoldes & mouldes & to lay under the plummers woorck		7	6
for makinge of settle beetles			8
to Tonnes for 10 wiekes worck at 7s 6d the wieke	3	15	–
to Thorne for 10 wiekes at 6s	3	–	–
to Johnsons for 10 wickes at 6s	3	–	–
to William Lyttle for 9 wiekes 4 dayes		58	–
to olde Lyttle for 5 dayes		5	–
to Piffe for 10 wickes		55	–
to Browne for 4 wyekes at 7s 6d a weeke		30	–
to Hugh Russell for 3 wiekes at 8d a daye		28	–
to Margon for 5 wyckes at 12d a daye		30	–
to Charles Hewes for castinge and layinge the gutters		30	–
to Bradbury to help him		2	–

129

Morgan for sklattinge over the porche, for lathe & nayle		2	–
Bradbury for taking up the sheetes of lead over the newe woorck			12
for glasinge the wyndowes of that newe woorck		27	–

This was not doen by him and is charged in the next accompt as doen by John Paynter

Laid out in amendinge the sowthside of the churche on the yle

Tonnes and Bradbury for pluckinge out weedes of the wall in the sowthe ile		2	–
to Tonnes & his men for makinge the battlement, mending the gutter & the wall of that ile		24	–
for 8 barrelles of lyme & smithes cole		9	–
for heare for the same			18
to Charles Hewes for castinge the gutter, making the spowte & solder for the same		13	4
Bradbury for helpinge the plummer			12

Laid out in sklatting the sowthside along the body of the churche

Hickes for goinge to the quarre to buy sklatt			12
for 10 lodes of large sklatt	3	6	8
for 3 lodes of small sklatt		18	–
for carriage into the churche			16
for 1000 of tyle		18	–
for 13 bundles of lathe		6	6

	£	s	d
to Dixon for dubbing rafters		28	–
for nayles		10	7
for lyme and heare		5	8
to Tyler for halling tyle lyme and sand		2	–
to Hugh Russell to attend the sklatter		3	4
to Morgan sklattinge & betinge on that side		36	8

The whole charges expended appeareth   85   14   10

Owinge by this accompte to the churchewardens besides 8s miscasted in the seates

130   Also these churchewardens undertooke to sett a battlement of stone uppon the topp of the tower as nowe it standethe where before was none, but stoode as it was at the fall of the spier of leade which happened on Easter daye in the first yeere of the Quenes Maris raigne which was a beawtifull woodden battlement[1]

This battlement of stone they adventured uppon themselves by makinge of martes with suche as woulde take of them, only was licensed them for that yeere, to devise some meetinges to be had within the towne for their helpe therein which they after practised by settinge further 3 severall stage playes within the abbey on the 3 first dayes of Whitson weeke anno domino 1600 havinge begun that woorck in lent before of which charge they acquainte the bailiffes & parishe as followeth

	£	s	d
They accompt to have gotten by gifte within the towne & countrey ⟨a⟩ neere aboute in wheate & malte viz. wheate 16 bushels at 3s 4d a bushels & of malte 31 bushels at 2s 6d rated	6	10	10
of which they gained by utteraunce of the same at their playes so muche as made the the [sic] same amount to	12	2	10
for the gaine of the playes	12	7	2
of free gifte above martes		15	–
for lead that was spared from the topp of the tower		18	15
for spare tymber		22	–

Summa   45   2   –

Expended aboute the same battlementes and playes as followethe

	£	s	d
for making a whele to drawe up stone to the tower		41	–
for takinge up the lead & wyninge & the tymber woorck		22	3
for wynding up stones to the masons	3	11	–
for baskettes, cradles & necessaries		8	8
for 19 lodes of stone from Coscombe quarr	5	4	–
for hallinge over stones from Stanwey hill	4	–	–
for sand hallinge it & lyme and timber & morter		44	2
131 to the masons	31	–	12
Bradburye to attend them		14	–
for yron woorck for bothe battlementes and pynnacles		43	4
for carpenters woorck & nayles to laye the lead on the tower		12	–
for castinge gutters laying & soldringe		32	3

Summa   54   13   7

---

[1]   The year is in error. The battlement fell in the first year of the reign of Elizabeth (that is, on Easter 1559).

Laid out aboute the playes

for the place to playe in	13	4
for attendantes & other thinges	11	10
to T. B. for his charges	30	–
for hier of apparell	20	–
for 3 trumpetters	15	–
for musicions all the tyme	33	4
for ⟨i⟩ butte⟨s⟩ of beare and brewing our malte	40	–
for fruites & spices	17	–
for coockery	12	8
for meate for the players	30	6
for wayters in the seller & cuppes	9	–

All of the receiptes towardes the makinge of the battlementes	45	2	–

The whole charges upon the battlements and playes	66	6	3

By which accompt appeareth that the churchewardens have in this woorke expended more then they gained by theire playes the sum of £21 4s

This £21 4s is to be compared with the martes which they adventured

132 Moreover these churchewardens undertooke the newe repayringe of the schoolehouse in 1600 and after £5 13s 4d layd out by John Smithe aboute the wyndowes filled with stone & makinge of the chymney whereof £5 was frely geven by Mr William Riche of London they accompte forthe rest as followethe

	£	s	d
of Mr Edward Cole in money by him & the said churchwardens			
collected of benevolence of certen persons towarde those reparacions	5	12	8
for 4 trees geven towardes the flouringe and bourdinge of the schoole		27	8
Summa	7	–	4

Layd oute aboute the same

	£	s	d
for 21 hundred of bourdes	6	8	–
for bringinge them by water from the hawe, for goinge to buy them at			
Rydmarley and watchinge them 3 nightes		6	6
spent in wyne uppon the gent at sundry tymes which gave the trees		3	8
for fellinge the trees		3	4
for sawyinge		18	–
to Fletcher for tymber for the galleries there set upp		12	–
for turninge the pillers		11	–
for makinge holes in the wall			12
for hallinge tymber & bourdes from the loade		3	6
for nayles of all sortes		11	–
Dixon & Hanbage for their woorcke carpenters there		3	14
Summa	13	12	–

	£	s	d
By this accompte the churchewardens laide out & were chargeable			
above receiptes	6	11	8
In discharge whereof Mr Parry the scholemaster hathe agreed to paye			
in 2 yeeres		4	–

Also the bayliffes & councell have allowed 2 yeeres rent for Mrs
    Wyattes landes to be ended at Michaelmas 1601 to be paied to them   53   4

This charge allocat allocandum on all partes   Quiet

133   Anno domino 1602

Thaccompte of John Coocke & Thomas Deacons contynuinge churchewardens from the daye of their last accompte 11º Aprilis 1602 unto this present 17th daye of Aprill 1603 anno regni regis Jacobi primo. And then yelded upp in the churche before Conon Richardson and John Vicarage bailiffes and other their coburgesses and many others of the parishe beinge as followethe; viz.

Receiptes	£	s	d
in stocke as in their handes remayninge nothinge because the churche was to them indebted		nihil	
of My Lye for the churchyard rent at St Mary Day 1602 1603		20	–
of Richard Mathewe for his fathers gifte to the churche		20	–
of William Allen for licence to build and enlarge his howse uppon the churchyard uppon the yerely rent [ ] the fine in hand		3	6
of Thomas Ridgedale for one yeeres rent of his howse ended at St Mary Day 1603		46	8
of John Orrell for one yeeres rent for the halfe acre of meadowe paid before hand for this yeere 1603 followinge		10	–
of Mrs Cotton for her husbandes buryall		6	8
of Thomas Plevie for his wifes buryall		6	8
of Mr Vicarage for his fathers buryall and the belles		8	8
of Mrs Brayforde for her husbandes buryall and the belles		8	8
of John Tyrrett for his wifes rome in the [ ] seate & [ ] rowe			12
of William Croste for his rome seate [ ] rowe [ ]			12
of Henry Tonye for his rowme & his wifes seate [ ] rowe [ ]		3	–
of Edwarde Tonye for his rome seate [ ] rowe [ ]		2	8
of Edward Holshippe for his rome seate [ ] rowe [ ]		2	6
of Thomas Gelfe for his rome seate [ ] rowe [ ] and for his wifes rome seate [ ] rowe [ ]		9	–
of James Wooddinge for his wifes rome seate [ ] rowe [ ]		5	–
of Richard Wheeler for his romme seate 7 rowe 3		6	–
of wadowe Willis for her seate [ ] rowe [ ]		2	–
of Roberte Smithe for his roome seate [ ] rowe [ ]		2	–
of William Fowke for his rome seate [ ] rowe [ ]		2	8
of Thomas Pulton for charges spent against him at Gloucester		2	6
of Mr Lye more then his yeeres rent		10	–

134 (appears beside "of James Wooddinge" row)

1602 (handwritten note in right margin)

Summa totalis   8   17   2

Layd oute by these churchewardens duringe this last yeere unto the daye of this accompte as followethe;

Expenses	£	s	d
Bradbury for his yeeres wages for the bell & clocke		26	–
to Paynter for glasinge the wyndowes which Charles Hewes was paied for before hand as appeareth in the last generall accompte but leavinge the same undoen		30	–
him for glasinge in the chauncell		6	8
for 2 newe belropes this yeer		11	–
for pentecost money this yeere		3	6

at the visitacion for paritors fees & the booke of articles			22
for the Register & clarckes fee to our presentment			16
for our & the sidesmen dynner		5	–
for lyme & woorck to stop up the abbey doore		2	–
for a barrell of lyme to the glasyer			11
to Nicholas Allen for whitleather		2	6
to Mr Cottrell for 2 olde males		4	–
Hanbage for mendinge the greate bell whele			12
William Dixon & others for movinge the monkes seates into the chauncell		5	–
for parchment and yncke to make the Register booke delivered to Gloucester			18
for receving the register at Gloucester and our charges		2	6
135 Thomas Cockes for wrytinge the register booke		5	–
for delivery of our presentment & charges at Gloucester		2	–
Bradbury for oyle for the clocke & makinge 4 baldrickes			20
for licor for the belles			6
for wasshing the surples & tableclothes		2	–
Mr Cottrell one pipe that fell to staves & hapinge 3 other pipes		7	–
Mrs Braford for 3 hoggesheades		8	–
to John Tonnes for nayles			4

Summa	6	11	3

Memorandum that these churchewardens are allowed in this accompt as money paied to John Paynter for glasinge the wyndowes neere the churche dore when the wall was newe made 2 yeeres past 30s which said wyndowes were before set to Charles Hewes to be glased and he before hand receaved of the churchewardens for the same 26s as in their formor accompt is to them allowed which they remember in their notes and would have allowaunce so that we shall then geve dowble charges for that woorck is to be considered

136 Anno domino 1603

The accompte of Fraunces Pace and John Raye beinge elected churchewardens the 17th daye of Aprill 1603 anno regis Jacobi 1 and continuinge in that office for one whole yeere viz. untill the 24th of Aprill then next followinge anno 1604 And then geven upp in the parishe churche before Thomas Hilley and William Parsons the bailiffes and other the burgesses and parishoners there present as followeth;

Receiptes	£	s	d
they acknowlege not any money receaved in stocke		nihil	
of William Cowles for exchaunge of his rowme to sitt in the 7 seate of the 7 rowe		4	–
of Thomas Hoare for a rowme in the 3 seate of the 3 rowe		3	–
of Mrs Willis for 2 rowmes in her seate for Thomas Perkins wife and Martha Perkins in 12 seate of 5 rowe		6	–
for 2 rowmes for John Deaves & his wife viz. 10: seate 7 rowe		4	–
of John Parker for exchange of his rowme into 6 seate 2 rowe			20
of Richard Flucke for his rowme in 6 seate of 6 rowe		5	–
of Henry Hasard for his rowme in the 6 seate of the 3 rowe		3	4
of Richard Pearse for 2 rowmes for himself & his wife in the 11 seate 2 rowe		4	–
of John Geast for his wifes rowme in the 10 seate of the 5 rowe		6	8
of Christofer Kannar for his rowme in the 2 seate of the 3 rowe		3	–
of John Sassell for exchaunge of his wifes rowme into the 18 seate of 3 rowe		2	–
of Richard Mathewes for ringinge of the belles			22
137 of Mr Cater for ringinge of the belles and his wifes buryall		8	8
of My Lye for the belles ⟨and⟩ for Mrs Coles ⟨buryall⟩		2	–

of Patrick Porter for ringinge the belles for goodwife Gregge	2	–
of John Shawe for the belles	2	–
of Mrs Braford for a stone for her husbandes grave	5	–
of Thomas Churchey for his wifes grave in the churche	6	8
of Thomas Rudgedale for a yeeres rent of his howse	46	8

Summa totalis	5	17	4

Layde out by these churchewardens during their yeeres office unto the daye of this accompt, as followeth;

Expenses	£	s	d
spent at the visitacion		8	10
for whitleather			18
for licor for the belles			2
for shuttinge the second bell clapper		11	–
for 3 keyes & mendinge the buckell for a bawdrick			12
for shuttinge the 3 bell clapper		15	2
for our charges a Cheltnham			12
for a communion booke		8	–
charges at our meetinge			3
for hanginge up the fore bell			8
for the greate bell rope		7	–
Bradbury for makinge 3 bawdrickes			12
for a barrell of lyme & cariage to the churche			14
for pavinge where Mr Brafordes stone was taken uppe			6
of mendinge the greate bell brace and hanginge him upp			12
Bradbury for 2 dayes woorcke at the leades			18
for a bagge of coles to solder			6
for 11 poundes of solder		7	4
the plummer 5 dayes woorcke			9
for a barrell of lyme and cariage			13
for caryinge home a bell clapper to Ashchurch			2
Bradbury & Mappe for 2 dayes woorck		2	6
for heare to make morter			6
for half a hide of whitlether		2	–
for oyle for the clocke			1
for makinge 2 baldrickes			8
for a rope for the third bell		5	4
for paper for Bradbury			1
for wasshinge the surplesse & churche clothes at twise		2	–
for nayles for the leades and for mending the churche doore keye			12
Bradbury for his yeeres wages		24	–

138

Summa totalis	5	7	9
Receiptes	5	17	4
Expenses	5	7	9
In stocke remaining to be delivered to the next churchewardens		9	7

Memorandum that this yeere and in these churchewardens tymes the leade rowfe over the chauncell was taken upp and newe builded the charge thereof beinge commytted to John Coocke and Thomas Deacons which was begun the 7 of Maye 1603 and ended in June followinge

Charge

		£	s	d
for 2 tones of tymber		3	9	4
for ⟨the⟩ nayles to amend the wheele				4
for the shides for the same				2
for Cannar for hallinge planckes				3
to labowrers for certen dayes			15	–
the sawyers for 3 dayes			5	–
Dickson & his 3 men for 5 dayes			21	8
for hallinge			7	2
to the plummer of Woorcester				12
more to the sawyers for 6 dayes			10	–
to Dixon & his men for 12 dayes			10	–
Hanbage for 2 dayes				14
to labourers for woorck		3	8	8
for sand & ridlinge of it				18
Harres the carpenter for 24 dayes			20	–
olde Dickson for 6 dayes			9	2
for kipes and grease				8
for a barrell of lyme and half a hundred of bricke			5	2
for nayles				12
to Bradbury for tryinge the solder			4	–
to the plummer			11	10
to the plummer of Gloucester			22	–
for hanginge the bell				12
for drinck at helping up the bell				6
for hallinge pulles				12
Holder the carpenter			7	–
⟨Summa⟩		⟨18	5	–⟩
for the plummers dyettes			24	–
Summa		19	9	–
Received of Mr Bayliff Vickarage out of the booke taxed for those reparacions		17	2	6
Received also for ashes and chippes			16	8

139 appears in left margin beside "Harres the carpenter".

140 William Hytchis   Churchwardens
        Richarde Brawdforde

The accompte of William Hytchis and Richarde Brawdforde churchwardens of the parishe churche of Tewkesburie in the diocese of Gloucester from the feaste of Easter 1604 untill the feaste of Easter 1607 made and given up before the bayeliffes burgesses and cominaltie of the burroughe of Tewkesburie the 28th daye of June 1607

Firste the sayd churchwardens doe charge themselves to have had and receaved in their sayd time of theire beinge churchwardens to & for the use of the sayde parishe churche the particuler summes folloinge

In the accompte of Fraunces Pace and John Raye churchwardens laste before appearethe for stocke in theire handes 9s 7d not here acknowledged

	£	s	d
Receiptes			
of Peter Wharton for his wives buriall		7	8

	for Mr Moons buriall	10	–
	of Roger Gilberte for his mothers buriall	6	8
	of Thomas Rydgedale for rent	23	4
	of Mr Lyes for rente	26	8
	of Mr Lyes for his wives buriall	6	8
	of John Orrell for his fathers buriall	8	–
	of Andrewe Baughan for his childes grave	2	6
	of John Sycell for the bells	2	–
	of John Shawe for his wives rome in the thirde rowe & 17th seate	4	–
	of John Shawe for his roome in the 6th roome and firste seate	2	–
	of Mr Hilley in exchaunge for his own roome in the 5th reowe and 5th seate	2	6
	of Mr Roger Dowdeswell for his roome & his wives in the 5th reowe		
	& 4th seate	11	7
	of Thomas Hale for his wives rome in the 6th reowe & 6th seate	3	9
141	of John Combe for his wives roome and his owne his wives seate is		
	in the thirde reowe & 19th seate and his roome in the 8th seate	8	–
	Andrewe Poullams his wives roome in the third reowe & 19th seate		
	and his owne roome in the seconde reowe & seconde seate	7	–
	of Mr Coocke for his daughters roome in the 4th reowe & 7th seate	5	–
	of Nicolas Hollifaxe for his wives roome in the seconde reowe &		
	9th seate	3	–
	of Thomas Coxe for his wives roome in the 6th reowe & 6th seate	4	–
	his owne roome in the 4 reowe and 5th seate	5	–
	of John Mathewes for his wives roome in the 5th reowe and 17th seate	5	–
	of Andrewe Baughan for his wives roome in the 6th reowe & 6th seate	5	–
	of Mr Grime for his wives roome in the thyrd reowe and 16th seate	5	6
	of Thomas Reeve for his wives roome in the 6th reowe & 6th seate	5	–
	of Mrs Butler her husbandes gifte	20	–
	of Roberte Canner for his wives roome in the 7th reowe the 8th seate	5	–
	his owne roome in the seconde reowe the firste seate	2	–
	of Thomas Ridgedale for his rent	23	4
	for the exchaunge of aroome for William Cowles wife in the 6th reowe		
	the thirde seate	2	6
	of John Powell for his wives roome in the 5th reowe the 18th seate	4	–
	of Thomas Ridgedale for his rent	23	4
	of Mr Coocke for his daughter Elizabethe roome in the 4th reowe the		
	7th seate		20
	of Roberte Jennynges for the exchaunginge his roome to the thirde		
	reowe & 8th seate		18
	for the exchaungeinge of his wives roome in the 5th reowe & 7th seate		20
	of Edward Rudgdale for his wives roome in the 5th reow the 16th seate	4	–
142	of George Morrye for exchaunge for his wives roome in the third row		
	the 16th seate		20
	of Mr Edwarde Alye	26	8
	of Thomas Ridgedale	26	8
	of Mr Phelpes for a roome for his daughter Marie in the 4th reow and		
	5th seate	3	–
	of John Mayle for his wives roome in the 5th reowe & 16th seate	4	–
	for the exchaungeinge aroome for John Hawker for his wife in the		
	5th reowe & 16th seate		18
	of Mrs Brawforde for exchaunginge her roome in the thirde reowe &		
	16th seate		20
	of Mrs Toanye her husbandes ghifte to the churche	20	–
	more receaved of the oulde churchwardens	3	4
	for Mrs Kedwardes buriall	8	8
	of Mrs Mann for astone for her husbandes grave	6	8

of Mr Hilleye for his wives buriall astone and the belles	15	4
of Thomas Rydgedale for halphe ayeres rent	23	4
of Mr Edwarde Alye for ayeres rente	26	8
for three yeres rent for the halph acre	30	–
of Mr Hilley for the buriall of his childe	3	4
for Mrs Bishoppes buriall	10	–
of Mr Nansan for a seate beinge the seconde in the 4th reowe	15	–
of Mr Mathewes for aseate in the 6th reowe the 14th seate	13	4
of Mr Scullowe for aroome	5	–
of Katherne Hill for a roome in the 5th reowe the seconde seate	4	–
of Alice Geines for aroome in the 5th reowe the 16th seate	2	–
of William Davis for aroome in the 7th reowe the 13th seate		12
of Thomas Millarde for aroome in the 7th reowe the 7th seate	2	6
of John Kyrrye for aroome in the 7th reowe the firste seate		12
William Cartwrite for his wife rome in the second rowe	2	–
143 of William Allen for a seate in the 7th reowe the second seate	7	–
of Patricke Porter for aroome in the seconde reowe the 4th seate	3	–
of James Style for roome in the seconde reowe the 4th seate	3	–
of Mr Reede for aroome in the 4th reowe the 9th seate	5	–
of Thomas Whitle for aroome in the seconde reowe the 17th seate		12
of Richard Hewes for aroome in the seconde reowe the 7th seate	3	–
of Amye Downbell for her roome in the 5th reowe the 7th seate	3	–
Thomas Deacons exchaunged aroome in the 5th reowe the 8th seate	[	]

Somme totalle of all receiptes duringe the time aforesayd doeth amounte unto	26 19	5

Out of which some the sayd churchwardens do crave allowance for the some of moneye by them layd oute for and to the use of the sayd churche in the time aforesayde

	£	s	d
at the visitation		8	–
for sclat stones		10	7
for wier and cole		2	–
for two males & whitleather		3	–
for the deliveringe in of the firste presentment		4	–
payde Broadberrye		6	4
for aboocke of cannons			18
for two barrelles of lime and haullinge		2	6
for mendinge adoore keye			2
Broadberrye for worke		4	–
at the archdeacons visitation at Cheltenham		5	5
for two bell roopes		15	9
for 600 of quickesett			16
144 to John Saunders for nayles			12
to John Saunders for worke		4	–
to William Dixson for bordes timber and worke		8	–
Braudberie for five dayes worke		2	6
for 600 of quicksett			22
at a visitation in Tewkesburie		5	10
for setting them		3	2
for two barrells of lyme		2	–
Bradberie			2
for carriage			3
for apecke to carrye morter			3
for nayles			15

	for thornes and settinge them		16
	for nayles		15
	John Hickes and his sonne for 11 dayes worke	20	–
	to Braudberrie for wages & worke	17	6
	for mendinge and washinge the surplis		8
	to John Saunders		12
	at the visitation	2	8
	penticoste monye	3	6
	Braudberrie		18
	to the somner		6
	Braudberrie for worke and wages	10	6
	for 16 pound of bell roope	5	4
	for lycour for the belles		3
	for certifyinge the havinge of the table of degrees		16
	at the archdeacons courte in Tewkesburie	2	6
	for aboocke of articles and for warninge of us		16
	for the forebell clapper	5	5
	Braudberrie for wages and worke	13	–
	John Hickes for crestes and worke		12
	Thomas Reeve for the mendinge of seates	6	–
	to Braudberrie		12
145	for washinge surplisses & clothes		12
	for regestringe	2	–
	unto Mrs Brawdforde for three males	4	4
	to Broadberrie for mendinge the leades on the toppe of the churche	5	–
	for makinge baldrickes	2	–
	to John Saunders for iron worke & nayles for the belles	3	–
	to Braudberrye fo quartrige	5	6
	for a roope	2	6
	for abarrell of lyme		14
	for trees		16
	for hallyers for the bell roopes		12
	to Braudberrie for quartrige	5	6
	for mendinge of seates nayles and pavinge	4	–
	to the painter	4	–
	for abarrell of lyme		13
	to Braudberrie for worke	2	–
	for aroope for the clocke	2	8
	to John Shawe for apeece of aroope for the clocke	3	–
	to John Saunder for a dogge for the belles		4
	to Braudberrie for soder and worke	12	–
	for washinge the surplisses and the churche clothes		12
	to John Saunders for nayles and iron worke at the churche grate	2	8
	for washinge the surplisses		12
	for charcole		12
	penticoste monie	3	6
	for charges for the sydemen at the visitation	5	–
	to Scriven for weedinge the quicke & bryeringe the trees	2	4
	to John Saunders for nayles and mendinge the church dore keye		6
	at the archdeacons courte		16
146	for washinge the surplisses		6
	at the courte for charges	5	–
	to Braudberrie for wages	5	6
	for white leather		14
	for oyle		2
	to Braudberrie for mendinge the leades	3	6

to John Saunders for nayles		3
for shides to make leavers		3
for worke	2	–
for regestringe	2	–
to Braudberrie		6
to Braudberrie		8
to John Saunders for nayles		6
for trees		8
for thinges aboute the faunt		4
to Alexander Parrett		12
to Braudberrie		12
for herre		6
to George Cheapman		4
to William Scriven		8
to John Saunders for nayles		9
to William Scriven		7
for clothe to mend surplisses		2
for akeye		4
for mendinge seates		8
to Braudberries wife		7
for nayles		2
for watringe the settes		3
to John Midlewright for aboocke		12
for goinge to Gloucester	2	–
to Roberte Jaynes for aquarters wages	5	7
for washinge the surplisses		7
to Braudberrie		12
for aroope	3	4
to Alexander Parrett		12
to Braudberrie		12
for apottell of wine & suger	3	–
at Gloucester	4	6
to Braudberrie for solderinge the gutters	2	8

147

to Braudberrie for washinge surplisses		6
to Alexander Parrett		6
for licour for the belles		2
to Alexander Parrett for carringe rubble		10
for a table of degrees of marriage		6
for licour for the belles		2
to Braudberrie for his quartrige	5	6
to Braudberrie for foure baldrickes for the belles		16
for oyle		1
to Braudberrie		12
for mendinge seates		6
for amale	2	4
to William Dixson for mendinge the grate	11	–
to Alexander Parrett for three yeres wages	15	–
to the paynter	3	8
for carryinge gravell to the church grate	2	–
for white leather	2	–
to Braudberrie	10	–
to Alexander Parrett		12
for lathe & carriage	3	2
for nayles & oyle		6
for makinge castinge & ingrosinge this accompt	3	4
for whitleather	2	–

Some totall of all paymentes layd out in the yeres aforesayde to the
   use of the church doethe amounte unto   19   15   11

Which some of £19 25s 11d beinge deducted from the forsayde some
   of £26 19s 5d there remaines due to the church uppon this accompt   7   3   6

Out of which remainder of £7 3s 6d there is payd into the handes of George Morrye and
Thomas Gelfe the new churchwardens the some of fyftye 3s 3d soe the remainder due
is £4 10s 2d

148   Debtes due and owinge to the church in the yeres of William Hycthes and Richarde
       Bradforde churchwardens

1607	£	s	d
there is owinge by Mr Roger Dowdeswell for the buriall of his father		8	8
for the buriall of his two children		6	8
of Mrs Wyett for the buriall of Mr Cole		8	8
of Thomas Gelfe for the buriall of his wife & childe		10	–
of Mr George Dowdeswell for the buriall of his childe		3	4
of Mr Edwarde Wakeman for the buriall of his childe		3	4
of John Geines for the belles		2	–
of John Braudforde for the belles		2	–
of Fraunces Clare for the belles		2	–
of Richard Weaver for the belles and buriall of his wife		8	8
of Mr Cotterell for the buriall of his daughter		6	8
of Richard Mathewes for the belles for his two wives		4	–
The somme totall owinge is	3	6	–

1607

149   [Added]

The Blew Gallery built 1607

150   George Morrye   Churchwardens
       Thomas Gelfe

Received of the last churchwardens William Hycthes and Richard Bradforde the third
of Aprill 1607 in monie due unto the churche as followethe

	£	s	d
the 3 of April	7	3	6
of John Turbell for the buryinge of his wife		6	8
of Mr Cater for the buryinge of his childe		3	4
of Mr Alye for the halph yeres rent for the churcharde		13	4
of William Blancket for halphe yeres rent for the house in the high streete	1	6	8
of William Allen fo 7 yeres rent from Mr Cowles & Mr Tomes the 13th of October		2	6
of Mr Alie for the churcharde the 20th of Maye		13	4
of astraunger for the buriall of his wife		13	4
of Richard Woodley for the buriall of his father		8	8
of George Shaw for the buriall of Alice Bowle & his wives seate		7	4
of Thomas Sclicer for his seate		5	–
of Phillippe Surman for his seate		13	4
of Giles Hashard for his seate		6	8
of Mr Hewes for their seate	2	5	–

for the buriall of Mrs Morrye	6	8
of George Morrye for his daughters seate	5	–
of Mr Whitt for his wives seate	5	–
for halph an acre in the meadowe	10	–
of Mr Roger Dowdeswell for the buriall of his father	8	8
for the buriall of his two children	6	8
of Fraunces Clare for the belles	2	–
of Mr Cotterell for the buriall of his daughter	5	–
of Richard Hawleye for aroome in the 8th seat the 5 reowe	6	–

151 (margin, at line "of Mr Whitt for his wives seate")

A note what Thomas Gelfe hathe receaved for the churche as followeth

Anno domino 1607

for halph an acre of meadowe		10	–
of John Parker for his seate		6	8
of Thomas Powlton et uxor for their seates		13	4
of Thomas Bicke et uxor for their seates		13	4
of John James for his seate		6	8
of William Layght for his seate		6	8
of John Orrell for his seate		6	8
of Henrye Porter for his seate		6	8
of John Powltam for his seate		6	8
of William Warde for his seate		6	8
of Henry Lytle for his seate		6	8
of William Bundye for his seate		6	8
of Richard Turner for his seate		5	–
of Arthure Birte for his seate		5	–
of John Jordan for his seate		4	–
of John Turbell for his seate		5	–
of John Walle for his seate		4	–
of Mr Wackemane for his seate & for the buriall of his childe	2	10	–
of Margerie Kinge for her seate		6	8
of Thomas Hoare et uxor for their seates		10	–
of Thomas Sowtherne et uxor for their seates		13	4
of William Turbell for his seate		6	8
of Nicolas Hallyfaxe for his seate		6	6
of James Houllshippe et uxor for their seates		9	–
of Roger Rayer for his seate		5	–
of Edwarde Phelpes for his seate		5	–
of Mr Parrye for his roume in the 10th seat the 4th reowe		5	–
of Fraunces Clare for aroome in the 3 seate the 3 reowe		5	–
of George Whitledge et uxor for their seates		8	–
of William Rayer for arome in the 7 seate the 3 reowe		5	–
of James Greene for arome in the 8 seate the 3 reowe		3	4
of Mr White for arome in the 8 seate the 5 reowe		6	8
of Mr Mintrige et uxor for their seates		10	–
of the goodman Geines for the belles at the buriall of his wife		1	6
of Richard Flucke for the buriall of Mr Layght		6	8
for the buriall of William Turbelles child		3	4
of John Geaste for his seate		6	8
of Thomas White for arome in the 7th seate the 4th reowe		5	–

152 (margin, at line "of Arthure Birte for his seate")

153 (margin, at line "of Thomas White for arome in the 7th seate the 4th reowe")

Anno domino 1608

of William Blanckett for the halphe yeres rent of the house in the high streete	1	6	8

of George Shawe for his seate		6	8
of William Johnsonns for his seate		10	–
of James Greene for his wives roome in the 5th seate the 2 reowe		2	6
of Mr Poulton which his brother gave to the churche		40	–
for the buryinge of Mr Poulton & for the stone		10	–
of William Woodwarde for rent	1	6	8
of Mr Lyes for halph yeres rent for the churcharde		13	4
of Mr Mintrige for the buriall of his daughter		10	–
of Mr Powlton for his seate		6	8
of Mr Hewes for the buriall of Mr Atkins		12	–
of Mr Hytchis for the buriall of his mother		6	8
of Mrs Butler for the buriall of her husband		6	8
of William Allen for one yeres rent for his litle house			6
of Phillippe Chaundler for a rome for his wife in the 8th seate the 2 reowe		3	4
of Humferye Higines for his roome in the 2 seate the thirde reowe		3	–
of John Turrett for his roome in the 2 seate the 3 reowe		3	–
154 of Henrye Tovie for his wives roome in the 15 seate the 3 reowe		5	–

Anno domino 1609

of Mr Lyes for the rent of the churcharde		13	4
of Mr Cater for his wives roome in the 8th seate the sixt reowe		4	–
of Richard Turret for his roome		6	8
of Thomas Allen for his roome		2	–
of George Rogers for his seate		4	–
of John Hardinge for his roome		4	–
of William Woodwarde for halphe ayeres rent	1	6	8
of Braudberye for his garden for two yeres rent			8
of Pursevall for his garden			4
of John Higgins for his roome			5
of John Aston for his roome		4	–
of Henrie Woodward for his roome & his wives in the 17th seate the firste reowe		4	–
of Mr Carr for the buriall of his sonne		4	4

Somme totall is	46	11	8

Layd out for the church by George Morrey & Thomas Gelfe churchwardens 1607

	£	s	d
to Thomas Aston and William Cotterell for 12 barrelles of lyme		12	–
for the hawlinge to Roberte Canner		1	–
for the washing of the surples & table clothe			8
155 to Edwarde Parsonnes for 7 bushelles of cole		2	–
to John Even for two dayes worke		1	4
to William Whitledge for heare		1	4
to Edwarde Parsons for three bushelles of cole		1	–
to John Even for one dayes worke			8
to Fraunces Bradberye for three dayes worke		3	–

June 1607

for a kipe			3
to Henrye Feilde for two bushelles of shreedes			8
to Fraunces Bradberye for wood			4

	to Fraunces Bradberye for 6 dayes worke	6	–
	to John Evens for six dayes worke	4	–
	to Fraunces Braudberye and his man		2
	to Fraunces Braudberye for five dayes worke	5	–
	for ale for Fraunces Bradberye & his man		9
	to John Even for five dayes worke	3	9
	to William Hill for two bushelles of shreedes		8
	to Fraunces Braudberye for 6 dayes worke & ahalph	6	6
	to John Even for 7 dayes worke	5	3
	for ale for Bradberye		5
	to Henrye Turke for mendinge the bell clapper and for crampes of iron	3	9
156	to John Even for three dayes worke	3	3
	to Edwarde Parsons for three bushelles of cole	1	–
	to Fraunces Bradberye for three dayes worke	3	–
	to Fraunces Bradberye for his quartrige	1	3
	to Alexander Parrett for his quartrige	1	3
	to John Saunders for pines	1	–
	to George Cheapman for ale		3
	to William Whitledge for herre		8
	to Mrs Brauforde for wine	2	–

Auguste 1607

	to William Dixon for a boorde		1	4
	for whitleather for the belles			2
	for aloade of sclat stones		5	8
	to William Dixon	2	3	8
	for apinte of sacke & suger to Mrs Brawforde			6
	for bread			3
	to George Walker for athousande of nayles		1	4
	to Thomas Compayne for three barrelles of lyme		3	–
	for bread			3
	to the painter		2	2
	to Robert Charnocke for haullinge lyme & lathe			6
	to John Turbell for foure bushelles of herre		2	8
	to Fisher for the carryinge of morter			6
	to John Hickes for five dayes worke		5	–
	to William Dixon	2	–	–
157	to Alexander Parrett for quartrige		1	3
	to George Cheapman for ale			8
	to William Dixon	1	13	4
	to Henrye Turke for nayles			6
	to John Saunders for abuckle			4
	for the carryinge of water to slake lyme			4
	to Rowles & John Even		3	8
	for the carryinge of aleter		1	6
	for ale			6
	for one dayes worke to John Even			11
	to Alexander Parrett for the carryinge of gravell		1	1
	to Alexander Parrett for pavinge		3	6
	to John Even for two dayes worke		1	6
	to John Henburie for the carryinge of gravell		6	8
	to Alexander Parrett for pavinge & carryinge of stone		3	4
	to Fraunces Bradberye for two dayes worke		2	–
	for three dayes worke		3	4

to Fraunces Bradberye for carryinge of stone		8
to Alexander Parrett for quartrige & for his boyes	1	8
for white lether	1	–

158   1608

to William Greffin for bringinge of the trees into the churchyarde	1	8
to Fraunces Bradberye for the layinge of the leades	12	6
for the castinge of leade		6
to John Arpine for lathe nayles & boord nayles	2	4
to John Hickes & his sonne for 11 dayes worke	11	1
for beere		3
to John Hardinge for 8 bundelles of lathe	6	–
to George Morreye for foure bundelles of stone lathe & two of seelinge lathe	3	7
to William Bundye for quarrell & to the pavier	3	–
to Alexander Parrett for pavinge in the churche		12
for our ministers goinge unto Cheltnam to the visitation	2	2
at Cheltnam at our comminge thither		8
for our dinner	5	–
given to our minister	3	4
for penticoste moneye	3	6
for the forbearaunce of our presentment		10
for apottell of wine given to the archdeacon & aquarte to the other officers	2	4
for our supper at our comminge home	5	10
to William Bowyer for the carryinge of our clockes		6
spent before we went to Cheltnam		3
given to the parritor		6
for oyle for the cloke		1
the same daye to a poore man by the appointment of Mr Baylifes	2	–
159 for bryeringe the trees	2	6
for iron worke about the belles	3	–
to Fraunces Bradberie & Alexander Parrett for the mendinge of the same	1	7
for two roopes to make halliers		6
for licour for the belles and for paper		4
for the note to gather for the churches	2	–
for one rope of twentie nine feathome & foure other ropes	9	9

⟨A note layd out⟩

A note of more monye layd out by Thomas Gelfe

Anno domino 1608

at the archdeacons court in Tewkesburie		2	–
the bishoppes visitation in Tewkesburie for our articles		2	4
for penticoste monye		3	6
for our dinner		4	–
for apottell of wine given to the chauncellor & the archdeacon		1	4
to William Dixon	6	16	8
to Bradberrye & Parrett		2	–
for coullouringe the gallerie		2	6
for settinge two [ ]			6
to the plummer of Worcester for castinge & for new leade		7	6
for carringe of leade to Worcester & from Worcester		1	3

for carryinge of the lead to the churche			4
160 the ropier for arope		2	10
to Fraunces Bradberie for two dayes worke		2	2
to Fraunces Bradberie for worke		1	5
to Fraunces Bradberie and Pursevall for ale			3
to Scriven for bryeringe the trees in the churchyard			6
to Alexander Parrett for the mendinge of the buckettes		1	–
to Patrick Porter for partchment		5	–
for 41 pounds of pewter to make soulder for the churche		10	8
for two thousande of lathe nayles		2	8
for oyle for the clocke			3
to Fraunces Bradberye			2
to Fraunces Bradberie			8
to William Dixon	5	3	4
Fraunces Bradberie for worke		15	2
for settinge one tree			4
to Fraunces Bradberie for his quarterige & for worke		7	11
to Alexander Parrett & for pavinge in the churche		2	–
for penticoste monye		3	6
besides in the office		1	10
for our dinner the same daye		7	6
for apottell of wine & sugar for the archdeacon		2	–
for makinge two keyes for one chest & mendinge the churchyarde gate		1	6
for a barrell of lyme		1	1
for carryinge agreat stone to the upper end of the church			7
161 for oyle for the clok & paper			3
for one rope wayinge 9 pounds at 4d the pounde		3	–
to Fraunces Bradberye for workinge in the church		2	6
geven to Mr Nutt when he preached heare aquart of wine			10
geven to Mr Griffin at his preachinge heare aquarte of wine		2	–
geven to Mr Lowe at his preachinge heare aquart of wine		1	–
spent at the makinge of our presentment		3	4
for charcole for worke in the church		1	–
Fraunces Bradberie for his quarteridge		5	6
to Alexander Parrett		1	3
to Fraunces Bradberie for three dayes worke & ahalph aboute agutter & his boyes servinge the sclatter		5	6
for washinge the surples and the table clothes			8
for the makinge of one balricke			4
to William Dixon for mendinge the roofe & for timber		5	–
for payntinge the church	1	15	–
for oyle for the belles			2
for wine & suger geven to the bishoppe		3	–
for an aquittance unto Mr Powlton			4
to Fraunces Bradberie for adayes worke & ahalph		1	6
for coles & nayles			6
for helpinge up with lead			6
for washinge the surplis & for carryinge of lead to the keye		1	–
for the exchainge of leade	2	–	–
162 for oyle for the belles & paper			3
Frances Bradberye & Alexander Parret their wages		6	8
for one barrell of lyme		1	4
spent at Gloucester		10	9
Fraunces Bradberie for layinge sheetes of lead & makinge up awall & for sowderinge agutter			[...]

		£	s	d
to Persevall & his sonne for helpinge him			1	10
Bradberie & Parret their wages			6	8
for two lockes			2	–
for washinge the surplis & the towelles paper & oyle for the clocke			1	–
for an howre glase			1	–
for iron worke to put him in & one hinge for adore			2	4
geven amessenger for bringinge aletter from Gloucester			1	–
for 12 buckettes and the carriage		1	13	–
for the paintinge of them			3	6
for the mendinge of the grate			1	2
for two balwrickes				8
for one service booke for the church			8	–
Fraunces Bradberie for his quarters wages			5	6
to Alexander Parett at the same tyme			1	5
for makinge of two parchment boockes			1	–
for hinges for a doore & nayles & for settinge it up			2	4
163 to Fraunces Bradberie for mendinge aglasse windowe & for other thinges			2	6
for sand				6
for makinge our accomptes & two regester boockes			6	8
Some totall payd is		45	–	7
Soe that there remayneth unto the church		1	10	–

More money layd out after the datinge of our boocke

		£	s	d
geven to apreacher by the appointment of Mr Morreye beinge bayeliefe			3	4
for makinge our boocke anew			3	4
Soe that the whole due remayninge unto the church is		1	3	4

The which we did deliver up into the handes of William Cowles one of the next churchwardens[1]

164   **The accompte of Thomas Hoare and William Dixon churchwardens for fower yeares vid. from the second of Aprill 1611 untel the eleaventh of Aprill 1615**

Receipts	£	s	d
of the last churchwardens in mony		47	–
more from Peter Bell uppon their accompte		6	8
from Mr Hitches		13	4
from William Woodward part of his rent		15	–
of Mr Alie for his sonns grave and belles		8	8
of John Hardinge for his wives seate		9	–
of Arthur Burte for a seate for himselfe		3	4
of Mr Sculloe for seate for his wife		10	–
of John Kingesburie for a seate for himselfe and a seate for his wife		16	8
of Mrs Phelpes for her husbandes grave and bells		8	8
of John Holtom for a seate for his wife		8	–
of Richard George for his father in lawes grave & belles & for Kenelm Weavers grave		15	–
of Richard George for his seate and his wives		20	–
of John Sawle for his seate & his wives		8	–

---

[1] The accounts for 1609–10 are out of sequence; see p. 114 below. The accounts for 1610–11 are missing.

of William Wilson for a seate for himselfe	5	–
of John Man for his seate and his wives	18	–
of William Guylbert for thexchange of a seate for his wife	3	–
of Mr Bradford for a seate for his wife	10	–
of Mr Bradford for his wives grave	6	8
of Mr Bradford for a ston for his wives grave and a ston for his daughteres grave	20	–
for the hafe aker in avon ham	12	–
for the churchard	20	–
of Edward Phelpes for his sisters grave and ston	16	8
of Edward Phelpes for his seate	12	–
of Mr Hitches for Mr Greenewoodes grave and belles	8	8
of John Rayer for his wives grave	6	6
of Mrs Mathewes for her husbandes grave and belles	20	–
of Mr Hitches for Mr Cunisbie his grave	6	8
of Mrs Field for her husbandes grave	6	8
of Mrs Turbervile for her husbandes grave ston and belles	18	7
of Ralfe Bartholmewe for his seate	9	–
of Edward Hill for his wives seate	12	–
of Fraunces Clare for a seate for his wife	10	–
of Mr Hillie for his childes grave and ston	4	–
of Richard Machin for a seate for his wife	6	8
for the halfe aker in the ham	12	–
for the churchyeard	20	–
of the widdow Seaverne for her husbandes grave & for a seate for herselfe	15	–
of Mr ⟨Bradford⟩ Baughan for his seate	8	–
of Edward Mellechepe for his seate besides his owne two seates which hee delivered up to us	10	–
of Robert Fletcher for his mothers grave ston and belles	15	–
of Curtes of Southwicke for his seate	8	–
of Fleris Couper for his seate	4	9
of Mr Vaughan for his chiles grave and ston	4	–
of Mr Balden for his seate	20	–
of John Payton for his fathers grave & belles	8	–
of John Orrell for 2 seates for his wife	6	8
of John Hardinge for his wives grave	6	8
of Thomas Slyser for a seate for his wife	9	–
for the ashe in the churchyeard	4	–
and for the elme	8	–
of Edward Alie for a seate for himselfe and his wife	30	–
of Arthur Burt for a seate for his wife	15	–
of William Wilson for his wives seate	15	–
of Edward Toney for thexchange of his seate	20	–
of George Chapman for a seate for himself his wife and his sonne	20	–
of Mr Hitches for Mr Greenewoodes gifte to the churche	20	–
of Mr Cooke for 3 graves	20	–
of Mr Underhill for his wives grave	6	8
of Michaell Millington for his wives grave and ston	11	–
of William Viceridge for his seate	10	–
of William Leight for a seate for his wife	8	6
of Kenelm Merson for his wives seate	6	8
of Gyles Hassard for a seate for his wife	5	–
of William Winter for his seate	4	–
of Gedeon Hoare for a seate for his wife	8	–
of William Cornwall for a seate for himselfe and his wife	5	–

165

of Ralfe Terrett for a seate for himselfe	8	–
of Mr John Viceridge for a seate	10	–
of Anthony Webbe for a seate for himselfe and his wife	4	–
of Henery Steavens for a seate for himselfe	2	–
of Henry Porter for his wives seate	10	–
of Gyles Thomas for his wives seate	6	–
of William Watkins for a seate for himselfe and his wife	10	–
of Mr John Kinge for a seate for himselfe and his wife	26	8
of Gyles Parker for a seate for himselfe and his wife	30	–
of Mistress Ann Marrten for a seate	6	8
of Richard Goodman for a seate for himselfe	12	–
of Thomas Jeynes of Southwicke for his seate	13	4
of William Hatton for a seate for himselfe and his wife	16	–
of Heliodorus Peter for his wives seate	6	8
of Richard Goreles wife for her husbandes grave	6	8
of Mrs Baston for her husbandes grave	6	8
of Mrs Wood for her seate in the churche	30	–
of Mr Wilkes for thexchange of his seate	10	–
of Edward Bright for his seate	20	–
of Capteyne Tracie for his seate	40	–
of William Turbervile for a seate for himselfe and a seate for his wife	20	–
of John Wood for his seate	6	8
of Cristoher Canner for thexchange of his seate	9	–
of Steaven Tench for a seate for himselfe	10	–
of Thomas Leapper for a seate for himselfe	6	8
of Henry Hodges for a seate for himselfe and a seate for his wife	13	4
of John Greene for a seate for his wife		8
of Mrs Hiett for a seate for her daughter Margery	6	8
of Thomas Cole for a seate for himselfe	5	–
of Robert Jeynes for a seate for himselfe	4	–
of Edward Crondale for a seate for his wife	6	8
of Thomas Cowles for a seate for himselfe	3	–
of Gyles Maninge for a seate for his wife	3	–
of my partner Dixon for a seate for himselfe and a seate for his wife	16	–
166 of Richard Cotton for his seate	2	–
for a seate for my sonne Walter Hoare	4	–
for the halfe aker in Avon ham	12	–
for the churchyeard	20	–
for the rent of the house in the highe streate beinge for halfe a yeare	20	–
for the old bible	6	8
of the widow White for her husbandes grave	6	8
of William Allen for his rent beinge fower yeares	2	–
of Thomas Cole for his wife sete	10	–

Somm	62	11	5

Expenses layd out by us the sayd churchwardens which wee desire allowance for out of the sayd receiptes

	£	s	d
at the visitation 1611 for penticost mony and for the acquitance		3	10
for the book of articles			8
for a potle of wine to the archdeacon			20
for Mr Blackwell his dinner		2	–
for our dinners Mr Wardes and the sidemen		13	–
to the person for steyinge our presentmentes		2	–

at Gloucester for delivering in our presentmentes		20
for a new bell rope and for mendinge the ropes	8	10
Sanie Parret for makinge a new baldricke		4
for whitleather	3	–
to Thomas Hewes for chastinge 1 hundred & a halfe of lead	7	–
for 21 pounds of ⟨leade⟩ new leade	3	–
for seameinge 38 sheets at 8d the sheete	15	4
to Thomas Hewes for 69 pounds of solder and for workemanshipe	3	9
for coles	3	4
Robert Smith for washinge the surples and the churchclothes		18
the ropier four halliors & for 6° shutts	2	2
for 4 dayes worke and a halfe for 3 men abought mendinge the frames of the belles	13	–
to Parret for two baldrickes and for mendinge of one		9
Mr Powlton for bossinge the booke of Marters	5	–
for a deske for the sayd booke	10	–
to John Jenckes for helpinge to take up and braceinge the belles		18
for his diett		12
Robert Smith for a paper booke		2
to the ropier for a new rope and for shuttinge of ropes	8	2
to Henry Reeve for mending the clocke	2	2
to Layleland for a hide of whitleather	6	6
for a cussion for the pulpitt and for a cussion case	6	6
for the longe mattes for the chancesell	5	6
Parret for mendinge to baldwrickes		6
at the visitacion 1612 for a potle of wine to Docter Ridler		20
for Mr Losbie his dinner	2	–
and for our owne dinners and Mr Wardes	12	–
for penticost money and for delivering our bill and the booke of artickles	5	6
to James the clockmaker for his worke abought the clock and his man which was three weeks	41	6
for their diettes	26	8
to Sanders for his shopp and coles when James did worke there	10	–
for the windeing whele and tunbrell	5	–
and for other tymber abought the clocke and for a dayes worke for 3 men	3	6
for wyer for the clock	2	4
for iorne to mend the clocke	3	6
for ropes for the clock	9	6
to Richard Kinges and Henrie Reeve for theire worke abought the clocke	4	6
for iorne to mend the braces of the greate bell & for workemanshipp	3	6
for an old rope to make halliors	3	4
to Richard Kinges for stoppinge a great windowe hole over the porch		18
for two barreles of lyme	2	6
for two loodes of paveinge stone and for carringe of them	4	4
for a new whele for the greate bell	10	–
for mendinge the railes in the churchyeard		16
to Richard Kinges for a weekes worke for himselfe & a man abought poynting the tower	8	–
and for lyme	4	8
and for heere	2	4
more to him for five dayes worke for himselfe and a man abought poyntinge the tower and gutters	7	–
and for lyme & heere	6	–

167

for a new rope & for mendinge ropes		9	2
to John Paynter for 123 foote of new glase at 5d the foote		51	2
more for 29 foote of old glasse new ledded		6	9
for five hundred fiftie & seaven quarrels of glasse abought the windowes		40	–
for settinge in of old glasse in divers places		5	4
Thomas Hewes for castinge 1 hundred & a halfe of leade & sixe pounds		7	4
for him for seameinge 78 sheets of lead at 8d the sheete		52	–
Thomas Hewes for layeinge 138 pounds of solder with the workemanship	6	18	–
more of Thomas Hewes for 14 pound & a halfe of solder & for two dayes worke and for castinge of 3 quarteres of a hundred of lead		18	6
at Gloucester beinge cald in upon our presentmentes for our dinneres there		3	–
for horsmeate			4
for coles to solder withall		4	6
for washinge the churchclothes & surplusse			18
to the ropier for halliors and for shuttinge of ropes		3	2
Parrett for two baldrickes			8
Tucke for mendinge the third bell clapper		16	3
to John Paynter for glassinge the upper windowes one both the sides the churche	6	15	1
to his men for that they did take paynes extraordinary			12
to my Lord Bishoppes man when hee came to survey the church		2	6
for whitleather to John James		3	6
at the visitation 1613 for penticost money the booke of articles & delivering in of our presentments		5	6
for our dinners Mr Barrels & Mr Wardes		13	–
for worke don abought the churche at divers times by John Sanders		5	–
to a messinger that went for Farmer to Evesham abought the staple of the greate bell			12
to John Sanders for mendinge the staple of the great bell		10	–
to the ropier for a new rope and for mendinge the ropes		9	6
to Sani Parrett for paveinge in the church		4	6
for a gate post for the churchyeard and 3 rayles and for workemanshipp		6	–
for moveinge the pulpitt for tymber and for mendinge the seates		26	8
for two postes for the buttes and for the makeinge of them		4	–
for mendinge the rayles in the churchyeard		16	–
to Richard Kings for clensinge the gutters at divers times		2	–
for makeinge the new gallarie	5	–	–
to Robert Smith for wages due from the church for three yeares	4	–	–
for iorne worke abought the stockes at the churchygrate and for tymber and workemanshipp		7	6
for oyle at divers times for the clocke and belles		4	–
for makeinge a new deske		2	–
and for mendinge the deske whereon the bible & communion booke doth stand			12
for alteringe the seate under the pulpitt and Mrs Woodes seate		5	10
to Parrett for mendinge the flore at the tower end of the churche			12
for the church bible a communion booke and a booke of cannons	3	–	10
and for bringinge of them home			8
at the visitacion 1614 for a pottle of wine to the archdeacon			20
for penticost money the booke of articles and delivering in our presentments		5	6
for our dinners Mr Losbies with others		13	–

168 (margin note at "to a messinger that went for Farmer to Evesham abought the staple of the greate bell")

beinge cald in uppon our presentmentes at Gloucester for our dinners there	3	–
and for horsemeat		4
for a new rope for six halliors and for mendinge the ropes	10	10
for washinge the clothes at Cristmas		12
for mendinge two baldrickes		4
for liquor for the belles at sundrie times	2	6
for mendinge the vane of the clocke		6
for mendinge the clapper of the fore bell	4	–
the widdow Smith for this last yeres wages due from the churche	26	8
for makinge of all our presentmentes	5	–
for washing the churcheclothes against Easter		8

Somm	66	–	1
Soe there rest due unto us from the church the just somme of	3	8	8

⟨. . .⟩

[*Added*] to Page 165

[*unnumbered blank page*]

169   Mr Cookes gyfte. He died much about the yeare of our lord 1558 being the first yeare of Queene Elizabethe raigne

I give & bequeath unto John Butler my fellow bayelyfe of Tewkesbury & to my other trusty frends Thomas Wytherstone William Cole William Alie & Richard Carricke of Tewkesbury aforesaid all that my messauge or tenement with agardin thereto lieing with the apertinancis now in the occupation of on Richard Mathew at the yearely rent of £1 10s per annum sittuat lieing & being & knowen in the high street within the borrough of Tewkesbury to have and to hould the said messwage or tennement & gardyn with the apertenancis unto the said John Butler Thomas Wytherstone William Cole William Alie & Richard Carricke thair heires & assignes from & emediatly after my decease for evermore of the cheife lords of the fee thereof by the serveng therof due & accustomed. To the use & behofe of the reparations of the parrish church of Tewkesbury or to Gods devine service with in the same as Mr Baylifes of the said borrough for the time being with the more part of the discretest burgages of the said borrow shall devise & apoynt for the further & full establishment there of

[*ten blank pages foliated 170–174*]

175   Churchwardens   William Cowles
         ellected for this yeare 1609   Roberte Jenynges

The accomptes of William Cowles elected churchwarden with Roberte Jenynges the third of May 1609 and geven upp by him alone Robert Jenynges beinge deceassed before John Cooke and William Hitches beinge bailiffes taken the one and twentithe of Maie 1610 for one whole yeare then ended

	£	s	d
Receptes			
in stocke of the last churchwardenes	1	3	4

June 1609

of Michaell Millington for a seate for him and his wife beinge the			
8th seate & second rowe		2	6

of John Mann for his roome in the ⟨second⟩ first seate in the ⟨gallery⟩ 3 rowe		4	–
of Mr Henery Jefferies for a roome for himself in the second seate in the gallery		6	6
of Richard Pumfrey for roome for himself & his wif in the 10th seat & and second rowe		5	–
of Richard Phinch of Wallton for roome for him & his wif in the 13 seate & second rowe		5	–
of Mr Allye for the buriall of 2 of his chilldren in the church		6	8
of ourselves for the half acre in Avon Ham		12	–
of Thomas Harris for himself & his wief Henery Feildes wief Benjamin Bailies William Feild & of ould Grine for their places in the seate where the preacher goeth through		4	–
of Leonard Ellis for a rome for himself in 3 seat: and 2 rowe in the gallery		6	8
of John Tailers wif and Andrew Severnes wif for their roomes in the 20th seate in the 6 rowe		3	–
of William Woodward for half a yeares rente for his howse in the high streete	1	6	8
of Mr Ally for half a yeares rent for the churchyard		13	4
of Mr Thomas Ward for a roome for himself in the 8th seate & 3 rowe		5	–
Somm	6	3	8

176 October

of Richard Woodley for a rome for his wief in the 17th seate: & 5th row		5	–
of Richard Woodley for a rome for himself in the first seate & 3 rowe		4	–
of James Collet for the buriall of his wief in the churche		6	8
[Sum]		15	8

November

of Richard Terret for the buriall of his wif in the church and for the bells		8	–
of Thomas Freebanck for the buriall of his father in the church		6	8
[Sum]		14	8

January

of William Allen for the howse that he holdeth on the church yard sid beinge the church land			6
of James Weaver for a rome for himself in the 6 seate in the second rowe		3	–
of George Rogers for a roome for his wif in the 16th seate in the 5th rowe		4	6
[Sum]		8	–

March 1610

of Mr Allye for half a yeares rente in the churchyard nowe due		13	4
of Mrs Slaughter for the buriall of hir daughter in the churche & for the bells		8	8
of William Woodward of half a yeares rente nowe due		26	8
of Henery Shawe for the bells		2	–
[Sum]	2	10	8

Aprill

of Thomas White for a rome for his wief in the 14th seate & 3 rowe		5	–

of William Whitledge for a roome for his wief in the 10th seat & 3 rowe	5	–
of John Sisell for exchainge of his seate unto the 3 seate in the fowerth rowe	4	6
[Sum]	14	6

of Richard Weaver for a debt he owed to the church for the burial of
his wif   a flaggan pott

Maie

of George Crumpe for a roome for his wief in the 18th seate & fifte rowe	3	4
177 of David Floyd for a roome for him his wief in the 11th seate and 3 rowe	4	–
of George Inis for a rome for his wif in the 7th seate & 2 rowe	3	4
of Samuell Whitledge for a rome for his self in the 7th seat and the 3 rowe	5	–
of John Hale for a rome for him self in the 7th seate and 3 rowe	5	–
of John Saunders for a peece of ironn that I found in the vestre		18
of my self for a stone that was in the vestre	2	6
of Fraunces Clare for a peece of brasse that was in the vestre	6	–
[Sum]	33	–

Summ totall	12	17	10

Expenses

Laid out by theise churchwardens to bee allowed them uppon this accompte as followethe

	£	s	d
spente upon Mr Archdeacon at his visitacion in wine		3	–
for penticost monie		3	6
for fees of the visitacion		2	11
for a sermon booke			18
to Saunders for mendinge the ironn worke of the greate bell		2	6
to Persevall for bryeringe the trees in the churchyard		1	–
for oyle for oyle for the clock			1
for two barrells of lyme		2	4
to Bradbery and Parret for worke		3	–
Parret for a daies worke			12
to Mr Ward and spente at makinge of a presentmente		3	2
spente at Gloucester at the delivery of it in and for fees that was paid for havinge adaie over for amendinge it		3	5
Somm		27	4

June

to Bradbery for mending the chaunsell windowes	5	–
him for whitinge the portch	2	–
for paintinge the kinges armes	8	–
Richard Toms for mendinge the church wall	3	8
for a rope for the third bell wayinge 9 pounds	3	2
for the ministeres dinner & our wine at the visitacion	3	6
the same time for fees	3	–
[Sum]	28	–

178   July

for mendinge the grate bell irons	12	–

to Bradbery: for balwricks		16
to Parret for pavinge		3
for coales		3
for 10 pounds pewter to make souder	6	1
for liquor for the bells		2
to Bradbery: for souderinge and mendinge the leades on the backe iles		21
[Sum]	10	10

August

for fees at my Lord Archbushops visitacion	6	10
geven to the chauncellor a pottle of sacke and suger	2	–
for our dinners & the sidmen	6	4
for oyle for the bells & clock		4
Bradbery for tuckinge up three shetes over the chaunsell & for nailing some others	2	4
for nailes to Saunders		5
for a labourer to help up with the sheetes		4
for coales		6
to the ropier for one pound 1/2 of rope		6
[Sum]	19	7

September

to Bradbery for himself & his boy for 2 daies worke in plumming	2	8
for 2 sackes of coales	1	–
[Sum]	3	8

October

Bradbery for mendinge the windowes in the abbie syde		18
to him & his boie for one dais soalderinge		16
to him & Parret for half yeares wages	13	4
to Parret for a daies pavinge		9
for a rope for the quarter cloke		16
for 4½ pounds of rope for halliers		18
for spisinge of the ropes		2
for oyle for the bells		2
Parret for pavinge in the church	3	–
Bradbery for souderinge over the chaunsell		15
[Sum]	23	6

November

to a labourer for pinchinge up of stone		12
for half a thousand of sklatt	3	6
179 for one to serve the slatter		6
to Parret for labor		8
for oyle and liquor for the clock and the bells twise		8
for a peece of rope for the 3 bell	12	–
for 1 daies worke for the slatter	2	–
[Sum]	9	4

December

for stones for to wale the newe grate and to pave the church	30	–

to Edward Williames for the makinge the grate and the yate and			
findinge the tymber		30	–
for digginge of the grate			17
for wallinge the grate & for labourers to fetch them stone		5	–
to the pavier for pavinge at the church grate beinge 40ti yardes		5	–
for 3 daies worke for Fisher			10
John Hickes for slattinge over the pigion howse		7	–
for half a thousand of slate		3	6
for half a bushell of heare			3
for two thowsand of lath nailes		3	–
for 3 bundell of lath			18
for 8 gutter creastes			8
for five daies worke for Fisher			15
for a barrell of lyme & hawlinge			16
to Fisher for a daies worke to pick slate			3
for halliers for the bells			4
to Saunders for 34 pounds of iron for the newe gate at 3½d		9	11
[Sum]	5	1	1

January

for mendinge the vane of the clock		4
Parret for worke and pavinge		12

March

Bradbery for a ballwrick		4
for makinge another ballwrick and for whitleather		7
to him for layinge the plankes in the chauncell & for nailes		8
for one hinge and two staples for the back iles dore		4
for washinge the church clothes		12
Bradbery for mendinge the church windowes on the abbye syde		15
him & Parret for ½ yeares wages	13	4
[Sum]	18	11

180   Aprill

Bradbery for a ballwrick		4
him for plumminge on the upper iles on the abbie syde		19

Maie

for a newe rope for the quarter clock	2	4
for a boored in the quire		2
for a cheasell for takinge up the strapps of the bells		6
Saunders for the pinn to hold the gigg of the grate		5
to Parret for carringe of stone to the church and pavinge		20
Persevall for bryeringe the trees in the churchyard		12
Parret for layinge the stones at the porch doore	3	–
Bradbery for takinge up 16 sheetes of lead & layinge them againe on		
the lower iles on the churchyard syde	4	8
Saunders for 40ti nailes to naile the same leades		8
for the church doore and a plate of iron		8
for keepinge & writinge of the regester bookes and for writinge these		
accomptes to Mr Ward	4	6
Somm	21	6

Somm totall	13	1	3[1]
Memorandum that the receipte of this churchwarden is truly accompted to by just	12	17	2
His layinge out is	13	4	43
So that there resteth owinge unto him		7	1

[*two blank pages foliated 181*]

182   Anno domino 1615 1616 and 1617

William Whitledge   Churchwardens
Kenelme Mersonne

The accomptes of William Whitledge and Kenelme Mersonn churchwardens of the parishe church of the burrow of Tewkexburie within the dioces of Gloucester from the feaste of Easter 1615 untill the feaste of Easter 1616 & from thenne untill the feaste of Easter 1617 & soe remayned untill the feaste of Easter 1618 & soe gave up their accomptes before Mr Vicaridge and Mr Hill beinge baylieffes

	£	s	d
Receiptes			
of Umferye Russell for ringinge at the funeraull of his wife			12
of Robert Dower for a rome for him selfe		4	6
of Roberte Mince for a rome for him selfe		4	6
of John Kingsburye for astone for his child		2	6
of George Crumpe for arome for himselfe		5	4
of Thomas Junes for arome for himselfe & his wife		11	6
of George Shaw for afuneraull		3	4
of Edwarde Milicheape for arome for his wife		13	4
of John Turett for arome for his wife		6	–
of John Kingsburie for exchaunging arome for himself		9	–
of Mr Higgins for exchanginge arome for his wife		12	–
of Fraunces Smyth for arome for her self		4	6
of Fraunces Jefferis for arome for himselfe		3	8
183 of Mr John Geaste for his fathers funeraull		13	4
of Edward Bowland for a rome for his wife		5	–
for the funeraull grave and belles for John Haszard Mr Whittes man		8	8
of William Whitledge for the church halphe aker		12	–
of John Hignell for a rome for himselfe & his wife		5	6
of Thomas Hickes for the five rommes that are up at the roofe for himselfe & some others		16	–
of William Bartley for arome		9	10
of Richarde Pearce for arome		3	4
of Mr Hilliard		2	–
of John Hardinge the baker for the pavinge of his wives grave			18
Mr Baldwine for a rome		6	–
of Henry Turke for arome for himselfe		2	–
of Nicolas Mersonne for arome for himselfe		5	–
of Richard Turner for arome for himselfe & arome for his wife		17	7
of Thomas Clarke for arome for himselfe & arome for his wife		37	–
of Edward Hill for arome for himeselfe		10	–

[1]   Cash figures are in Arabic numerals henceforth.

	of John Sadler for arome for his wife	9	6
	of Mr Cowles for the exchaunge of arome for his wife		12
	of Mr William Hill for arome for his wife	10	–
	of Nicolas Nuttinge for arome for his wife	2	6
	of Thomas Hoare for halph ayeares rent for the churchard	10	–
	of the widowe Reeke for her husbandes funreaull in the church	6	8
	of William Allen for rent		6
184	of Thomas Layght for arome for himself & arome for his wife	5	–
	of Richard Mince for arome for himselfe	6	8
	of John James for arome for his wife	12	–
	of William Turbervile for his wives funeraull	12	4
	of Henry Edwardes for arome for himselfe	10	–
	of William Sheene for the funeraull of his sonne	6	–
	of William Toavye for arome for his wife	2	6
	of Mrs Cotterell for her husbandes funeraull	6	8
	of Mr Hille for astone for his childes grave		18
	⟨of Mr Baughan⟩ for a seate ⟨for the use⟩ of Gabriell Johnsons	12	–
	of Richard Crumpe for arome for his wife	4	–
	of John Davis for arome for himselfe	4	–
	of Mrs Barston for her husbandes funeraull & stone	13	3
	of Giles Brawforde for arome for himselfe	16	–
	of George Whitledge for the exchaunge of arome		20
	John Walles for arome for his wife	4	–
	of John Greene for arome for himselfe	13	4
	of Mrs Tomes for her husbandes funeraull	6	8
	of Richard Michell junior for arome for himselfe & arome for his wife	8	–
	of John Shurle for arome for himselfe & arome	⟨17	10⟩
	for his wife	19	10
185	for the funeraull of Mr Warde and his wife	10	–
	of John Whineat for arome for himselfe & arome for his wife		22
	of Mr Harth for aseate	3 10	–
	of Roberte Geines for arome for himselfe & arome for his wife	49	–
	of Thomas Hoare for rent for the churchyarde	15	–
	of Mathew Hawkinges ⟨in parte of paymente⟩ for arome for his wife	4	–
	of Alexander Parret for the rent of his garden		4
	⟨of Mr Wiett for Mr Millingtone towardes the glasinge of a windowe	10	–⟩
	of John Hale for arome for himselfe & arome for his wife	24	–
	of John Shawe for arome for himselfe	17	–
	of John Ockle for arome for himselfe	8	–
	of Andrew Baughan junior for arome for himselfe	5	–
	of Micaell Woode for arome for his wife	10	–
	of Gedeon Whoare for the funeraull of his child	3	4
	of Mr Morrisonne for arome for himselfe	4	–
	of William Winter for arome for himselfe & arome for his wife	18	–
	of Thomas Crumpe for arome for himselfe	17	6
	of Thomas Perkinges for arome for himselfe		[...]
	of Richard Hiet for arome for himselfe	4	[...]
	of Jone Garne for arome for her selfe	3	4
186	of Phillipe Harbage for arome for himselfe	8	6
	of Mr Henrye Tracye for aseate in the neweste gallerye as longe as the wainscoote backe goeth	8 –	–
	of Mr Alye in money foure poundes & more in two thousand of sclates	13	4
	of Thomas Allen for arome for his wife	4	–
	of Thomas Harris for arome for himselfe & his wife	10	–
	of Mr John Wiett for his rome	15	–
	of George Aulcycke for arome for his ⟨selfe⟩ wife	8	–

of Thomas Fisher senior for arome for himselfe	10	–
of Mrs Sellers for her husbandes funeraull	6	8
of the widowe Sclicer for her husbandes funeraull	14	8
of Andrewe Wullams for the funeraull of his sister	6	8
of Thomas Fisher aforesayd for his wives rome	11	–
of William Crafte junior for arome for himselfe	7	6
of Mr Tracye senior for arome for himselfe	20	–
of Mrs Decons for her husbandes funeraull	8	4
of Mr Hitchis for the rent of halph an aker	14	–
of Nycolas Smissens for arome for himselfe	25	–
of Charles Geines for arome for himselfe	8	4
of Mrs Thorne for arome for her selfe	10	–

187	of Mr Morrisonne for his daughters rome	2	–
	of John Franckcome for arome for himselfe	2	6
	of Arter Burte for the funeraull of his wife	7	8
	of the widowe Gilberte for her husbandes funeraull	8	8
	of Henrye Porter for the exchaunge for aroume for himselfe	3	–
	of Mr Vaughan for the funeraull of his childe	3	4
	of William Allin for arome for his wife	8	–
	of James Weaver for arome for himselfe and his wife in the new gallerie	33	–
	of Henrye Edwardes for arome for his wife in the ould gallerye	10	–
	of Water Williams for a rome for him selfe in the new seate one the abye side	2	6
	of Roberte Lytle of Walton for arome for his wife	7	–
	of Mrs Windsmore for a rome for hir selfe under the pulpitte	16	–
	of Fraunces Jefferis for a rome for his wife	8	–
	of Carolus Geines for a rome for his wife	8	–
	of Thomas Barthe for the use of the belles	2	–
	of William Dixon for rent and for rubbell stone	23	8
	of John Powlton for a rome for his wife	17	–
	of the widowe Kinges for the use of the belles for the funeraull of her brother William Bundye	2	–
	of Mr Hytchis for rent for the halfe aker that doeth belonge unto the church	14	–

	of Mr Pauncefootte for his seate in the church	4	–	–

188	of John Lyes for a rome for his wife	3	–
	of James Weaver for the funeraull of Mrs Deakines	8	8
	of William Dixon for halfe yeres rent for the house which doeth belonge unto the churche	20	–
	of Thomas Carte for a rome for his wife	7	–
	of George Shaull for the funeraull of his childe	3	4
	of Roberte Lytle of Walton for a rome for himselfe	10	–
	of Thomas Smissens the sonne of Jone Smissens for a rome for himselfe	10	–
	of Giles Hermer for the exchaunge for a rome for him selfe and for the funeraull of his wife	19	9
	of Thomas Tayler for a rome for his wife		12
	of Thomas Jeninges for a rome for himselfe	10	–
	of Thomas Hale for the exchaunge of a rome for himselfe	11	–
	of John Fisher junior for a rome for himselfe	5	6
	of Thomas Whoare for ayeres rent for the churchyarde	18	–
	of Thomas Whoare for the funeraull of William Turbervile	8	8
	of Andrewe Wallames for the exchaunge of a rome for himselfe	18	–
	of John Ockle for a rome for his wife	8	–
	⟨of James Bubb for a rome for himselfe	6	–⟩

of Thomas Fisher for a rome for himselfe	6	10
of Fraunces Jefferis for the exchaunge of a rome	3	–
of Richard Windowes for arome	2	8
of Mr Dowdeswell for the funeraull of his child in the churche	3	4
189 of Richarde Salker for a rome for his wife	5	8
of Henrye Edwardes for the funeraull of his father	6	8
of Mr Packer for a rome for his sonne Nathaniell	10	–
of James Woraull and Thomas Welles for eyther of them a rome in the newe seate twardes the abye	4	–
of Mrs Johnsons for the funeraull of her husband	6	6
of Gedeon Hoare for a rome for himselfe	6	–
of John Wood for a rome for himselfe	4	4
of Mr Hille for astone for his childes grave	2	4
of Cristopher Charnocke for aseate for himselfe and his wife in the new gallerie	12	–
of Thomas Hilliard for aseate for himselfe & his wife in the same gallerie	8	–
of Thomas Haines for the use of the belles at the funeraull of his mother	2	–
of Thomas Jeines for mucke in the churchyarde againste the barne dore	2	–
of Kenellme Merssone for the exchaunge of his rome in the churche	4	–
of Roger Plevie for aroume in the churche for him selfe	12	–
of Micaell Millingtone for the exchaunge of arowme for his wife	9	–
of Mr Price for a roume for him selfe	7	–
of Mr Henrye Tracye for mucke that was in the churchyarde over againste the barne dore	2	6
190 of Mr Dowedswell for the funeraull of his childe in the churche	3	4
of Thomas Haynes for a roume for himselfe and his weife	6	–
of Mr Millingtone for the glasinge of awindowe	20	–
of Mr Clarke of Twininge for the rent of the church house for halfe ayeares rent	20	–
of Mr Henrye Tracye for the funeraull of his child in the churche	3	4
of Mr Bradforde for the funeraull of his father inlawe Watter Portman	6	8
of Alice Mince for aroume for her selfe	5	–
of John Fisher junior for a rome for his wife	10	–
of Gabriell Johnsonns for a rome for his ⟨. . .⟩ sister Margerie Johnsons	10	–
of William Bauldwine for the funeraull of his wife	7	5
of Mr Whitt for a rome for his daughter Martha	11	–
of Niicolas Allin for a roume for himselfe	3	4
of Richard Hanleye for a roume for his wife	2	9
of Mr Baylye Hill in parte of payment of Mr Parkers funeraull	8	–
more of Mr Hill for the full satisfaction of Mr Parkers funeraull	18	8

The summe totall receaved by Mr Whitledge & Kenelme Mersonne churchwardens is foure score & eleven poundes nine shillinges & two pence

[*blank unnumbered page*]

191 ⟨Expenses⟩   Paymentes

Layd out by the aforsayd churchwardens William Whitledge & Kellume Mersone to be allowed them uppon this accoumpte as followethe

	£	s	d
to John Hickes and his sonne Thomas Hickes for sclattinge		27	–
for six crestes			12

	for seaven bundels of lathe	1	27
	for nayles	3	4
	for foure barrelles of lyme	4	8
	to Alexander Parrett for helpinge the sclatters	2	6
	to Thomas Davis for plumminge	6	3
	to Alexander Parrett for helpinge the plummer	5	–
	to John Parrette his sonne for helpinge the plummer	2	–
	to Alexander Parrett for whashinge the communion clothes		6
	to Roberte Barker for the mendinge of seates		10
	to Thomas Davis for sowder and worcke	11	–
	to Alexander Parrett for helpinge the plummer	2	–
	to Alexander Parrett for pavinge in the churche	3	3
	at the visitation	7	2
	for apottle of wine that was bestowed uppon the archdeacon	2	–
	for Mr Looesbye his dynner	4	–
	for apecke of sclate pinnes to John Hickes		12
192	to Thomas Geines for worke in the firste gallerye	13	4
	for our dinners & the sydmen with others	15	6
	for apottelle of wine that was bestowed uppon Mr John Reade for eight		
	loades of planckinge stone	2	2
	for nayles	1	4
	for mendinge of the floure behinde the church	1	6
	of John Parrett for helpinge the sclatters	2	–
	to Roberte Barker for mendinge the seates in the chauncell and		
	lyminge of rafters over the bodye of the churche	2	8
	to Roberte Charnocke for hawllinge of lyme & sclate	1	6
	for haire		1
	to Alexander Parrett for pavinge in the church and emtyinge of the		
	grate		20
	for bere for the worckemen		12
	for leavellinge of the floure behinde the churche	2	6
	for foure shides to line the rafters		7
	for nayles for the mendinge of the chauncell seates	1	6
	for bere for the woorcke men at sundrye tymes		14
	to Alexander Parrett for pavinge in the church	2	6
	to Roberte Barker for the mendinge of adoore		4
	for bere for the men that brought stone from the whooe hill		6
	Roberte Barker for the makinge of adoore		6
	to Thomas Godfree for hinges & hoockes & for the churcharde gate		
	& mendinge the barres of the grate		15
193	for the carriage of seaven loades of stone from the whooe hill	7	1
	to John Tycie for the loadinge of stone		8
	to John Bradforde for the carriage of two loade of stone		16
	to John Bradfordes man for the carriage of stone		3
	to Alexander Parrett for pavinge the waye in the churcharde	58	2
	to Roberte Barkers sonne for the carriage of stone		3
	at the Bull when the archdeacon did visite for aquarte of wine & sugar		12
	for beere for the worckmen at sundrye tymes	3	–
	to Alexander Parrett for his quartrige	6	8
	to Alexander Parrett for pavinge & whashinge the churche lynnen	4	–
	to Alexander Parrettes sonne for worcke		16
	to Henrye Turke for mendinge the clapper of the firste bell	2	6
	to John Barneslye for two barrelles of lyme	2	4
	to Thomas Mayde for three trees bought from Waltons woode	16	–
	to William Thornburye for the faullinge of the same trees		18
	to Alexander Parrett for pavinge in the lower end of the church	3	–

for three peckes of heaire		6
at Antonye Webes for beer for the worckmen		18
for five yeu trees		10
194 for ayounge elme tre & settinge it in the churchyarde		6
for two bushelles of heere		16
to Alexander Parrett for pavinge in the church	6	10
to John Barneslye for two barrelles of lyme	2	4
to William Winter for sclate		15
to John Woode the smithe for mendinge the keye of the churche dore		3
to Thomas Greenowe for sclate & carriage from his house to the church	2	6
for the carriage of foure barrelles of lyme		8
to John Parrett for foure dayes worke		16
to Roberte Barker for the mendinge of the bayeliefes seate		4
to Thomas Hickes for sclattinge uppon the iles of the churche	9	8
to Alexander Parrett for his quarters wages	6	8
for sclate		20
to Richard Kinge for worke	7	–
for certaine yew trees		16
to Alexander Parrett for two balriges		8
to Alexander Parrett for pavinge		6
for abushell of heaire		3
for timber twardes the gallerie	4	3
to Richard Kinge for worke	6	8
for the sawinge of certaine timber	4	2
for haire		11
to William Moppe for worcke	2	6
to Alexander Parrett for worcke	2	4
195 to Richard Kinges for worcke	3	–
to William Cornewall for hawllinge of tymber		12
to the sawyeres for the sawinge of timber	4	2
to Richard Kinges for worcke	3	–
to John Parrett for worcke		12
more to the sawyeres for the sawinge of tymber	2	6
for the carriage of lyme	2	4
to Henrye Turcke for the mendinge of the firste bell clapper		12
for two bushelles of haire		6
to Richarde Kinges for worcke	10	–
to Alexander Parrett for worcke		16
to John Parrett for worcke	2	–
to Gilberde Tundye for roopes	7	–
to John Barneslye for two barrelles of lyme	2	4
to John Parrett for worcke	2	1
to Giles Parker for the yealdinge up of his rome in the churche	10	–
to Richard Kinges for worcke	8	–
to Alexander Parrett for worcke		12
to Giles Millerde for turninge of pillers for the gallerye		12
to William Griffine for worcke		16
to a tincker for two poundes of sowder		16
to John Parrett for worcke		20
to Giles Robertes for the hawlinge of lyme		4
to Giles Robertes for the hawllinge of timber from Waltons wood to the churche	6	3
for beere for the worckmen		16
for the carriage of bordes		2
for three bushelles of haire	2	–

	to Thomas Geines senior for worcke	20	–
196	to Richard Kinges for worcke	5	–
	to Thomas Hickes for worcke	5	–
	to John Parrett for worcke		20
	to Giles Myllerde for worcke	4	–
	to John Barneslye for lyme	14	8
	to Thomas Geines senior for worke	40	–
	for two bushelles of haire		16
	to Giles Myllerde for worcke	2	6
	to Alexander Parrett for quartrige	6	8
	to Thomas Geines senior for worcke	14	–
	to Richarde Kinges for worcke	7	–
	for two bushelles of haire		16
	to Alexander Parrett for the whashinge of the churche lynnen & for worcke	2	6
	to Thomas Hickes for worcke		18
	to Richarde Windowes for two whoopes that were set uppon the roodlafte		6
	for beere for worckmen		12
	to William Dixon for worck	3	8	–
	to Henrye Reeve for worck	3	17	–
	to Richard Kinges for worck	5	9
	to John Hickes for worcke	5	–
	to Henrye Reeve for worcke	10	8
	to William Griffine for the carriage of stone		12
	to Richard Kinges for worcke	4	–
	to Roberte Barker for worcke		16
	to Henrye Turke for iron worcke		14
	to Richard Kinges for worcke	6	–
	to Thomas Hickes for worcke	6	–
	to Richard Kinges for worcke	6	–
	to Roberte Barker for worcke		8
	to Thomas Hickes for worcke	4	–
	to Thomas Godfreye for iron worcke	19	8
	to Ricard Kinges for worcke	4	–
197	to Henrye Turcke for iron worcke	8	6
	to Richard Kinges for worcke	5	–
	to Robert Barker for worcke		12
	to Richard Kinges for worcke	5	6
	to Richard Hiet for lathe	4	–
	to Richard Kinges for worcke	13	–
	to John Parrett for worcke		8
	to Thomas Hickes for worcke	12	–
	to Richard Kinges for worcke	2	–
	for the puttinge in of our presentment	3	–
	for penticoste monye	3	10
	to John Barneslye for lyme	4	6
	to Alexander Parrett for the washinge of the churche lynnen		6
	to Thomas Hickes and Richard Kinges for worcke	9	–
	to Giles Myllerd for worcke	2	2
	to John Parrett for worcke		20
	at the Bull for beere for the worckmen		8
	to Thomas Hickes Richarde Kinges & Alexander Parrette for worcke	11	8
	at severall tymes for bere for the worckmen		21
	to Thomas Geines and his sonne for worcke aboute the gallerie	14	–
	to Thomas Godfreye for iron worcke aboute the great bell	3	6

		£	s	d
	to Richard Kinges for worcke		6	–
	to John Parrett for worcke		2	–
	to Thomas Geines senior for worcke		13	–
	to John Hickes & his sonne for foure dayes worcke		6	5
	for lathe		3	6
	to Henrye Turcke for iron worcke		2	4
	to Gyles Robertes for the haulinge of lyme			6
	to Richard Mason for worcke			3
	to William Dixon for worcke			6
198	to Thomas Hickes & Richarde Kinges for whitlyminge the chancell	3	7	–
	to John Barneslye for acable roope & for lyme		20	–
	to Henrye Reeve for worcke abought the new gallerie		20	–
	to Gilberte Tandye for the mendinge of one of the bell roopes			12
	for beere at severaull tymes for worckmen			12
	to Henrye Reeve for worcke		10	–
	for Mr Loosebees dinner at the visitation		3	–
	to Patricke Porter for the hawlinge of lyme			6
	to Henrye Reeve for worcke		15	–
	to John Paynter for the glacesinge of awindowe for master Millingtone		20	–
	to Alexander Parrett for his quarters wages		6	3
	to Wager the glasier for worcke		3	–
	to Richarde Kinges for worcke		3	–
	to John Parrett for worcke			12
	to Alexander Parrett for worcke		7	2
	to Gilberte Tandye for abell roope		10	–
	to Edwarde Braune for beer for worckemen			8
	to Richard Kinges for worcke		3	–
	to John Parrett for worcke			12
	to John Hale for aboorde			12
	to Alexander Parrett for worck		4	–
	for the hawlinge of lyme			6
	for abushell of haire			8
	for mendinge the key of the churche dore			4
	to Alexander Parret for worcke			34
	to Richard Kinges for worcke		8	–
	to Alexander Parret for his quartrige		6	8
	to Richarde Kinges for worcke		7	–
	more to Richard Kinges			6
199	to Richarde Kinges for worke		6	8
	to John Parret for worcke			3
	to Alexander Parret for worcke			12
	to Gilberde Tandye for roopes			22
	to John Arpine for nayles			20
	to William Allin for bere for the worckmen at sundrye tymes		3	6
	for coles			8
	to John Ockle for whitt leather to macke balriges		3	2
	to Richard Kinges for worcke		5	2
	to Turcke for mendinge the great bell clapper			16
	to Alexander Parrett for worcke		5	–
	to Richard Kinges for worcke and sowder		13	10
	to John Paynter for glasinge		22	–
	to Patricke Porter for haulinge foure barrelles of lyme & apeece of tymber			14
	to Richard Kinges for worcke		7	–
	to William Bartlett for the surrendringe of his wives rome		5	–
	for oyle and caullours for the kinges armes uppon the new gallarye		6	2

for two bucket payles			7
to Alexander Parrett for pavinge in the church		3	–
to Richard Kinges for worcke		2	–
to Thomas Hilliard for the drawinge of trees from the wood to the churche		4	–
to John Paynter for glasinge		14	–
to Gyles Robertes for the haullinge of lyme			12
to Alexander Parrett for his quartrige		6	8
to Henrye Porter for hoockes and hinges for the chauncell dore		2	–
to John Barnesleye for sixteene barrelles of lyme		16	–
⟨to Mr Loosebee in money that was borrowed of him for to paye worckmen⟩	3	–	–

200

to Gilberde Tandye for mendinge the bell roopes & for halliers		11	10
to Thomas Godfree for iron worke aboute the belles		3	2
to Thomas Dixon for two dayes worke aboute the belles		2	–
to Alexander Parrett for his quartrige		6	8
to John Parrett for foure dayes worke			16
to John Paynter for glasinge	2	10	–
to Alexander Parrett for worke		5	8
to Cristofer Charnocke for the haullinge of eighte barrelles of lyme			12
to the surveior of the churche		2	11
to Alexander Parrett and Richarde Kinges for worke		20	8
to Thomas Godfree for iron worke		4	7
for abuckett payle			4
to Alexander Parrett for his quartrige		6	8
unto Alexander Parrett for worke and for washinge the churche lynnen		4	8
to Henrye Reeve for makinge the wainscote in the chauncell	10	–	–
to the archdeacon at the visitation for dues belonginge to him and his officers		6	–
to Henrye Reeve for worke		26	7
to Henrye Reeve for worke		30	–
for achaine for the boocke of martyris			4
for nayles at our fayre for the scollers gallerie			16
to Alexander Parrett for the makinge of two balriges			12
to John Barnesleye for three barrelles of lyme		3	–
to Alexander Parrett for mendinge the leades and for mendinge some seates that were amise		6	–
to Micaell Millingtone for nayles & hoockes and hinges about the chauncell & gallaries		10	5
to Alexander Parrett for his quarters wages		6	8

201

Alexander Parrette for adayes worke			12
to William Dixon for the gates as you goe in to goe behind the church		40	–
to Alexander Parrett for pavinge in the churche		33	4
to Richard Kinges for sowder		7	10
to Nicolas Phelpes for the yealdinge up of his romme & his wifes		6	8
to Devoraxe Goodwine for mendinge the great bell clapper		10	–
for haire for the scollers gallarie		2	9
to John Barneslye for onne barrell of lyme			12
to Thomas Dixon for anew wheele for the great bell		22	–
to Henrye Reeve for the scollers gallarye		40	–
to Henrye Reeve for the new seates of wainscotte in the chauncell & for iron worke belonginge to the same		16	4
to Mr Loosbee for his dinner at the visitation		3	8

The summe totall payd by Mr Whitledge & Kenelme Mersonne churchwardens is foure score & twelve poundes seaven shillinges & apennye

Richard Pearse doeth remayne indebted unto the church for his
    childrens sittinge in the scollers gallarie   8   –

Thomas Dixon doeth remayne indebted unto the churche for his
    ⟨wives⟩ daughters grave in the church & for the belles   7   8

202   13th of November 1618
Anno Jacobi Regis 16

Md This day Mr Edward Alye aged 63 yeeres one of the principall burgeses, and a
justice of the peace within this borough did freely give to the church, a fayre silver cup
for the communion table waying twentye ounces a halfe and 2 quarter & cost 5s 7d the
ounce, which came to £5 12s 4d & withall hee gave a leather case for the said cup
which cost 2s 6d in toto £5 14s 10d

Also there is now remaynig in the church, one other communion cup of silver gilded
with a cover to him which wayeth 18 ounces

John Cooke   Baylifes
Thomas Vaughan

Edward Milichep   Churchwardens
Thomas Hale

20th March 1619

Md This present day I have seene the licence graunted by Mr Loosebye the minister of
this parishe unto Elisabeth the wife of Edward Wakeman gent. for her eating of flesh,
by reason of her weake estate of body, dated the 13th day of this instant month & doe
heere recorde the same according to the statute in that case provided witnes my hande
subscribed the month & yeere above written

Edward Millichep

The like licence graunted to Edward Alye of Tewxbury esquire

Edward Millichep

The like to Anne Slaughter of Tewxbury widow both in respect of her age & other
    infirmites

Edward Millichep

The like to Anne Cooke of Tewxbury widow

Edward Millichep

The like to Usly Wiat widdowe for the like infirmity

Edward Millichep
Thomas Halle   Churchwardens

The like for Edward Aly esquire for the weaknes of his body

Edward Millichep
Thomas Halle

The like for Mr Richard Whillar balife for the like infirmity

Edward Millichep

203   1622

All somes graunted

The accountes of Edward Millicheape and Thomas Hale churchwardens the 7th day of Aprill Anno domino 1618

	£	s	d
they acknowledge not any monie receaved in stocke		[	]
of Mr Kennet of Stoke Orcherd for his sonne in lawes funerall		13	–
of Mr William Witledge for the halfe acre 1618		14	–
for ringinge the bells at sundry times		7	–
for the scollers gallerye		2	–
of Anne Walker quartridge for Mr Meeresonns wives rome			4
of George Shaw Mr Nansan widow Beale Roger Wiett for there			
4 sonnes in the scollers gallery		4	–
of Anne Walker quartridge			4
of Mr Robert Turner for his childes funerall		3	4
of Mr Andrew Baughan for his childes funerall		3	4
Michelmas rent of the widow Kinges for the churchyeard 1618		9	–
Michelmas rent for the house 1618	1	–	–
of Kellan Meersone for Dukes sonne of William Gilbert for Josepth			
Slicer of Henry Shaw for his sonne of William Cartwright for his			
sonne of Mr Barnefield for his sonne in the schollers gallary		4	–
for the iron barres of the churchgrate		13	5
for the ould clapper of the great bell		11	6
St Mary rent for the churchyeard 1619		9	–
St Mary rent for the house 1619	1	–	–
of Mr Bradford for Mrs Butlers funerall and stone		10	–
of Mr William Whitledge for his wives funerall and tombestone		13	4
rent for the gardens in the church yeard			10
more for Mr Barnefeildes sonne in the schollers gallery		1	–
for the halfe acre at midsummer 1619		14	–
of Henry Porter for his fathers funerall		6	8
of Mr John Wiatt for his mothers grave and belles		8	8
of Mrs Geast for her Husbandes funerall and stone and ringinge	1	–	–
of Mrs Morry for Gyles Brafords funerall and stone		11	–
of William Jennynges for his sonnes funerall		1	–
The some is	11	4	5

204   Receipts   1619

	£	s	d
Michelmas rent for the church yeard		9	–
of Richard Wattes for his sonne in the schollers gallary		2	–
of Mr Andrew Baughan for his sonne Richardes funerall and belles		8	–
of Robert Sprat and Thomas Lewes for theire sonnes in the schollers gallary		2	–
Michelmas rent for the house 1619	1	–	–
of Mrs Morry thyonger for her husbandes grave and belles		8	8
of Mrs Winsmore for her cheildes grave and stone		6	8
of the widow Bradfford for her ⟨son⟩ husbandes grave stone and belles	1	2	–
of John Sicell for a country boy in the schollers gallary		2	–

of Mr Pledwelles sonne for the schollers gallary		2	–
St Mary rent for the house to domino 1620	1	–	–
St Mary rent for the churchyeard 1620		10	–
for ringing of the belles halfe aday		1	–
of Mrs Hilly for her husbandes grave tombestone & belles	1	–	–
of Thomas Smysines for his mothers grave		6	8
of Mr Slaughter for the halfe acre 1620		14	–
for the ould butterlead out of the south ile 10s 2d per hundred	4	6	3
Michelmas rent for the house 1620	1	–	–
Michelmas rent for the charchyeard		9	–
of George Alcocke for his wives grave & stone	1	6	–
for Humphrie Higgins grave		6	8
of Conway Whithorne for his childes grave		3	4
of Mrs Hilly for her childes grave		3	4
of Joyes Allen rent for her house ayeare 1620			6
of Mr Meeresonne for his daughteres grave		6	8
of Mr Edward Wakeman for his childes grave & stone		6	–
of Mr Richardsonne for his wives grave		6	6
of Edward Phelpes for his childes grave		3	4
of widow Chapman for her husbandes grave		6	8
of John Sicell for his wives grave & belles		8	8
of John Saule for his wives grave		6	8
of William Wilsonne for his 2 sonnes in the schollers gallary		2	–
of Robert Charnocke for his sonne in the schollers gallary		1	–
St Mary rent for the house to domino 1621	1	–	–
of Henry Reeve for his brothers grave		6	8
St Mary rent for the charchyeard 1621		9	–
of Thomas Smisines for his childes grave		3	4
for Phillip Hodgeses grave		6	8
of Thomas Dicsonn for his wives grave		6	8
of Henry Tracy for his wives grave		8	8
The some is	19	19	17

205   Receiptes

for Elner Frebankes grave in the church		6	–
of Jakob ⟨Garnett⟩ Poulton for his childes grave & belles		4	2
of Robert Charnocke for the halfe acre 1621		16	–
of William Jenninges for Michelmas rent for the house	1	–	–
of William Driver for the rent of the church yeard 1621		9	–
of Mrs Anne Cooke for her husband & her two sonnes graves in the church the belles & two stones	2	10	–
of Mrs Turbervile for her husbandes gift to the church	2	–	–
of Thomas Clarke for his wives grave & stone & for his childes grave & the belles		19	–
of William Jenninges for St Mary rent for the house 1622	1	–	–
of William Driver for St Mary rent for the church yeard 1622		9	–
of Mr Edward Wakeman for his mothers grave in the church		6	–
of John Hardinge for his wives grave		6	–
for rubble stone		1	–
of Thomas Turbervile for a grave & stone	1	–	–
of Edward Millichep for 2 tombstons	1	10	–
of the church land £2 per annum for 5 yeare	10	–	–
The some is	22	16	–

Anno domino 1618

Edward Millichep and Thomas Hale beinge churchwardens foure yeares have layde out upon the church £116 11s 06d of which they have receaved but £95 3d for they given to the church £21 11s 3d

Anno domino 1622

		£	s	d
206	The accountes of receipts for the seates			
	of John Arpine for his wives rome		7	–
	of John Davis for his wives rome		7	–
	of Robert River for his rome & his wives		3	10
	of Richard Hale for his roome		4	6
	of John Butler for his wives roome		3	–
	of William Baldwine for his wives roome		5	–
	of Richard Hale for his wives roome		4	–
	of Henry Williames for his roome		1	8
	of John Fisher senior for his wives roome		4	–
	of Robert Charnocke junior for his wives roome		4	–
	of Laurance Kinges for his wives roome		4	6
	of Margrett Laight junior for her roome		12	–
	of John Wattes for his wives roome		4	–
	of Frances Rickardes for his roome		4	–
	of William Baldwine for his roome		6	–
	of William Land for his roome		4	–
	of John Hale for exchanging his roome		2	3
	of Thomas Hale for exchanging his wives room		1	6
	of Conway Whithorne for his wives roome		11	–
	of Thomas Bartlemew for his roome		7	–
	of John Slicer for his roome		7	–
	of Richard Underhill for his roome		5	–
	of Thomas Beavans for his wives roome		2	–
	of John Poulton for his roome	1	–	–
	of William Wilsonne for exchanginge his room		18	–
	of John Stile for his roome		5	–
	of Thomas Coole for his wives roome		10	–
	of William Gilbert junior for his roome		8	–
	of Thomas Whitledge for his roome		5	–
	of Jacob Garrett for his roome		5	–
	of Alles Pitt for her roome		10	–
	of Roger Wiatt for his roome		3	–
	of Hughe Notte for his wives roome		14	–
	of Thomas Allen for his wives roome		1	6
	of Thomas Huson for his wives roome		1	6
	of Mr William Cowles for his mothers roome		10	–
	of Richard Mannynge for his wives roome		6	–
	of Conway Whithorne for his roome		15	–
	of William Showell for his roome		5	–
	of John Sicell thyonger for his roome		6	8
	of Frances Stokes for his roome		6	8
	of Bartilmew Smith for his wives roome	1	–	–
	of Thomas Welles for his wives roome		8	–
	of Michell Millington exchangde for his roome		11	–
	of Humpry Mosse for his roome		13	4
	of William Sheene for his roome		12	–
	of William Mince for his wives roome		6	–
	⟨of Richard Fare for his rome⟩		⟨6	8⟩
	of one Rowland Coole for his wives roome	1	–	–

of Thomas Higgins for his roome	1	–	–
of Richard Baylis for his roome		10	–
of John Downebell for his roome		6	–
of Thomas Hale junior for his roome	1	–	–
of Thomas Sklicer for his roome exchanged			6
of Mr Richard Dowdswell for his roome	1	4	–
of Frances Godwine for his roome		5	–
of Richard Viner for his roome		2	–
of John Jenckes for the whole seate		4	–
of Anne Porter widow for her roome		3	–
The some is	22	16	1

207   Receiptes for seates

of Richard Underhill for his wives roome		5	–
of Richard Slycer for his wives roome		4	–
of Thomas Smisins for his wives roome		15	–
of William Turbervile for his roome	1	–	–
of Christopher Canner for his wives roome exchanged		10	–
of Richard Baylis for his wives roome	1	–	–
of Richard Yerrow for his roome		12	–
of Mr George Shaw for his wives roome exchanged		10	–
of the widow Anne Beale for her roome		10	–
of Thomas Greene of Walton for his rome		5	–
of Thomas Greene for his roome		13	–
of Gyles Harmer for his wives roome		14	–
of Edward Arndell for his sonne in the schollers gallary		1	–
of George Underhill for his wives roome		5	–
of Floris Cooper for his wives roome		2	–
of Edward Jones for his sonne in the schollers gallary		1	–
of Henry Stevens for his sonne in the schollers gallary		1	–
of Henry Vicarage for his sonne in the schollers gallary		2	–
of Thomas Turbervile for his roome		9	–
of William Wilsonne for his roome exchanged		2	–
of John Downbill for his wives roome		5	–
of Thomas Chester for his wives rome		5	–
of Elizabeth Weaver widow for her rome		12	–
of Ralfe Bartilemew for his wives roome exchanged		1	–
of Mary Bartilmew for her roome		1	–
of Margery Kinges widow for her roome exchanged		6	8
of Thomas Wardes wife for her roome	1	2	–
of Jeffry Bradford for his roome		5	–
of George Smith for his roome		5	–
of John Jordaine for his roome exchanged		2	–
of James Braford for his roome & to serrender it up to Mr Parry when			
he comes to church		10	–
of Mr Roger Dowdswells wife & Mrs Elizabeth Geast thyonger			
widow for one rome ⟨. . .⟩		12	–
of Thomas Bartilmew for his wives rome		12	–
of Anne Mathews for her rome exchanged		5	–
of Edward Mellichep junior for his roome		12	–
of William Craft for his wives roome		13	–
⟨of William Cooke for his roome⟩		⟨10	–⟩

[*Marginal note*]
William Couels seat [...] & Edward Hilly

of Robert Jenninges for his roome	2	–
of Edward Jennyngs for his roome	2	–
of Robert Charnocke for his roome	2	–
of Knelme Chanber junior for his roome	2	–
of Thomas Higinge for his wiffes rome exchanged	2	6
Some is	15 17	2

208   Receiptes for seates

of Henry Stevens for his roome	2	–
of Thomas Bache for his rome & his wives	3	–
of Hughe Sanders for his wives rome	2	–
of John Sumner for his roome	5	–
of Humphry Mosse for his wyffes roome untell George Alcotes wife comes	2	–
of Thomas Greene for his wives roome	7	–
of Edward Baylis for his roome	6	8
of William Alline for his roome	3	–
of William Driver for his roome	3	–
of Thomas Bache for his roome	5	–
of John Wattes fore his rome	2	–
of William Fillde fore him & his wife	2	–
of John Teyler fore his rome	3	–
The some is	2 9	2

Laide out by these church wardens duringe their yeares of office unto the day of theire accountes beeinge the 7th day of Aprill Anno domino 1618

Charges	£	s	d
for paveinge at the chirch grate & there aboutes		4	10
for mendinge the paul & for cloth for him		17	9
for the great bel rope & mendinge ropes		12	6
for 18 barrells of lime & hallinge him at 1s per barrell		18	9
for makeinge the house at the church grate	4	16	2
for castinge lead, charcole & sowdring the lead over the chancell & rafters for the ruffe & walpletts for the ruffe & for the carpenters workemanshipe	3	13	9
for abarr for the chansell dore & for nayles for the leads & for keyes for locks		8	8
for slattinge over the porch & backe iles	1	6	7
for mendinge the clock & stayers		9	9
for mendinge the seates in the chancell		4	–
for mattes for the chancell		4	–
for the communion table clothes	1	2	3
for postes & rayles about the churchyard		4	–
for the visitation dinner pentecost booke of articles & our othes 1618	1	5	10
for heare		3	4
the sextons midsommer wages 1618		6	8
for 8 dayes worke to Richard Hanbidg		8	–
Henry Reeve for wainscott in the chancell		3	4
for hinges lockes & nayles		5	4
for broomes & oyle			6
The some is	12	16	–

209   Charges laide out

more for a locke	1 [...]

for 6 trisells for the cradle		1	[...]
for 18 barrels of lime & hallinge them		19	[...]
for the cooberinge the churchgrat house		3	[...]
for 3 lade payles & the seate booke		1	[...]
for our dinners in the archdeacons court in August 1618		8	[...]
for ropes to make atacle for the cradle and other ropes	1	–	[...]
Thomas Hickes & Richard Kinges towardes whitinge the church August 5	7	2	[...]
for diaper to make communion table cloths		13	[...]
for 2 napkins for the communion bread		1	[...]
for 1 barrell of lime & hallinge it		1	[...]
for the mendinge of 3 bell ropes & halfe a hide of whitleather		3	[...]
for makeinge covenantes & bandes for Hickes & Kinges		1	[...]
for 2 horslode of cole to soulder		3	[...]
for 18 pounds & ½ of soulder at 9s per pound		14	[...]
for souldringe the tylles	1	–	[...]
for 10 barrells of lime and halling		10	[...]
for 2 longe ladders		11	–
for abarrell to make parjettinge in			6
for 2 hundred of sweet lead at 15s per hundred	1	10	[...]
for abow to hall to the dore at the churchgrate			[...]
for 2 barrelles of lime & hallinge it		2	[...]
William Dicsonne for worke		18	[...]
for 16 feathums of rope		6	2
for nayles & lade pailes			8
Hanbidge for a dayes worke		1	–
for 2 loggers for the bells		1	–
the sexton for Michelmas quartridge – 1618		6	8
for coulers for & about the Starre		2	3
for beare for the ringers at the comminge of the Lord Presdence		1	6
my Lord Bishopes servayer of the churh		2	8
for 3 bundle of lath		1	6
Thomas Hickes & Richard Kinges for mendinge the ribes about the stair & makeinge ribes & stoppinge the hole by the clocke	1	10	1
for mendinge bell ropes & hallyers		1	–
for a pottle of secke for the counsell at the receavinge Mr ⟨Lytl⟩ Alys cupp		1	8
the sexton his Christmas wages 1618		6	8
Kinges toward paintinge	1	15	–
for a gues boord & mendinge the south yle			10
Parrett for worke		1	–
Thomas Harris for apeece of timber		2	2
The some is	21	13	[...]

210 Charges paide

spent when wee went to Gloucester to my Lord Bishopes about paintinge		1	10
my Lords Secretary for makeinge directions about paintinge		2	–
for 3 barrells of lime		3	–
for a horselode of charcoale		1	8
for 214 of sheet lead at 13s per hundred	1	8	7
for ropes to hang the pulles & ladders		2	–
for 2 bushells of heire		1	4
for boardes to make scaffolds		6	–
for ropes & hallyars & mendinge ropes		11	9

for 2 horseloade of scharcole	3	8
for 3 boardes to putt over the ladders to stand to worke oon	2	4
for mendinge 2 seates in the middle row	1	9
for a locke & 2 partisions to save the leade		10
for 4 mattes & washinge the communion clothes	2	–
for 8 barrells of lime	8	–
for hallinge of lime		10
for 2 pailes & 2 loggers	1	8
for nayles for the lead	1	10
for 6 ropes to fasten the ladder		6
for hewinge astone for adiall in the churchyeard	1	–
for fastninge the diall one the crosse	1	–
for mendinge window barres		5
for a barrell of lime & hallinge	1	2
for 3 crampes of iron to fasten the plumehouse wall	1	1
Richard Kinges for paintinge	5	–
for 2 loade of charcole	3	8
Thomas Hickes for slatting the backe yles	1	8
Parratt for paveinge in the church	3	4
for nayles for the leads	2	2
for thorneinge & pruning & for 2 yow trees	1	4
for a locke for the dore in the abbye & for a paire of hinges	3	8
for 2 crampes & manding window barres		5
for nayles for the dore next the abby & mendinge him	1	2
The some is	5 8	8

211   Charges paide

to Thomas Hickes for quyninge and mendinge the church walles in the inside next the abbye	8	[...]
for shides to make ronges for ladders		[...]
for a side for a ladder & a whope for a coule	1	[...]
Richard Kinges for a dayes worke	1	[...]
for 2 locke stockes		4
for 18 pounds of sowder	13	6
for wateringe the walke behinde the church		6
for helpinge to make cleane the church		3
Richard Kinges for a dayes worke	1	–
for makeinge cleane to lower roomes		8
for a locke for Warwickes chappell	1	–
for a ladder		8
for a barrell of lime & halling	1	2
for washinge sheetes that saved the gallaryes from lyming	1	4
for the little bell rope	1	10
Richard Kings for parte of a day		[...]
for the great bell clapper	3 –	–
for hallinge 5 barrells lime		5
for 20 pounds of soulder	14	5
for 2 barrells of lime & halling	2	3
to a mason for hewinge tombestones	3	1
Alixander Parrett for worke	1	–
Richard Kinges for paintinge	5	–
Richard Kinges for 3 dayes worke	2	3
Hanbidge for 2 dayes worke	1	8
for 8 barrells of lime	8	–
for 2 barrells of lime & halling	2	5

for a dinner for Mr Barwell minister & Mr Cox the sexton & his wife			
at the Bull		5	–
Alixander Parrett St Mary wages – 1619		6	8
Thomas Hickes toward his last payment for whitinge	1	–	–
Richard Kinges toward his last payment for whiteinge	1	–	1
for whitleather to make baldwrickes		1	8
for helpinge downe with the mast & ladders		1	6
The some is	9	9	1

212   Charges paide

for a paile & 2 bosses of iron & whitleather		1	4
for broome & slipes to hange the ladders			4
for a 11 pounds of lead at 1½d the pound		1	2
for 2 iron barres for the ⟨little⟩ window		1	3
for iron eares for abuckett			3
for mendinge the booke of common prayer		2	6
for mendinge 5 window barres			4
for hallinge to & from the church		1	9
Thomas Hickes for parjetinge towardes his last payment		7	–
Richard Kinges for pargetinge towardes his last payment		7	–
for mendinge the wedding house window & for iron barres for the			
window	1	18	8
more paid Thomas Hickes towards his last payment		10	–
more paid for our visitation dinner the last of May 1619		3	8
for 7 barrells of lime		7	5
for aload of charcole		1	11
for 4 window barres		2	1
the smith for worke			3
for the iron pinn for the balwricke of the great bell			8
for 6 speekes for Mrs Bayliffes wives seat			4
for a plate to mend a ladder & a crampe			4
for hallinge 5 barrels of lime to the church			4
for hewinge atombestone		1	–
for 9 barrells of lime & hallinge it		9	6
Parrett for makeinge 4 balwricks		1	6
for mendinge the coule			7
Thomas Hickes toward his last payment	6	10	–
John Paynter toward glasinge window	1	–	–
for 4 barrells of lime & hallinge it		4	4
for a horseload of charcole		2	–
for 2 hallyers			6
Richard Kinges toward his last payment for whiting		10	–
for 2 bundles of lath			10
Thomas Hickes for slattinge the body of the church 4 dayes		4	–
for 2 bushell of heire		1	4
for 3 barrells of lime & halinge it		3	3
for 2 iron cleetes for the south dore goeinge into the church			3
the sexton for adayes worke			8
for 4 whookes to hange ladders one the church wall			3
the sexton midsummer wages 1619		6	8
The some is	8	5	5

213   Charges paide

the sexton for mendinge the bench walls about the church		8	[...]

for pentecost the 13 of May 1619 & other charges	3	10
for ringinge the bells at my Lord Bishopes visitation	2	–
for the booke of articles presentments & the parretters fees the 13 day of May 1619	3	4
for 8 barrelles of lime & hallinge it downe	8	[...]
for 2 load of charcole	4	[...]
Richard Kinges for paintinge	10	[...]
for nayles for the leads & broomes	3	[...]
for quininge the walles within the church one both sides	8	[...]
for lead for the volt over the schoolhouse	4	[...]
for a peece of timber over the volt & plasinge hime	10	[...]
for boultes iron that houldes up the voult	1	16 [...]¹
John Painter for glasinge one the churchyeard side	1	– –
for 6 pounds of soulder		4 4
for brazinge the boultes heades in the voult		8
Thomas Hickes & Richard Kinges for 19 dayes worke at the voult over the clocke house	2	10 [...]
for bell ropes		5 2
the sexton Michelmas wages – 1619		6 8
the sexton for 3 dayes worke		3 –
for a peece of timber that makes a ribb for the vault		2 6
for mendinge the church key		4
for 2 lade payles with iron to them		1 6
Kinges for paintinge	1	– –
for a smale spowt & the putting him in		2 3
for 2 barrells of choyce lime & hallinge it		2 8
for makeinge of 3 balwricks		1 –
for nayles for the leads		1 –
for 6 barrells of lime & halling		6 6
for lattice windowes at the clocke house		5 –
Richard Kinges towardes whitinge		10 6
Thomas Hickes & Richard Kinges fore payntinge & putting in of stones about the walles		14 6
John Painter for glasinge	10	12 –
for makinge iron barres for 4 windowes		5 11
The some is	13	17 5

214 Charges paide

for levelinge the gardens in the churcheyard		2 –
for hewinge a tombstone		1 –
for balwrickes & a gudgin		1 –
for liquar for the bells & mendinge awheele		1 –
Thomas Hickes for whitinge	1	– –
Richard Kinges for whitinge	1	– 6
for carryinge aladder home & atree to sett		6
for 2 balwrickes & greece		6
Parrett for adayes worke & makeinge cleane		1 2
for 60 nayles for the leades		1 8
for alocke for the church dore		4 –
Richard Kinges his last payment for whitinge		3 –
Thomas Hickes his last payment for whitinge		4 –
the sexton wages 1619		6 8

---

¹ The page has been cropped for binding and the last figure has been lost for these eight entries.

for abarrell of lime & hallinge		1	2
for halfe a hundred of nayles for the led		1	–
for 2 dayes worke & ahalfe for mendinge the leades		2	6
for the second bell rope		2	6
for washinge the communion table clothes		1	–
for alonge ladder		10	–
the servayers of the church in September 1620		5	–
for bell ropes		4	8
for abarrell of lime		1	–
for 157 dussens of quarrells at 2d the dossen	1	6	–
for hallinge them from the winyard & carryinge them in		2	8
for liquor for the bells & oyle for the clocke			7
the sexton St Mary wages anno domini 1620		6	8
for timber & planckes lath nayle & lath & for other nayls & for 2000 of slatts & for masonis worke & carpenters worke for the south yle & for the gutter	4	19	5
Mr Peeresonne for his fees at times		5	–
Parrett for paveing the quarrells in the church		7	8
for 42 footes of gutter lead in length for the south yle at 12s 6d per hundred	5	7	–
the plummer for soulder & workemanshipe	1	5	–
The some is	18	15	8

215   Charges paide

for 20 pounds of soulder at 10d per pound		17	–
aman for tendinge per plummer aday			[...]
for 3 dayes worke to a carpenter		3	–
for mendinge the seates in the 3 row upper end			9
for nayles for the lead		1	–
for 4 barrells of lime & halling it		4	4
for pentecost the booke of articles & acquittance in July 1620 ⟨& oathes⟩		3	[...]
the parretter his fees		1	[...]
Mr Peeresonne the register fees		3	[...]
the archdeacon a pottle of wine		1	4
for our visitation dinner		3	6
for Mr Loosebees dinner at the visitation		1	6
the sexton midsummer wages 1620		6	8
for 4 barrells of lime & hallinge		4	4
for carryinge the lead to & from Bristoll		2	8
the carpenters for worke & boards to putt under the broad leades in the yle next the warkey		9	1
for 4 hundred of lead for the same place 11s 6d per hundred	2	6	[...]
for mendinge the forebell clapper twice		10	5
for mendinge the clocke		2	4
for sarchinge for Mr Turberviles will at London for £2 he gave the church		6	8
for oyle for the clocke & bels			6
for the churchwardens & sidesmens dinners		2	[...]
the sexton Michelmas wages 1620		6	–
for slattinge in the longe yle & other yles		5	–
to two minesters at 2 severall times		8	8
for the candlestickes for the church		7	8
the sexton Christmas wages 1620		6	8
Alexander Parrett for mendinge the leades		6	–
for paveinge on the church and at the grate		2	–
for abow & astringe for the churchgrate dore			7

for ahide of whitleather		5	8
for 4 braces a gudgin & a iron pine to goe through the cannon of the great bell		6	9
the sexton for makinge 3 balrickes		1	–
for 4 hallyers & shuttinge the great bell rope		1	6
for 2 new sides for the beire & mendinge him		2	10
The some is	9	14	2

216   Charges paid

for alocke & nayles for the dore next thaby			11
for the visitation in Aprill 1621 for pentecost dinner & a pottle of wine to the archdeacon		8	4
the sexton St Mary wages 1621		6	8
Parrett for 4 dayes worke on the leads		4	–
Mr Vaughan for iron for the church	2	–	6
Mr Pearesone at the archdeacons court all dutyes 1621		7	2
the parretter for our oathes also		1	–
for a hinge & nayles for the beare			6
for a pine for the great bell clapper			2
the sexton Midsommer wags 1621		6	8
for 3 barrells of lime & hallinge		3	5
for iron worke for to hange the great bell & for 4 mens worke		8	7
for mendinge the window behind the church next thaby		1	10
for a new spout in the long yle		1	5
for mendinge the window over the church porch		1	5
Parrett for 8 dayes worke one the leades		8	6
for a bushell of heire & a mans worke		1	–
the sexton Michelmas wages		6	8
Alexander Parrett for 6 dayes worke one the leades		6	–
Mr Parker for slatt		3	–
a mans worke at severall times			8
for nayles for the leades		4	4
for mendinge the wainescott over the chansell dore & over Mr Tracyes gallary		3	–
for mendinge the starr for abow & stringe for the dore at the church grate		2	10
for a hide of whitleather for balricks		5	4
for makeinge 3 balrickes			10
for mendinge the clocke		8	6
for mending the leads & sowder	1	5	–
for adore lock hinges & a bushel heir		2	–
for charges for the great bell		1	4
for makeinge the gutter next Beards chamber		13	2
for sowder lead & worke		9	–
the sexton Chrismas wages 1621		6	8
the ropear for arope for the great bell for hallyers & shuttinge ropes		14	–
John Parrett sexton St Mary wages 1622 & for worke		10	9
the widdow Aline for beare for worke men at sundry times		3	–
3 men to help with the leads		1	–
Godfry the smith for worke		1	6
for washinge the communion clothes against Ester 1622		1	–
The some	11	11	2

[*two blank pages foliated 217*]

218   Anno domini 1622

Edward Phelps
Richard Mynce   Churchwardens

The account of Edward Phelps and Richard Mynce churchwardens of the parishe church of the burrough of Tewksburie within the dioces of Gloucester, from the feaste of Easter 1622 untill the feaste of Easter 1623 geven up before Mr Bradford and Mr Whitledge being bayliffes

Receipts	£	s	d
of John Aston for his wives rome		10	–
of John Shawe & John Tyler for their roomes		24	–
of the goodwife Kings for a yeares rent for the churchyard		16	–
of Mr Shawe for John Beale his childs grave		3	4
of Mr Slaughter for his wives grave & for the bells		8	6
of John Laight for his owne roome		16	–
of Mr Parker for his daughters childs grave		3	4
of Samuell Whitledge for his mother in lawes grave		6	8
of Thomas Arpin for a seate		1	6
of Richard Yerrow for his wives roome		12	–
of Mr Georg Dowdswell for Phillip Surman his grave & for the bells		8	8
of Mr Jeynes for his childs grave		3	4
of Gedeon Hoare for a strangers grave		6	6
of Mr Wheeler for his wives grave		6	8
of Mr Wilkes for his childs grave		3	4
of Thomas Hale for his brother John his grave		6	–
of John Payten for his mothers grave		6	8
219 of Richard Viner for John Raye his roome yf he come not agayne			
within the time lymitted		10	–
of Giles Hazard for the halfe acre in Avon Ham being flouded		3	4
of John Sklicer for his roome		16	–
of Mr Henry Tracey for the mucke in the churchyard		2	–
of Joice Allen for a yeares rent			6
of William Wilson for Mrs Tomes her grave		6	8
of John Wilde for his roome		1	6
of Mr Pauncefoote for Mr Tracey his grave		10	–
of Mr Higgins for his wives roome		13	–
of Mr Andrew Baughan for the exchange of his roome & for his childs grave		22	4
of Henry Tonye for his roome		20	–
of Connon Smyth for his roome		4	–
of Thomas Clarke for his two childrens graves		6	8
of John Orrell for his wives grave		6	8
of John Wilson for Eckington for John Hews grave		7	5
of Thomas Laight for his owne roome & his wives rome		15	–
of John Kingsbury for his wives grave		6	8
of Mr Vaughan for his wives grave		6	8
of Edward Flemming for his wives seate		2	–
Some totall	15	2	11

220   Expences

Laid out by these churchwardens to be allowed them upon this account as followeth

	£	s	d
laid out for repayring of the great bell the 27th of Aprill		15	–

for one barrell of lime	1	2
at the visitation for pentecost money & for an acquittance	2	10
for wine & sugar bestowed upon Mr Sutton at the visitation	2	–
for owne dynner and the sidesmens dynner at the visitation	10	6
to the ringers at the visitation	1	4
to John Parrat the 29 of June for his quartedge	6	8
for the booke of articles and the putting in of our presentment	3	2
for 2 barrs of iron for 2 windowes	1	4
for 4 barrells of lime	4	6
for 3 bushells of haire	2	–
for mending the forebell roope	2	–
for mending the leades and for nailes for the same	6	–
for expences at Gloucester	2	–
to John Parrat for two daies worke	1	8
for 4 barrells of lime	4	10
for 4 bushells of haire	2	8
to Walter Trumper for surveying of the church	3	–
for halliers & mending a roope	1	6
to John Parrat for 3 daies worke	2	6
to John Parret for 1 quarter	6	8
for 3 bagges of charcole	10	–
for wyer for the clocke	1	8
for boordes to laie under the leades	2	2
for nailes		6
for soulder	4	–
for 2 pound of pewter to make soulder	1	4
for five daies worke to Thomas Arpin and his sonne	8	2
for 4 halliers	1	4
for 3 hundred 1 quarter & 16 pound of lead	41	–
for licour for the bells		4
for wood & coles	1	2

221 for five pound of pewter to make soulder	3	9
to Thomas Arpin for 2 daies worke for himselfe & his sonne	3	4
for a barrell of lime and a bushell of haire	2	–
for halfe a hundred of lead	5	10
for 6 pound of soulder	4	6
for 6 daies worke to Thomas Arpin & his sonne	10	–
to John Parrat for poynting the leads of the church	1	4
for 4 pound and a quarter of soulder	3	2
to Thomas Arpin and his sonne for five daies worke	8	6
for wood & cole		6
for 6 pound of soulder	4	6
to Thomas Arpin and his sonne for 6 daies worke	10	–
for coles		4
to Wassell for 1 daies worke		8
to William Dixon for his wives roome	6	–
to John Parrat for 2 daies worke	1	8
to John Parrat for one quarter	6	8
for a bauldrige for the great bell	3	6
for peecing the third bell roope & one hallier	1	3
for one pound of candles and for licour for the bells		4
for 1 barrell of lime	1	4
for a newe roope for the litle bell	1	8
to John Parrat for 2 daies worke	1	8
for fencing the trees sett in the churchyard by Mr Smyth	2	2
for 4 halliers and for nailes	1	5

to John Parrat for one quarter		6	8
to John Parrat for washing of the table clothes		1	–
to Georg Alcock for wryting the books		3	–
Sum totall	12	2	7

[two blank pages foliated 222]

223   Anno domini 1623

Michaell Millington
William Wilson   Churchwardens

The account of Michaell Millington and William Wilson churchwardens of the parish church of the burrough of Tewksburie within the dioces of Gloucester, from the feaste of Easter 1623 untill the feaste of Easter 1624 geven up before Mr Cowles & Mr Myllicheape being bayliffes

		£	s	d
Receiptes		£	s	d
in stocke		3	8	–
of William Sheene for the exchange of his wives roome			5	–
of Thomas Yend for a roome in a seate for himselfe			5	–
of Giles Hassard for the church halfe acre			13	–
of Mr John Wiatt for Mrs Collins buriall in the church			6	8
of Mr Clarke for the buriall of his child			3	4
of John Shawe for the buriall of his child			3	4
of John Wilson for the buriall of his child			3	4
of Mr White his buriall in the church			6	8
of Robert Kedwards for his wives roome in a seate			16	–
of the widow Allen for the rent of the ground of her house				6
for the buriall of the goodwife Jorden			6	8
for the buriall of Mr Poultons child			3	4
for the buriall of Mr Kingsbury his child			3	4
for the buriall of Mr Hill his child			3	4
for the buriall of Conway Whitterne his child			3	4
for the buriall of James Braford his child			3	4
for the buriall of John Orrell			6	8
for the buriall of Mrs Cowles			6	8
224	of John Payton for a roome for his wife in a seate		22	–
	of Mr Clarke for his daughter in lawes buriall		6	8
	of Henry Shawe for the exchange for a roome for himselfe in a seate		12	–
	of Gedeon Hoare for the buriall of his child		3	4
	of Mr Wilkes for the boyes gallery		16	–
	of Nicolas Mearson for his wives roome		5	–
	of John Fisher junior for a roome for himselfe		20	–
	of Thomas Fisher junior for his owne roome & his wives roome		14	–
	of John Beale for a roome for himselfe & a roome for his wife		20	–
	of Anthony Rowles for his wives roome		10	–
	of Georg Whitledge for the exchange of a roome for his wife		15	–
	of Giles Blissard for a roome for himselfe & a roome for his wife		5	–
	of Jacob Garrett for his wives roome		6	–
	of John Orrell for a roome for himselfe		10	–
	of Thomas Yend for his wives roome		12	–
	of Anthony Web for the rent of the churchyard		14	–
	of Richard Cotten for his wives roome		2	–
	of John Stile for the exchange of a roome for his wife		4	–
	of William Staight for a roome for himselfe		9	–

of John Tyler for his wives roome	12	–
of John Pierce for his wives roome	7	–
of Robert Clarke for rome	10	–
⟨Suma totalis⟩	⟨19 12	6⟩
Somm totalis	22 7	6

225   Expences

Laid out by these churchwardens to be allowed them by this account as followeth

to the archdeacon for pentecost money	2	6
for the booke & an acquittance	1	4
to Mr Pearson for his fee	3	2
for the archdeacons dynner at the Bull at the visitation	12	–
to John Millwright for his fee	1	–
to the ringers upon the visitation daie	2	–
for mending the clapper of the forebell	1	2
for 9 pound of soulder at 9d a pound	6	9
for 8 pound of lead		8
unto John Parrat for 6 daies worke for mending the leads	6	–
for 2 bushells of charcole	1	–
unto a boy that did worke with John Parrat for 6 daies worke	2	–
for 8 pound of soulder at 9d a pound	6	–
for 1 bushell and halfe of charcoles		9
unto John Parrat for 4 daies worke for mending the leads of the church	4	–
unto the boy that did worke with John Parrat for 4 daies work	1	4
for 1 bushell & 1 peck of charcole		8
for 5 pound of soulder	3	9
for rasen		1
for Mr Shawe for 8 pound of nailes and to Henry Turke for pointing them	1	6
unto John Parrat for 3 daies worke and a halfe	3	6
unto the boy that did worke with John Parrat for 3 daies worke and a halfe	1	2
for 3 pound of soulder at 9d a pound	2	8
for 1 bushell of charcole		6
unto John Parrat for 4 daies worke and a halfe for mending the leads of the church	4	6
226 unto the boy that did worke with John Parrat for 4 daies worke and a halfe	1	6
for 6 pound of soulder at 9d a pound	4	6
for halfe a bushell of charcole		3
unto John Parrat for 5 daies worke upon the leades of the church	5	–
unto the boy that did worke with John Parrat for 5 daies worke	1	8
for oile for the clocke		2
unto John Parrat Myddsomer quartredge	6	8
unto Mr Pearson for his fee when we did deliver the presentment at Gloucester	2	6
for expences at Gloucester	1	5
for a roope for the third bell	6	–
unto Jeffe Paynter for mending the glasse windowe & 1 iron bar	1	10
for a buckle and 2 keys to hang the great bell	1	–
unto John Parrat Michaelmas quartredge	6	8
for 1 pound of candles		4
for mending the wheeles and the watch of the clocke	2	2
for 2 barrells of lime and the halling of them	2	3
for licour for the bells		2

for ringing the great bell mornings		10	–
for 6 halliers for the bells		1	9
unto John Parrat for Christmas quartredge		6	8
unto John Parrat for St Mary daie quartredge		6	8
for 2 yewe trees and the setting of them		1	–
for 11 elme setts and the thorneing of them		4	–
unto Giles Blissard for 63 postes and nailes for the churchyard			
at 8d a peece	2	2	–
unto the workmen for setting up the railes		26	–
unto John Parrat for the washing of the clothes		1	–
227 unto Georg Alcock for wryteing the bookes		3	–
Suma totalis	10	15	9
Delivered by Michaell Millington and William Wilson unto the newe			
churchwardens in stocke	⟨8	16	9⟩
the full sume of	9	11	9
More to be receved from Mr Sysell for the funerall of Mr Reede		6	8
More for Thomas Turberville his funerall		6	8

INDEXES

EDITORIAL NOTE ON THE INDEXES

Each entry indicates the page or pages on which the name or topic shown occurs; multiple entries are not distinguished. For reasons of space, entries on runs of consecutive pages are shown thus '47–51'.

The main version of each surname is either the usual modern spelling or the version closest to it which appears in the text; major variants are given in parenthesis. No attempt has been made to indicate the most common contemporary usage. Where the spelling is so much at variance with the usual modern form that the reader might have difficulty in locating or identifying the name required, the usual modern spelling has been provided in square brackets and the entry thereby placed where the modern reader would expect to find it. No attempt has been made to discriminate between different individuals bearing the same name. As explained in the introduction, the text faithfully reproduces original spelling except for 'u' and 'v' and 'i' and 'j' where modern style is given, but this convention proved to be a source of difficulty in dealing with surnames in which either 'u' or 'n' were equally acceptable readings, such as Tony/Tovey. In this instance further research showed that 'Tony' is probably correct, despite the two instances where the 'v' is clearly written, which have been retained in the text (pp. 105, 120). It has been thought helpful for certain types of studies to indicate the existence of references to unnamed women by using the form 'wife of'.

Christian names are given in the index with modern spelling though in the text they are rendered as in the original manuscript. Other designations such as 'Mr', 'Goodwife', 'widow', etc., are listed in alphabetical order amongst the Christian names.

For the index of subjects a hierarchical structure has been adopted in the hope that the reader will be the more readily guided towards related topics of interest. Thus, for example, all the various trades are grouped alphabetically under the generic main heading 'Occupations', and cross-referencing has thus been kept to a necessary minimum.

Caroline Litzenberger
David Smith

INDEX OF PERSONAL NAMES

Abesone, John, 70
Acleytone, Thomas, 32
Adames, Edward, 13, 21, 23, 27, 38
Addis (Addyce), Humphrey, 30, 33, 38, 40–42,
    45–47, 50–52, 55, 57, 59, 62, 63, 66, 69, 71,
    74, 75
Alcocke (Aulcycke), George, 120, 130, 133, 142,
    144; George (wife of), 120, 130, 133
Allen (Alyne), Goodwife, 48; Joyce, 130, 140; Mr,
    26, 72, 75; Mrs, 26, 63; Nicholas, 36, 88, 89,
    96, 122; Nicholas (wife of), 36, 89; Thomas,
    88, 105, 120, 131; Thomas (from Westen-
    cote), 32, 54; Thomas (wife of), 3, 5, 13, 17,
    19, 31, 35, 39, 42, 44, 120, 131; Widow, 139,
    142; William, 95, 100, 103, 105, 111, 115,
    120, 121, 126, 133; William (wife of), 121
Alye, Edward, 56, 99, 100, 110, 128; Edward (wife
    of), 110; Kedwards, 73; Mr, 103, 109, 115,
    120, 134; William, 114
Androwes, Thomas, 61
Arkell, Mrs, 18, 23, 89; Richard, 29, 41, 58, 59,
    64; Richard (wife of), 29, 64
Arndell, Edward, 132; Harry, 36; Harry (wife of),
    36
Arpine, John, 107, 126, 131; John (wife of), 131;
    Thomas, 140, 141
Ashelworth, Hugh, 73; Hugh (wife of), 73
Asson, Ann, 54; Robert, 54
Aston (Ashton), John, 105, 140; John (wife of),
    140; Robert, 49, 64; Thomas, 105
Atkins, Mr, 105
Aunton, William, 36; William (wife of), 36
Awdrey, Mr, 76

Bache, Thomas, 133; Thomas (wife of), 133
Backe, Henry, 8
Bailie, Benjamin, 115; Benjamin (wife of), 115;
    John, 59; John (wife of), 59
Baker, Robert, 17, 19; William, 12, 13, 15, 32
Baldwin, Balden, William, 110, 119, 122, 131;
    William (wife of), 122, 131
Balthrop, Edmund, 81; Mr, 73
Band, John, 6, 15, 22
Banke, Thomas, 21; Thomas (wife of), 21
Bankes, Parson, 32, 38
Barbon, John, 29; John (wife of), 29

Barker, 91; Richard, 29, 49; Richard (wife of), 29,
    49; Robert, 123, 124, 125
Barkley, John, 26; John (wife of), 26
Barnard, Richard (of Hardwicke), 88; William, 18
Barnefield, Mr, 129
Barnesley, John, 123, 124, 125, 126, 127
Barrel (Barells), Mr, 113; Simon, 26; Simon (wife
    of), 26
Barrett (Barrite), Peter, 44, 59; Peter (wife of), 59;
    Richard, 27, 33, 39, 40, 41, 42, 45, 46
Barston, Edward, 59; John, 35, 64, 67; Mr, 78;
    Mrs, 120
Barthe, Thomas, 121
Bartholomew, Bartlmew, James, 27, 29; James
    (wife of), 27, 29; Mary, 132; Ralph, 70, 88,
    110, 132; Ralph (wife of), 70, 132; Thomas,
    131, 132; Thomas (wife of), 132
Bartlett, Bartlete, Mrs, 48; William, 126
Bartley, William, 119
Barwell, Mr, 136
Baskerville, Mr, 49; Mrs, 48
Baston, Edward, 23, 28, 29, 30, 36; John, 36, 44;
    John (wife of), 44; Mr, 35; Mrs, 111
Batten, Jarvis, 53; Jarvis (wife of), 53
Baughe see Vaughan
Baylis, Edward, 133; Richard, 132; Richard (wife
    of), 132
Beale, Anne, 129, 132; John, 140, 142; John (wife
    of), 142
Bearde, Sir, 60, 91
Beaste, Francis, 6; Thomas, 88
Beavans, Thomas, 131; Thomas (wife of), 131
Bell, Peter, 109
Bennett, Mother, 29, 43
[Berkeley] Barkley, John, 26; John (wife of), 26
Besant (Beysan), 64; John, 29; John (wife of), 29
Bicke, Thomas, 104; Thomas (wife of), 104
[Biddle] Byddell (Byttle), Ralph, 20, 27, 34, 35,
    37, 50, 57, 89; Ralph (wife of), 20, 27, 35, 89;
    William, 82; William (wife of), 82
Bishoppe, Mrs, 100
Blackwell, Mr, 111
Blancket, Richard, 81; William, 103, 104
Blissard, Giles, 142, 144; Giles (wife of), 142
Blomer, Mr, 67, 89
Boche, Mr, 59

80; George (wife of), 10, 48; Margery, 49; Mr, 26, 29, 53; Thomas, 23, 38, 42, 44, 49, 51, 52, 115; Thomas (wife of), 44; William, 49

Frewen (Freun), George, 61, 70, 73, 76; George (wife of), 61, 70; Leonard, 72

Frith, 45

Garrett, James/Jacob, 131, 142; James/Jacob (wife of), 142

Garne, Joan, 120

Garner, Harry, 24

Gase, John, 3

Geaste (Gest), Alexander, 3; Alice (Mrs), 26; Elizabeth, 132; Giles, 26, 29, 37, 45, 88; Giles (wife of), 26, 29; John, 96, 104, 119; John (wife of), 96; Mr, 49; Mrs, 129; Thomas, 31, 54, 58

Geines see Jeynes

Gelfe, Thomas, 95, 103, 104, 105, 107; Thomas (wife of), 95, 103

George, Richard, 109; Richard (wife of), 109

Gibbes, Widow, 70

Gibson, Thomas, 64; Thomas (wife of), 64

Gilbert (Gilbte), Roger, 99; Roger (alias Guye), 17-20, 23, 59; Roger (alias Guye, wife of), 20, 59; Widow, 81, 121; William, 68, 73, 74, 76, 77, 80, 110, 127, 131; William (wife of), 73, 74, 77, 110

Godfrey, Thomas, 123, 125, 127, 139

Godwin (Goodwin), Devoreaux, 127; Francis, 132; Thomas, 3, 5, 13, 14

Goodman, Richard, 111; Thomas, 37

Goreles, Richard, 111; Richard (wife of), 111

Goughe, Richard, 7, 11, 12

[Green] Grene (Grean), Alexander, 5, 6, 8, 9, 22, 32, 61; Alexander (wife of), 61; Henry, 3, 9, 10, 13, 17, 31, 34, 39, 42, 44; James/Jacob, 37, 43, 49, 61, 67, 68, 104, 105; James/Jacob (wife of), 37, 43, 64, 68, 105; John, 111, 120; John (wife of), 111, 120; Mr, 36; Richard, 68, 70, 82; Richard (wife of), 68; Robert, 5, 6, 27, 44; Thomas, 132, 133; Thomas (wife of), 133; Thomas (of Walton), 70, 132; Thomas (of Walton, wife of), 70

Greenowe, Thomas, 64, 82, 124; Thomas (wife of), 64, 82, 124

[Greenwood] Greanwoode (Grenwod), 52; Henry, 19; Mr, 39, 40, 41, 42, 44, 63, 67, 110; Mrs, 88; Nicholas, 5, 9, 14, 34, 35, 53; Thomas, 10, 18, 24, 30, 32, 33, 46, 47, 50, 57

Gregge, Goodwife, 32, 56, 97; Richard, 36, 43, 48, 49; Richard (wife of), 48

Gregsone, Edward, 50, 52

Grettane, 4

Greves, Mr, 12

Griffin, Mr, 108; William, 107, 124, 125

Grime, Mr, 99; Mrs, 99

Grindle, John, 29; John (wife of), 29

Grine, John, 70; John (wife of), 70; Old, 115

Grubbe, 10

Grundye, 91

Grymer (Grinner), Thomas, 2, 3, 73; Thomas (wife of), 73

Gubbins, John, 73; John (wife of), 73

Guildinge, Richard, 76, 77; Richard (wife of), 76

Habbock, James, 61; James (wife of), 61

Hale (Hall, Hawle, Hawley), 39; John, 32, 36, 37, 54, 82, 88, 116, 120, 126, 131, 140; John (wife of), 32, 36, 37, 54, 88; Richard, 3, 104, 131; Richard (wife of), 131; Robert, 36; Robert (wife of), 36; Thomas, 58, 68, 71, 72, 73, 82, 84, 91, 99, 121, 128, 129, 131, 132, 140; Thomas (wife of), 68, 99, 131; Widow, 81

Hallyfaxe (Hollifaxe), Nicholas, 99, 104; Nicholas (wife of), 99

Hanbage (Hanbidg), 78, 79, 94, 96, 98; Richard, 133, 134, 135

Handforde, Mr, 88

Hanley, Richard, 122; Richard (wife of), 122

Harbage, Phillip, 120

Hardinge, John, 54, 59, 80, 105, 107, 109, 110, 119, 130; John (wife of), 109, 110, 119, 130

Harley, John, 54; Richard, 5, 13, 17, 19, 31, 34, 39, 42, 44

Harmer (Hermer), Giles, 76, 88, 89, 121, 132; Giles (wife of), 89, 121, 132

Harris, 98; Thomas, 115, 120, 134; Thomas (wife of), 115, 120

Harth, Mr, 120

Harvard, Thomas, 37; Thomas (wife of), 37

Hasard (Hassarde, Hashard), Anne, 47; Giles, 103, 110, 140, 142; Giles (wife of), 110; Henry, 96; John, 49, 56, 64, 68, 69, 119; John (wife of), 64, 68; Mr, 76; Mrs, 73

Hasson, Richard, 70

Hatle, Thomas, 53

Hatton, William, 111; William (wife of), 111

Hawkins (Hawker, Hawkinges, Hawkes), Goodwife, 49; John, 73, 99; John (wife of), 73, 99; Matthew, 120; Matthew (wife of), 120; Thomas, 65, 68, 76; Thomas (wife of), 65, 76

Haynes (Heaynes, Henies, Heynes), 46, 47, 51, 52, 62; Goodman, 71, 90; Thomas, 48, 50, 55, 60, 86, 122; Thomas (wife of), 86, 122; William, 39

Henbury, John, 72, 73, 106

Hews see Hughes

Hiatt (Hiett, Hyett, Heiet), Father, 10, 11; John, 44, 45, 54; John (wife of), 44; Margery, 111; Mrs, 111; Richard, 61, 120, 125; Richard (wife of), 61; Thomas (of Walton Cardiff), 10, 63, 67; William, 54, 70, 81, 88; William (wife of), 54, 88

see also Wyett

Hickes, 92; John, 101, 106, 107, 118, 122, 123, 125, 126; Thomas, 119, 122, 124-126, 134-137

Hicox, Robert, 11

Higges, Alice, 88; Ann, 88

Higgyns (Higines), Humphrey, 105, 130; John, 105; Mr, 119, 140; Mrs, 119, 140; Robert, 10; Thomas, 132, 133; Thomas (wife of), 133

Hignell, John, 119; John (wife of), 119

INDEX OF SUBJECTS